Eleana Vaja
Epilepsy Metaphors

Lettre

To my parents: Harald, Georgia, Dionissios

Eleana Vaja (PhD) taught American literary and cultural studies at the University of Cologne. Her research interests include U.S. American literature, philosophy and disability studies.

Eleana Vaja

Epilepsy Metaphors

Liminal Spaces of Individuation in American Literature 1990-2015

[transcript]

This study was accepted as a doctoral dissertation by the Faculty of Arts and Humanities of the University of Cologne.

Bibliographic information published by the Deutsche Nationalbibliothek
The Deutsche Nationalbibliothek lists this publication in the Deutsche Nationalbibliografie; detailed bibliographic data are available in the Internet at http://dnb.d-nb.de

Cover layout: Marie Arndt, Bielefeld
Printed in Germany
Print-ISBN 978-3-8376-4118-9
PDF-ISBN 978-3-8394-4118-3

Contents

III. Epilepsy Metaphors in American Literature (1990-2015)

Acknowledgments

I want to thank my supervisor Hanjo Berressem for giving me the opportunity to teach and research at his chair, for believing in my topic from the very beginning to its end, and for his constructive criticism along the way. I would furthermore like to thank my second supervisor Norbert Finzsch for his unconditional support, enthusiasm, commitment and encouragement, and for providing me with the strength to pursue my research's aim with confidence and determination. I would also like to thank the other members of the committee, Roman Bartosch, Wolfram Nitsch, Elisabeth Schäfer-Wünsche and Andreas Speer for their interested, thought stimulating and critically engaged questions and the scientific as well as humorous atmosphere they created in so doing, and which gratifyingly framed these four years of research for me. And I want to thank Bärbel Eltschig, the heart and soul of the English Seminar I.

Being part of the a.r.t.e.s. *Graduate School for the Humanities Cologne* I am thankful for the curricula, conferences, reading circles, and the interdisciplinary outline that embedded my project in a nourishing environment. In particular, I want to thank Sabine Folger-Fonfara, Frank Hentschel, Artemis Klidis-Honecker, Florian Petersen, Katrin Schaumburg, Stefan Udelhofen and Aiko Wolter for their support. A special thanks goes to Johannes Schick for including me in every session, trip and reading circle on Gilbert Simondon. I would also like to thank the whole crew of Prof. Berressem's colloquium as well as Prof. Anne Waldschmidt's colloquium for reading essential parts of my drafts and for their valuable feedback. Since my time at the University of Berkeley not only defined the starting point of my writing process but also allowed me to study and research at this politically progressive institution, I want to thank Beverly Crawford Ames, Brit Sperber and Gia White for this once-in-a-lifetime experience.

A special and eternal thanks goes to my patient and brilliant lecturers Kelly Kawar and Anja Schmidt-Ott. Knowing that two such remarkable researchers were looking at my thesis really calmed me down in those many moments of doubt. Thank you both from the bottom of my heart, for your work, feedback and reassurance. I want to thank you, Kelly, for being as unstoppable, precise, and focused as you were; and thank you, Anja, for your dedication and your perfectly timed persistence as well as for the visual digitalization of my graphs and speeches. I would also like to thank my colleague Jasmin Herrmann for her constructive remarks on my project; thank you for your meticulousness and honesty.

To my father, Harald Schmidt-Ott, for his unconditional love and for his adamant belief in me and this project long before even I knew I could or would write a dissertation; and for making sure that I accepted doubt as a necessary step and motivator on this journey, instead of affirming my fears, which read it as an evidence of a bold, wrong choice. I want to thank my mother, Georgia Kotsialou, for her unconditional love, her witty insights, curious questions, relentless hours of patient listening as well as her brave heart, making her the best role model I can have. I want to thank my father, Dionissios Vajas, for those times of unbreakable support and guidance that allowed me to benefit from his exceptional dedication and relationship to writing and thinking that define him as the philosopher that he is.

I am so grateful to have you in my life, I want to thank each one of you individually for your own way of comforting me, listening to my ideas and doubts, sharing as well as pretending to share—which makes it even more loveable—my enthusiasm about my research as well as your unique loveable personality: To those of you, who I consider family: Elena Ntikbasani, Janelle Kempe, Ratko Salostey, Giannina Terriuolo. To those of you giving me shelter when I had no home: Joana Bürgin, Maike and Martin Cosler. To those of you, who live freedom and embraced me for who I am: Alysha Colburn, Jeff Dimock, Cecelia Littlepage, Andreas Raspotnik. To those of you I asked to guide me: Sensei Ogawa, Markus Fochler. To those of you, whose concern was directed to anything but academia, making sure that I eat, sleep, laugh: Vasiliki Karouta, Gregorios Karoutas, Lambrini Kotsialou, Georgia Ntikbasani, Jutta and Hartwig Fricke, Deniz Firat. And finally to my little sister Clara Henrike Schmidt-Ott, whose remarkable inner peace, laughter, audacious acrobatics and intimidatingly intelligent questions about life, love and death lightened up even my darkest days.

Introduction

The implicitness and frequency in which epilepsy appears in documents as early as the Egyptian hieroglyphs (4000 B.C.),[1] the Babylonian *The Code of Hammurabi* (1750 B.C.) as well as the *Diagnostic Handbook* (1070-1050 B.C.),[2] the Indian *Ayurveda,*[3] and the Hippocratic treatise *The Sacred Disease* (400 B.C.) underlie this books' overarching hypothesis that epilepsy is

1 For further research see Hans-Werner Fischer-Elfert's *Abseits von Ma'at. Fallstudien zu Außenseitern im Alten Ägypten* (2005).

2 See also "A Dialogue with Historical Concepts of Epilepsy from the Babylonians to Hughlings Jackson: Persistent Beliefs" (2011) by Umair J. Chaudhary, John S. Duncan, and Louis Lemieux, as well as J.V. Wilson's and E.H. Reynold's essay "Texts and Documents. Translation and Analysis of a Cuneiform Text Forming Part of a Babylonian Treatise on Epilepsy" (1990), or *Epilepsy in Babylonia* (1993) by Marten Stol.

3 "Ayurveda, based on the Vedas was developed systematically more than 3000 years ago" (Kurup 3). It cannot be dated back to one specific era; in contrast to the other documentations, the Ayurveda was continuously adapted and refined so that it still serves as a philosophical treatise on the Indian "science of life"; it describes the ancient Indian holistic psycho-somatic interdepence which, in terms of epilepsy, resonates with nineteenth and twentieth century Jacksonian psychomotor-epilepsy and the "dreamy state" (Govindaswamy 204ff.). For further research consider Satish Jain's "Ayurveda: The Ancient Indian System of Medicine" in Orrin Devinsky, Steven C. Schachter and Steven Pacia's *Complementary and Alternative Therapies for Epilepsy* (2005), as well as Saligrama Krishna Ramachandra Rao's "The Conceptual Context of Indian Medicine" (1987).

intrinsically connected to our understanding of life.[4] Looking at the dominant disciplinary methods for explaining epilepsy in its relation to life, one is confronted with biology and medicine on the one hand and religion and metaphysics on the other hand. This has held true over the millennia, for even today responses to the riddle of epilepsy tend toward the legitimization of this respective epistemological outline, be it medical researchers in search of "one of the 'holy grails' of modern neuroscience" (Cavanna 1) or neurotheologists working to articulate an interdisciplinary account of religious, if not spiritual, experience.

"Epilepsy" derives from the Greek word "epilepsia" which means to seize or attack (Livingston 5). It defines the "occurrence of unprovoked seizures," where seizures define "the disorderly discharges of interconnected neurons in the brain that temporarily alter one or more brain cells."[5] In drawing attention to the delicacy of consciousness, epilepsy poses significant challenges to our notions of life, death, pain and in/dependence. The vague quality of the definition of epilepsy given above is largely due to the fact that epilepsy remains a conundrum, leaving scientists, given the status of neurological progress, still in agony. At the end of the twentieh century Robert A. Gross, although appreciative of recent achievements in this field, points out that

> "[e]nthusiasm for the state of the art should be tempered, however, by the realization that we have yet to elucidate fully the ways in which seizures start, spread or terminate, or whether these mechanisms are the same as those underlying the development of epilepsy. Not surprisingly we have yet to come to an understanding of all the mechanisms by which antiepileptic drugs prevent the disorderly neuronal activity that causes seizures." (40)

It is worth reiterating this statement's core—physicians can neither fully capture the origin nor the concept of epilepsy, or rather *epilepsies*, but are limited to a symptom-based treatment—which leaves us with a rather basic questions: What is epilepsy, and how many forms, varieties and degrees are there? Even here, the state of the art is caught in a circuit. Regarding the

4 See also Peter Wolf's "Sociocultural History of Epilepsy" (2010).

5 <http://www.brainfacts.org/diseases-disorders/epilepsy/articles/2012/seizures-and-epilepsy/> consulted: 10/22/14, 3:00 p.m.

etiology of epilepsy, the International League Against Epilepsy (ILAE) relies on Henri Gastaut's (1915-1955) classification, which was first formulated in 1969, in the form of the categories "idiopathic," "symptomatic," and "cryptogenic" (Berg and Scheffer 1059). These categories were revised by Anne T. Berg and Ingrid Scheffer in 2011 as "genetic," "strucutural/metabolic," and "unknown" (ibid.) in order to take into account new scientific findings in the fields of genetics and hormone metabolisms. They, nevertheless, but fail in their aim of clarifying what, exactly, epilepsy is. In layman's terms, Berg and Scheffer's categories mean that epilepsy can either be inherited, developed in life through the different hormonal adjustments of the body, or simply acquired through some other means.

Provocatively speaking, but in line with what disability studies scholars have heard Lennard J. Davis continuously emphasize, merely being born, merely *living* could induce some form of disability/epilepsy. Walter J. Friedlander coined the term "seizure-threshold" (107) to capture this immanent, ontological potential of epilepsy in humans. Strangely enough, the "seizure-threshold" found strong support in 1997 in the 38th episode of the *Pokemon* series, whose flickering screen triggered seizures in many of the children watching. This event encouraged researchers to further investigate the correlation between seizures and epilepsy (Okumura et al. 981). Scholars are in agreement to try and distinguish between seizures and epilepsy. Yet, a clear-cut demarcation between the two is almost impossible. Seizures, tremors, shivers, and spasms are the hints of an upcoming epilepsy, blurring the boundaries of the two. Concludingly, let it be stated that this outline shall suffice to provide a working definition of epilepsy, as any further look into the medical understanding of it opens a Pandora's box of classifications and etiologies that outreaches the course of this thesis by far.

The goal of this book is to look at epilepsy from the interdisciplinary perspective of literary and cultural disability studies. Since the previously mentioned approaches, such as medicine and religion, share common ground in the overall effect they have on the life of people with epilepsy by perpetuating its stereotypes and thereby securing a notion of "normal," this book seeks to learn the degree to which literature participates in this tendency. It also works to understand if the trope of metaphor is capable of generating an approach to epilepsy that respects rather than stigmatizes the individual. Moreover, I work to disclose the mechanisms of stigmatization through metaphor, offering a theoretical means for disentangling the various forms of metaphors that structure our understanding of epilepsy. This method can also serve as a novel approach to representations of other classified disabilities in literature.

It is metaphors, in particular, that are at stake, since metaphors constitute a trope of literary expression as much as they form idiomatic language, possessing, thus, the ability to mirror and reinforce a cultural zeitgeist. Concerning the stigmatization of epilepsy, metaphors are, as Michael Andermatt points out, in reference to Susan Sontag's by now classic research on metaphors, a "Vehikel [vehicle]" (Andermatt 107) to account for the lack of information of mystified diseases, shaping "modern fantasy" (Sontag 11). Since epilepsy still remains to be scientifically demystified, it abides in metaphors in the socio-cultural sphere be it on the level of daily language or fiction. Gerhard Sauder and Steffi Ehlebracht allow for other readings of the strict pathological materialism in Sontag's theory of metaphor that account for the integration of social norms (Sauder 10) as well as the hermeneutical potential of literature to encompass and envision existential human experience (Ehlebracht 33).

Taking these considerations as a starting point, the question arises as to why the two and a half decades, from 1990 to 2015, the time frame this book explores, are of interest. These years mark an exciting, unexplored period for a theorization of epilepsy metaphors, because they feature the discipline of neuroscience in its heyday as well as the political and academic establishment of cultural disability studies.[6] With the beginning of the 1990s, research focuses on exploring brain disorders and diseases such as Alzheimers, autism and epilepsy. It was former president George Bush who announced in 1990, "The Decade of the Brain" and promised significant scientific breakthrough in this area. It is this announcement that sensitizes scholars such as Jeannette Stirling, whose book on the cultural negotiation of epilepsy is a landmark in the field, to the metaphors that define disorders as "enemies" yet to be "conquered." At the same time, the "Americans with Disabilities Act of 1990" (ADA) secured economic and social equality for people with disabilities, arguing, in contrast to the enemy-rhetoric of

6 On the conceptual metaphors of war that dominate the Presidential Proclamation 6158, see <http://www.presidency.ucsb.edu/proclamations.php?year=1990> consulted: 11/23/14, 2:42 p.m.; see also Jeannette Stirling's *Representing Epilepsy. From Myth to Matter* (2010).

Bush's declaration, on behalf of the multiplicity of bodily and mental varieties. The neuroscientific core, on the one hand, and the promotion of corporeal diversity and alterity on the other hand, stand as reason enough for exploring the literature of this period as a cultural product of its time and to discern to what degree it mirrors, juxtaposes or goes beyond this ostensible tension.

Another ground for this timeframe can be found in Irma J. Ozer's essay which dates the beginning of the integration of people with epilepsy into the "part of the continuum of what we consider normal" (798) at the beginning of the 1990s, leaving open the decade following for adjacent research. Perhaps most convincing, however, is the increased thematic presence of epilepsy in fictional and nonfictional writings, namely in the genres of illness and life narratives. With Anne Fadiman's *The Spirit Catches You and You Fall Down: A Hmong Child, Her American Doctors, and the Collision of Two Cultures* (1997) and Terry Tracy's *A Great Place for a Seizure* (2013), readers receive the exhausting and depressing exposure to the bureaucracy of the health care system and the lethal outcomes of its cultural belief systems. Fadiman's work, in particular, sensitizes readers to the drastic consequences she witnesses in the Lee family after ten years of struggle. *A Great Place for a Seizure* focuses on the daily struggles a person with epilepsy faces, including the longing for integration into the 'normal continuum.'

My first chapter deals with the history of epilepsy, traces its literary presence and identifies it as a disability by looking at its historical and cultural heritage. Chapter I.A identifies five recurring motifs that define epilepsy throughout history—*sleep, falling, danger, intelligence, religiousness*—forming the foundation of its social stigma. Based on these motifs, Chapter I.B scrutinizes the contemporary American literary corpus on epilepsy and its critical reception in order to discern to what degree and by what means literature reiterates these motifs and thereby partakes in discriminatory attitudes toward people with epilepsy. The research affirms what cultural disability studies scholars suspect—namely, that metaphors are the central rhetorical device at work in strengthening rigid belief systems. This is due to the fact that metaphors rely on the interplay of known concepts. These concepts inhere in a certain stability, as mirrored in history on the one hand and the reference to epilepsy on the other hand.

As epilepsy is classified as a disability in society, Chapter I.C offers a general outline of cultural disability studies and juxtaposes this academic field with the cultural notion of epilepsy. Concepts which crystalize disability and, thus, epilepsy as 'undesirable,' are namely 'the normal' and 'the able.' As the discrimination against disabilities goes hand in hand with their deviation from the normal, epilepsy metaphors mirror this intimacy. However, between the 1990s and 2015 novel approaches to epilepsy metaphors enter into literature, promising a shift away from this fetishization of ability and the normal.

Chapter II deals with the theorization of epilepsy metaphors in order to renegotiate the concept of epilepsy and, thus, approach the individual on three levels: society, body and language. Central to this task is an analysis of the implied stability of epilepsy's associated concepts found in motifs of its history and of the normal. While the motifs transport a historical stability, the normal designates a social and somatonormative stability. Stability is, nevertheless, required in order to account for epilepsy and the person living with this disorder. People with epilepsy experience auras, pain, fear, seizures and the exposure of their vulnerability on a daily basis. These experiences define the individual and thereby play a stable factor in his or her life. To ignore the effects these experiences have on the individual, is to display an indifference to his or her emotional states. Furthermore, the notion of stability is required by the rhetorical trope of metaphor per se, whose success depends on recognition.

The recognizable, the known, is, however, the criterion that ultimately sustains discrimination: referring to the person with epilepsy as a genius displays the same mechanism as the association of epilepsy with possession. Still, it is via metaphors that novel ways of viewing epilepsy and disability are introduced. Since stability cannot be completely abandoned or sustained, it forms the kernel of this theorization of epilepsy metaphors. Along the literary corpus three renegotiations of the stable are addressed and applied: the *flexible,* the *relational* and the *metastable*. The *flexible, relational* and *metastable* moment describe how novel epilepsy metaphors position themselves in relation to the stable (discrimination) and renegotiate the individual through emerging liminal space. Each of these moments grounds in a different theory and embeds the respective metaphors accordingly.

Flexibility, as discussed in Chapter II.A, allows for a social renegotiation of epilepsy metaphors. These metaphors still function within the realm of a quantitative normal and a clinical notion of epilepsy. Jürgen Link's theory of proto- and flexible normalism answers the question 'who is normal?'. This notion of the normal is introduced in connection with Michel Foucault's observation on the clinic and aids in the formulation of *protometaphors* and *flexmetaphors*. Following this, in Chapter II.B, George Canguilhem's biosocial approach dissolves the connection between the normal and the statistical in favor of a *relational* materiality of the body and its environment. His leading question is, therefore, 'what is the normal?'. Metaphors of this second theory focus on novel interpretations of epilepsy because Canguilhem emphasizes the individuality of each body by liberating them from any comparison. Gilbert Simondon's notion of the *metastable* forms the concluding chapter, II.C, of this section. The metastable helps to reveal the hidden potentiality of daily—normal—language through the consideration of epilepsy as a new ontological "event structure." Here the cognitive linguistics of George Lakoff and Mark Johnson enter the discussion in the form of what they coined "conceptual metaphor."

Chapter III turns to the literature, structuring the nine works it examines according to the theorization of epilepsy metaphors in the preceding chapter. This means that the first three works in Chapter III.A offer, through their respective epilepsy metaphor as *proto-* or *flexmetaphor*, a platform from which to decipher the social mechanisms of exclusion and inclusion and their relation to the individual, answering, thereby, the question of 'who is normal?'. As this section's underlying theoretical bias rests on a statistical approach to define a society's normal or anormal participants, these metaphors mirror this outline in terms of what I call *calculated individuation*. Chapter III.B looks at individual bodies as metaphors and defines the normal as individual, arguing for a necessary alterity. As epilepsy is "the disorderly discharges of interconnected neurons," electricity defines the phenomenon from which these three texts build their *relational metaphors*, delineating, I argue, what comes to be an understanding of *electric individuation*. Chapter III.C scrutinizes idiomatic language and focuses on the utterances, expressions and motifs usually associated with a signification and deprication of epilepsy but now contributes to its renegotiation. As these last three novels display a poetics that seeks to introduce epilepsy as metastability, they come to terms with what Gilbert Simondon calls a "transindividual."

The three literary works addressed in Chapter III.A are Lauren Slater's *Lying: A Metaphorical Memoir* (2000), Audrey Niffenegger's *The Time Traveler's Wife* (2004) and the poetry collection by Dennis Mahagin, *Grand Mal* (2012). These publications mark the end of "The Decade of the Brain" and are thus offered to the audience two decades after the ADA, promising insight into the nexus of scientific research and its socio-cultural negotiation. *Lying*, furthermore, is the only book in this selected corpus that initiates a cultural disability studies discussion of its epilepsy metaphor, emphasizing even more so the need to address it in this chapter. As Audrey Niffenegger's debut secured her a huge audience, Lauren Slater relies on a fanbase established with the successes of *Welcome to My Country* (1996) and *Prozac Diary* (1998). Dennis Mahagin's work is the only one in this section whose publication and audience remains scarce prompting the question as to why. What resonantes quite vividly in these works are the calculations according to which these metaphors operate, elevating mathematics, among the historical reiteration of motifs attached to epilepsy, as necessary lenses for understanding the means of their operation.

Chapter III.B begins with Thom Jones' short story collection *The Pugilist at Rest* (1993), before it discusses Rodman Philbrick's *The Last Book in the Universe* (2000) and then closes with Reif Larsen's *I Am Radar* (2015). This section formed itself, however different their various epilepsy metaphors are, because they all rely and play in some form or another with the connection of epilepsy and electricity. As these metaphors stress the relational aspect—that is, how the protagonists evolve to become themselves due to their epilepsy—it is electricity that further defines the *relational*. In line with the variety of bodies, epilepsy and electricity open up a cluster of readings that, at their core, destigmatize the individual as he or she acts out his or her own norm. These epilepsy metaphors include a reading of epilepsy in terms of boxing and compassion (*Pugilist at Rest*, and its eponymous short story), epilepsy as denoting instead of threatening the brain's archive function (*The Last Book in the Universe*), and finally epilepsy as a means to communicate with the world on a level of electric wave lengths (*I Am Radar*). As these books cover the entire timespan my thesis examines (1990-2015), this suggests an affinity of epilepsy with electricity worth unfolding.

Chapter III.C argues that within Siri Hustvedt's oeuvre a new conceptual metaphor of epilepsy manifests, which simultaneously discloses her poetics along her rhetoric and which destigmizes the disorder. A reading of Hustvedt's literary debut *The Blindfold* (1992) marks the beginning of this final section on epilepsy metaphors. It is followed by readings of her second novel *The Enchantment of Lily Dahl* (1996) along with one of her more recent publications, *The Summer Without Men* (2011). Although these three novels provide only a glimpse into her oeuvre, they capture her unique style.[7] What is at center stage are the allegedly inconscipcuous usages of three concepts: falling, shaking and the em dash; the em dash denotes the moment of a pause. While terms such as falling, collapse, and dropping will lead to a new means of addressing experienced fragility, they form the lens for zooming into *The Blindfold.* Shaking, trembling, shivering, and spasms define the means for addressing *The Enchantment of Lily Dahl,* before the various grammatical positions of the em dash explore the possibility of endurance. Hustvedt subtly and slightly but ever so effectively redefines these concepts by reintroducing them, almost unnoticeably, into daily—normal—language, and thus tackles discrimination and stigmatization practices at their very core.

7 Siri Hustvedt's entire body of work—fiction, non-fiction, art—would require a dissertation of its own in order to be grasped in its philosophical, psychological, phenomenological as well as psychoanalytic and neuroscientific outreach and interconnectedness. For an updated look onto the author's continuously growing oeuvre, please consider her website <http://sirihustvedt.net/> consulted: 07/17/17, 8:45 a.m.

I. The Folklore of Epilepsy

I.A Falling Asleep: The Stigma of Epilepsy in History

This chapter deals with the socio-cultural history of epilepsy and explores reasons for the persistence of its stigmata. To do so, I employ Erving Goffman's notion of "stigma"—as an individual's feature that clearly "disqualifie[s] from full social acceptance" (9)—along with Lerita M. Coleman Brown's refinement of it. For her, social stigmata are highly effective in their discriminatory power because they operate on five levels of personal and social interaction. These levels include the "affective," "emotional," and "linguistic level," as well as the "level of social conduct" and the "cognitive level" (182ff.). They ensure the persistence of discrimination over time because each level legitimizes the fear of the unknown in its own subversive way. A closer look at the history of epilepsy will show that epilepsy, in the continuous challenge it poses to researchers, not only works on these five levels, but also adds another one to them: *spiritual-rational*. Its history displays a certain set of stable motifs that remain attached to epilepsy despite scientific research.

These motifs, thereby, define the stigmata of epilepsy by disguising the ephemeral character of scientific truth and, likewise, religious belief. It is for this reason that the history of epilepsy given here seeks neither to retrace the medical achievements in the field,[1] nor does it claim to provide a

1 A genuine medical analysis would misconstrue the thesis of this book by affirming a leading explanatory model which considers any other approach inferior. For further research on the medical history of epilepsy consider: Owsei Temkin, Walter J. Friedlander, Mervyn J. Eadie and Peter F. Bladin, as well as Marten Stol, and Hansjörg Schneble. This book also does not address the abundant

medically-detailed analysis or, even, follow a strict chronological timeline.[2] The foremost aim of this 'history' is to identify these motifs, analyze how they interplay with and reinforce each other in medical and cultural narratives, and to delineate how their refinement consolidates our knowledge of epilepsy as *epileptic*, an enduring image that fails to designate the individual with epilepsy. With these parameters I seek to highlight the bond between the evolution of our understanding of epilepsy in accordance with our understanding of ourselves as social beings, thereby providing the basis for an analysis of epilepsy in literature that captures the experiences of disability and expresses and utilizes varieties of human existence.

Although the English expression to *fall asleep*[3] has the potential to capture the liminal space of epilepsy, it chiefly emphasizes the stability of its stigma in history. 'Falling asleep' could point to the liminal space that arises between two corporeal states and thus serves well to describe the 'space' of an individual's epilepsy. In doing so, however, it conflates the two most stable motifs of epilepsy: falling and sleeping. Due to this double connotation, *falling asleep* appears to be not only a profound but also a vital attribution—profound insofar as it stresses the historically-rooted hierarchy of *sleep* and *fall* from which most of the dominant motifs in the history of

treatments, drugs prescribed or surgeries performed in this area, as each topic would require a book of its own. Jeannette Stirling, however, highlights, in her analysis of epilepsy and its cultural representations, that scientific theorizations contribute to the multitudinous facets of epilepsy folklore (ix).

2 A chronological approach, in particular, would not only be impossible to recreate, as the history of epilepsy exceeds human documentation, but would also mislead the reader by oscillating between motifs rather than facilitating an understanding of the manifestation of each motif throughout the millennia. The opening lines of Temkin's treatise on the medical history of epilepsy refer to Oliver Wendell Holmes' famous quote among researchers in this field. The following quote is also found in the prologue to Friedlander's and in Stirling's works: "'If I wished to show a student the difficulties of getting at truth from medical experience, I would give him the history of epilepsy to read.'" (Wendell Holmes qtd. in Temkin x).

3 See Siri Hustvedt's article "Failing to Fall" (2010).

epilepsy[4] derive. *Sleep* and *fall* connect two decisive features of epilepsy, merging into the theme of *falling asleep*:[5] While sleep defines the body's and the mind's necessity to regenerate, falling refers to the unexpected and involuntary change from one physical state into another. It thereby links the moment of corporeal inevitability with chance, and alludes also to its vital attribution. Moreover, *falling asleep* triggers, due to its metaphorical allusion with death, the notion of its antonym, life. Through this euphemistic conflation, the validity of dualisms such as life and death, health and illness, mind and body is put at stake. The dualism of interest, here, is consciousness/unconsciousness insofar, that it—as I seek to draw attention to the in-between phases of these two state—is the state that actually defines the daily routines of people with epilepsy, rather than, as the stigmata would have us believe, the presence or absence of seizures.

From this inconspicuous idiom, *falling asleep*, the main motifs of epilepsy are successively derived and put into hierarchy: *sleep, falling, danger, intelligence* and *religiousness.*[6] Since *sleep* and *falling* are pivotal to the formation of the following three motifs and define the leading theme's core, they form the onset of the historical delineation. In line with these five motifs, Irma J. Ozer and Michael Andermatt deduce their own respective set of epilepsy motifs which strengthen the findings of this historical overview. It only stands to reason that some of the concepts will affirm themselves in other researchers' work, thereby emphasizing the persistence of their stigmatizing power. Thus, the motif of *danger*, which Ozer identifies in her literary analysis as "evil" (798), exposes the allied discriminatory practices and stereotypes rooted in *sleep* and *falling* alike. *Intelligence*, congruent with Ozer's identified "genius" category, as well as *religiousness,* or "saintliness" (ibid.; Andermatt 107), have reinforced their own stigmatizing po-

4 The enumeration of all motifs ascribed to epilepsy throughout the millennia could comprise a book of its own; the stress, here, lies on those five motifs functioning as umbrella terms, capturing the general characteristic habitus of how epilepsy has been perceived.

5 Not only 'to fall asleep' trigger a strong alliance with epilepsy, but according to Hubertus Tellenbach 'waking up' and sleeping link easily with epilepsy and inspire numerous interpretation, especially in the work of Dostoyevsky (205).

6 For more on epilepsy as a sacred disease, see Julie Laskaris' *The Art is Long. On the Sacred Disease and the Scientific Tradition* (2002).

tential especially in the last three centuries, framing this motif-oriented historicity.

1. THE MOTIF OF *SLEEP* IN THE HISTORY OF EPILEPSY AND THE PERSISTENCE OF ITS STIGMA ON THE "AFFECTIVE" AND "EMOTIONAL LEVEL"

> "And I know that many persons in their sleep groan and cry out, while others seem to be choked and still others get up and flee outside and are deranged."
> HIPPOCRATES, *THE SACRED DISEASE*

To begin with the manifestation of the motif of *sleep*, epilepsy[7] is, in Babylonian and Indian writings, particularly attached to the notion of nightmares. In view of the fact that the Indian "Ayurveda means science of life . . . [and] defines life as the union of body, sense, mind and soul" (Kurup 3, 5),[8] it propounds a philosophical, psycho-somatic and theoretical conceptualization of health, understood as an "equilibrium of the Vedas" (Rao 13),[9] and illness as the corresponding distortion and disturbance of this equilibrium.[10] The Indian model, in its rationally-legitimized outline, appears rea-

7 For the various Babylonian terms that have been associated with epilepsy, Stol notes that only the Neo-Assyrian "bennu," "enables us to identify the demonic disease, associated with 'shivering' and 'cold' in the lexical tradition, as a form of epilepsy" (3). "Bennu" also appears to be the name of the analogous demon who can be tamed by Shiva as "divine dancer" <https://www.desitinpharma.com/art-at-desitin/gallery/the-epilepsy-motif-in-religious-art/the-epilepsy-motif-in-religious-art/> consulted: 01/13/14, 7:40 p.m. Other Babylonian terms such as the Sumerian "miquit same" mean "fallen from above" (7) and denote one of the central motifs of epilepsy.

8 It should be noted that the Ayurveda calls for a "eugenics" view on epilepsy almost two millennia before the actual scientific movement, coined by this name, enters the stage in eighteenth century Europe (Kurup 6).

9 "Veda" means "to know." For further information on the meaning of Veda, see Satish Jain's *Ayurveda: The Ancient Indian System of Medicine* (2005).

10 See Chapter II.C as well as Chapter III.C.2 of this book.

sonable from a present day perspective, considering the contrasting Babylonian concept of a mythical and supernaturally-based explanatory model for illnesses. The latter becomes ever more striking in light of the Akkadian cuneiform inscriptions mentioning "suripu," or "feverish shivering[s]," which prelude "terrors at night" (Stol 39), whereas the Ayurveda pushes forward the resemblance between sleep, dreaming and epilepsy (Manyam 473). Night terrors and the many other related motifs attached to epilepsy thus confirm the earliness of its stigma as an endured horror and exposed loss of control. This is how *sleep*, as a motif, comes to serve as the basis for future interpretations of epilepsy as danger, possession, divine punishment[11], and prophecy.

Looking into the tradition of epilepsy and possession that arises from the motif of *sleep*, one can see that the bond of epilepsy and demonic influence descends from the Babylonian demon Alu, who exercises his powers over night and enslaves the sleeping person. This notion of possession connects to *danger* and finds its correlation in the ancient Greek populace in the shape of the demons Ephialtes, Pan or Hecate, depending on the nightmare, as either evoking pure terror (Ephialtes) or ecstasy (Hecate, Pan) (Stol 41). In his distinguished work on the medical history of epilepsy, Owsei Temkin identifies contagiousness as another crucial aspect of possession (51)—namely, that epilepsy is the sign that a person has been invaded by a demon: "The epileptic himself was unclean; whoever touched him might become prey to the demon" (8).[12] To avoid the contamination and transmission of these demons, people with epilepsy are spat at or excluded from family life. To shelter themselves from blame and humiliation, they seek sanctuary as they anticipate their epileptic attacks. Moreover, in antiquity, nightmares, if not cured, are supposed to initiate epilepsy in the person. Temkin writes that,

11 For the relation between punishment and epilepsy see Nicole Kelley's "'The Punishment of the Devil Was Apparent in the Torment of the Human Body': Epilepsy in Ancient Christianity" (2011).

12 The issue of uncleanliness was also addressed by Fischer-Elfert (129), Stol (55), as well as in Eadie's and Bladin's *A Disease Once Sacred. A History of the Medical Understanding of Epilepsy* (2001).

> "[i]n particular, two pathological conditions, nightmare and vertigo, were seen closely related to epilepsy. In the book *The Sacred Disease*, nightly terrors have already been mentioned as a form of the disease . . . . And although a later author, Soranus, discusses nightmare in a separate chapter, he nevertheless calls it a forerunner of epilepsy . . . [and], according to Aristotle, in many persons the disease originated in their sleep and did not attack while awake." (43)

These readings of *sleep* and epilepsy as nightmares trigger the inclination of witchcraft and possession in the fifteenth century bringing *religiousness* into the mix. Between the fifteenth and the seventeenth centuries, the fear of demoniac possession spreads among leading religions, influencing medical practices and initiating contentious debates about the powers of the devil in all possible forms. Prominent at that time, the practice of exorcism was rooted in the proliferation of the scriptures of the epileptic boy who was cured by Jesus. Additional religious approaches to cure epilepsy include pilgrimages, relicts, prayers, "and a variety of other activities of religious significance" (Eadie and Bladin 166). The idea of epilepsy as divine punishment can likewise be parallelized to this development of nightly terrors and possession. It, too, roots in Babylonian and Egyptian times where the belief is that gods exercise their power over humans through demons as punishment for their sinful behavior (Fischer-Elfert 124).

Another traditional perspective from which to view the stigma of epilepsy with respect to *sleep* is epilepsy's resemblance to dreaming and dreaming's evocation of prophecy. The similarity between epilepsy and dream-like states, as presented in Ayurvedic medicine, resonates in Western culture and reassures this motifs' survival. It is the trance-like state and the alleged ability of prophecy, the ostensibly conscious moments experienced in sleep through dreaming, that are first formulated in the Ayurvedic understanding of the holistic mind-body relationship. These conceptualizations of epilepsy also appear in Plato's *Timaius* and *Phaidrus* (Temkin 6, 51), as well as in Aristotle's *On Sleep and Waking* and *On Divination and Sleep* (44, 157). The issue at stake is that the mind, during sleep, is free of mundane boundaries and thus has access to seeing the past, the present and the future.[13] This cognitive ability accessed in sleep is supported, too, in

13 Temkin refers to Aristotle's theory: "In sleep, in emotional states, or in disease, when the mind was not in control, man might be guided by what he imagined"

Jewish philosophy, namely by Moses ben Maimon who states that it is not the activity "as in a fit of epilepsy . . . [that] starts indicating the future . . ." but the ability to ". . . *focus* the power of conjecture to ascertain the future" (original emphasis Kreisel 250).

It is in this sense—through the ability to channel the rational and imaginative faculty (ibid.)—that prophets, in their superiority over philosophers, diviners, and rulers, distinguish themselves. Averroës cautiously affirms the epistemological value of sleep that mirrors Moses ben Maimon's view on epilepsy. It appears that both philosophers find the source of this epileptic ability in the individual itself and epilepsy as an expression of his uniqueness (Kreisel 393; Temkin 160). Still in the Middle Ages, Thomas Aquinas takes on a quite contrary position. He points out that epilepsy is akin to death rather than to *sleep*, thus reinforcing its etymological outline of *falling asleep* even further (Temkin 157). Besides the attributed prophetic ability of ancient figures such as the Akkadian priests of Baal, Saul, and the Sybils, the Middle Ages continue to relate the notions of ecstasy and possession to epilepsy (Detweiler 128). Another historical manifestation of the relation between prophecy and epilepsy, at least in Western culture, is rooted in Arabic tradition, where European scholars and researchers ascribed epilepsy to the prophet Muhammad, blurring the lines between ascribed possession and prophecy (Temkin 148ff.)

The notion of *sleep* and epilepsy as prophecy that is so closely related to the motif of *intelligence* takes on a decisive semantic turn in the nineteenth century. Although John Hughlings Jackson (1835-1911) identifies the "dreamy-state" by way of biochemical mechanisms, thereby attempting to dissociate the disorder from any behavioristic or psychological phenomena, the stigmata are too deeply embodied in the cultural knowledge (Temkin 316). In fact, by this era, they have been naturalized through the establishment of asylums and those respective epilepsy treatments still adhering to the ideas and texts of antiquity in which epilepsy and dream induce fear on the level of nightmares. As Temkin notes, the popular belief at that time

---

(156). And "Aristotle himself had likened the epileptic seizure to sleep, one of the conditions in which the mind failed to restrain the imaginative faculty, the Latin translation, consciously or not, remained within the sphere of Aristotelian thought. At any rate, epilepsy was acceptable as a disease that could lead to natural ecstasy marked by visions" (157).

relied on a bond between the spectacle of the epileptic fit and automatisms during sleep (190).[14] A platform from which to derive certain epilepsy-specific personality traits, such as anger and irritability, thus arises. Among the most prominent advocates are "Benedict Augustin Morel (1809-1879) and Jules Falret (1824-1902)"[15] (317), who push forward what will be known as the "epileptic character." This view on epilepsy describes one of the key aspects of the motif of *danger* which I discuss further on in this chapter.

2. THE MOTIF OF *FALLING* IN THE HISTORY OF EPILEPSY AND THE PERSISTENCE OF ITS STIGMA AT THE "LINGUISTIC LEVEL"

> "This face is an epilepsy, its wordless tongue gives out the unearthly cry
> Its veins down the neck distended, its eyes roll till they show nothing but their whites
> Its teeth grit, the palms of the hands are cut by the turn'd-in nails,
> The man falls struggling and foaming to the ground while he speculates well."
> WALT WHITMAN, "FACES"

The motif of *falling* appears cross-culturally in many variations as the most incisive characteristic of epilepsy, and it initiates a manifold nomenclature that relies on the consecutive stages of unconsciousness and consciousness (Schneble *Krankheit* 79). This nomenclature mirrors, above all, the popular mass' view on epilepsy, its folklore. In Babylonian cultures the Sumerian term "an.ta.sub.ba" implies that this disease is "what has fallen from heaven" (Stol 7) and stresses, foremost, the loss of consciousness, followed by

14 Epilepsy as automatism also appears in Sigmund Freud's "The Uncanny" (1919).

15 For further research on Morel and Falret with respect to epilepsy-related concepts such as madness and hysteria, see Michel Foucault's *Psychiatric Power. Lectures at the Collège de France, 1973-1974* (2005).

seizures and an increased saliva production. The Ayurveda qualifies the moment of *falling* as an indicator of a variation in the state of consciousness and establishes it as the key feature of their understanding of epilepsy. The term for epilepsy here is "apasmâra," a compound of the two consecutive states, "*apa*, meaning negation or loss, *smara* meaning recollection or consciousness" (Manyam 473). Hansjörg Schneble defines "apasmâra" as forgetfulness and refers to Leo Kanner who then interprets this forgetfulness as the loss of consciousness during a seizure and the loss of memory afterwards (*Krankheit* 11f.). These terms, despite slight changes in the interpretation, capture the essence of epilepsy which continues to puzzle researchers. In conceiving of epilepsy in terms of the loss of consciousness, followed by intermittent stages of and the eventual regaining of consciousness, Schneble's and Kanner's definition avoids reducing epilepsy to the seizure alone and thus works to define it as a general state of body and mind, highlighting its liminality.

Schneble's and Kanner's conception, however, has had little success in mitigating the impact that the mythological Babylonian, medical Indian and religious Hebrew and Christian interpretations have had in establishing *falling* as epilepsy's "cardinal symptom" (*Krankheit* 16). The Talmud refers to epilepsy as "nôphel," *falling down*, explicitly referring to the direction of the fall—namely to the ground—and thus adhering to the religious view of epilepsy as the ability of foresight, of receiving God's message. The message, which is received from above, overwhelms the individual through its unearthly power. Prophecy, henceforth, conjoins with *sleep* through *falling*, securing itself a firm position in the history of epilepsy. This interpretation includes, Balaam son of Beor (*Hebrew Bible*, Num. 24.3-17) and King Saul (*Hebrew Bible*, 1 Sam. 10.10, 16.15, 18.10) and accords epilepsy with a feature that continues to influence the portrayal of the Three Wise Men (*Hebrew Bible*, Ps. 72.11) and their devoted act of *falling down* before Jesus.[16] In the Middle Ages, *falling* becomes stigmatized in the New Testa-

---

16 Saint Valentin is one of the many patrons of epilepsy, but his very name refers, in particular, to the motif of *falling* as "the German word *fallen* sounded identical" (original emphasis Temkin 101).

ment when Jesus exorcises the demon out of the young boy[17] (*Krankheit* 42).

This last reoccurring notion, in particular, leads to diversified discrimination practices of people with epilepsy, a topic I discuss more thoroughly in the upcoming section on the motif of *danger*. Epilepsy as *falling down* also appears as the Arabic "ṣar'un," derived from the verb "ṣara'a" which means to throw to the ground (*Krankheit* 80). "Morbus caducus," one of the many Latin terms of epilepsy, also sustains the nomenclature of *falling*: morbus caducus, Averfall, fallender Siechtag, Fallsucht, falling sickness, falling evil (*Krankheit* 79; *Heiligen* 104). It is in this homogenous view on epilepsy that, from late antiquity throughout the Middle Ages and finally in the seventeenth and eighteenth century, leads to the fusion of epilepsy with the demonic and lunatic, insinuating the motif of *danger* (Temkin 138ff.).

17 For further information, see New Testament, Matt. 17.14-18, Mark 9.17-29, Luke 9.37-42.

3. THE MOTIF OF *DANGER* IN THE HISTORY OF EPILEPSY AND THE PERSISTENCE OF ITS STIGMA ON THE "LEVEL OF SOCIAL CONDUCT"

> "He [Ernst Jentsch] adds to this class the uncanny effect of epileptic seizures and the manifestations of insanity, because these excite in the spectator the feeling that automatic, mechanical processes are at work, concealed beneath the ordinary appearance of animation."
>
> SIGMUND FREUD, "THE UNCANNY"

The motif of *danger* takes on a leading role when it comes to the stigmatization of epilepsy, as it changes according to the respective zeitgeist.[18] It accumulates characteristics that form a canon of stereotypes, ranging from the unclean and contagious to the poor, stupid, and the mad, peaking, eventually, in the understanding of the epileptic as a threat to the genetic lineage of humankind. Analogous to these stereotypes are the discriminatory practices against the epileptic such as humiliation, exclusion, social decline, pity, segregation, criminal law enforcement, and sterilization (Friedlander 210). These practices evolved mainly around the mere sight[19] of the cramping body and the unconscious mind. Conceived of as Babylonian nightly terrors, epilepsy is rendered a malicious disease marked by severe seizures and contingent aftermaths incited by revengeful demons and prolonged by torturing nightmares which haunt the person while asleep and helpless. Here, the individuals are the disease's victims. The Assyrian term "sakkiku" emphasizes this idea of being a victim and adds the notion of dirt and uncleanliness, since another explanation for nocturnal seizures is the visit from a drowned person's ghost (Eadie and Bladin 84). The idea of epileptic

18 According to Eli S. Goldensohn, Roger J. Porter and Philip A. Schwartzkoin this can also be seen in the treatment of slaves in antiquity, being documented in *The Code of Hammurabi* (1750 B.C.) or in Plato's *Law II.* slaves whose epilepsy appears after they have been purchased can be "refunded," since they are "damaged goods" (124).

19 See Chapter I.C of this book.

individuals inflicting the disease upon themselves by sinning against the goddess of the moon and, later in history, attracting the spirit of the "unclean deaf and dumb" (Origen qtd. in Eadie and Bladin 87), thus becoming contagious themselves, fortifies this image of the 'harmful disease,' while partly blaming the individual's sinful behavior for attracting it. This commences a shift in the way people with epilepsy are perceived for centuries: the victim transforms into the malefactor, that is, into the object of emanating *danger*.

In the eighteenth century the *danger* radiating from the mere sight of an epileptic fit serves as the most prominent motif (Temkin 114ff.). This has two significant consequences. First, a movement of epilepsy imitators across Europe comes to life; these people fake epileptic fits and rely on the mesmerizing effect of this spectacle on the audience in order to rob the attracted observers (*Krankheit* 50). The exploitation of this voyeurism adds ploy and fraud to the already profound body of negative attributes. Second, it leads to segregation within the psychiatric facilities due to the fear that some inmates are too feeble, psychologically, to endure the supposedly disturbing view of a convulsing body without succumbing to epilepsy themselves. Persons with epilepsy thus come to be treated as capable of inducing a traumatic experience in the observer. This segregation and incarceration, then, replaces the ancient and medieval discriminating conduct of spitting as a means for the prevention of contagion.

From the eighteenth century up until the middle of the twentieth century, both psychiatry and psychoanalysis consolidate a pool of epilepsy stigmata, coining the concept of the "epileptic character" or "epileptic constitution" (Bladin "Historical" 97). These types characterize people with epilepsy as aggressive and strongly inclined toward irritability, feeblemindedness and compulsory sexual drives[20] (Friedlander 248). Such people require stricter law enforcement and, for children, home-schooling (242f.). The strength of this conception is evidenced in its service of the eugenicist movement which justified the compulsory sterilization of people with epi-

20 For further information on the tradition of epilepsy and sex in literature, particularly the resemblance between orgasms and seizures, see Burton Blistein's *The Design of 'The Waste Land'* (2008). Peter Maxwell Cryle's "The Aesthetics of the Spasm" (2008).

lepsy[21] on the grounds of a presupposed biologically-detectable physiognomy of people with epilepsy. The rising interest of the State in working upon these biological features is demonstrated in the establishment of colonies for people with epilepsy (264). Overtly, the tone of these tenets highlights the profitable lifestyle for people with epilepsy since special medical and social needs can finally be met. Covertly, these colonies held the firm conviction that people with epilepsy posed a natural threat to society and thereby justified their existence.

4. THE MOTIF OF *INTELLIGENCE* IN THE HISTORY OF EPILEPSY AND THE PERSISTENCE OF ITS STIGMA ON THE "COGNITIVE LEVEL"

> "It seems a fact that idiots are considerably prone to the development of epilepsy, inasmuch as epilepsy so frequently appears in conjunction with idiocy, and as the latter is a primary affection one must suppose some bond to exist between these two maladies."
> C. THEODORE EWART, M.B., ASSISTANT MEDICAL OFFICER, "EPILEPTIC COLONIES"

The history of epilepsy shows a constant oscillation between imbecility and genius. The Ayurveda initiates this view, connecting epilepsy with *intelligence*, wavering between cognitive ability and disability. The Ayurvedic lore, however, takes a definite standpoint in declaring the cause of this condition a deprivation of cognitive ability. This underlines the perception of epilepsy as a minor human condition. But it is the perspective of Plato and Aristotle that epitomizes the dichotomous conception of epileptic persons as of either lower or higher intellectual ability. While for Plato epilepsy is

21 People with epilepsy were often subject to clitoridectomy and castration. For further research see "A Dialogue with Historical Concepts of Epilepsy from the Babylonians to Hughlings Jackson: Persistent Beliefs" (2011) by Umair J. Chaudhary, John S. Duncan and Louis Lemieux.

considered a disruption of the most sacred ability of humans, namely thinking (Temkin 6f.), Aristotle stresses its similarity to sleeping and dreaming and hints toward the mind being freed from earthly distractions. Epilepsy as a marker of genius originates in the Aristotelean *Problemata Physica* (21). Hieronymus Gabucinius addresses *intelligence* as well, but as the result of possessive intervention (Chaudhary, Duncan and Lemieux 111). In spite of these voices and the affiliation of historical figures of epilepsy, such as Caesar and Napoleon Bonaparte who are commonly referred to in this context, the dominant perception of people with epilepsy as having lesser intellectual ability persists throughout the centuries. And with the eugenicist movement in the nineteenth and twentieth century, the extreme labels of "genius" and "mentally retarded" grow more acute (Lombroso 43).

5. THE MOTIF OF *RELIGIOUSNESS* IN THE HISTORY OF EPILEPSY AND THE PERSISTENCE OF ITS STIGMA ON THE *SPIRITUAL-RATIONAL* LEVEL

> ". . . such religious geniuses have often shown symptoms of nervous instability . . . ; and have frequently fallen into trances, heard voices, seen visions, and present all sorts of peculiarities which are ordinarily classed as pathological."
> WILLIAM JAMES, *THE VARIETIES OF RELIGIOUS EXPERIENCE*

The bond between epilepsy and religion is strong, contributing to the stigma of epilepsy throughout history. In alliance with the ancient term of epilepsy as a "sacred disease" or as the "disease of divination," the religious framework embodies one of the main pillars in the history of epilepsy. The subgenres of prophecy, ecstasy, divine punishment, and possession have already been discussed under the motifs of *sleep* and *falling*. In line with that, it should be noted that, in the context of epilepsy, *religiousness* refers to a person's general spirituality. *Religiousness* arises both from prophetic ecstasy and trance-like states and thus completes the holistic outline of this motif by conforming itself to the individual experience of divination. Thereby, the concept of the aura requires special consideration. As it describes precursory states of epilepsy, it is already known in Egypt as well as in India. The actual term, however, is first announced when Greek physicians in antiquity began to record and classify the different premonitory signs and subsumed them under the umbrella term 'aura.'[22]

The nature of an aura as an individualized experience withholds itself from clear categorization and thus continues to fascinate scholars today.[23] Individuals who experience this sense of forecast or religious insight are subjects of scientific interest. This interest peaks with the rise of psychiatry defining the "epileptic character" and the "intellectual aura" by Jean-Pierre Falret (1794-1870). It is within this model of the epileptic character that, alongside irritability, aggression, and madness,[24] an inclination toward an intense *religiousness* is observed. Psychiatrists begin to scrutinize "epileptics" for common denominators, *religiousness* being one of them. This model persists and stigmatizes people with epilepsy until the middle of the twentieth century. It calls for physicians like Samuel Livingston to question the imposition of certain ostensibly "epileptoid" (30) features and to reverse this biological model in favor of a behavioristic one.

With the appearance of neurotheology on the scientific stage in the twenty-first century, researchers are finally able to locate the experience of auras and thus 'religiousness' in the brain. This means that, for the first time, one of the most mystic features of epilepsy can be empirically confirmed. Hence, medicine and religion merge into one agent (Trimble 133), blurring the demarcations between belief and science. It is in these notions of neurotheology and neuropsychoanalysis that the motifs of *sleep* and *falling* find themselves conflated, affirming their role in shaping the image of people with epilepsy. The explanatory models of medical, religious and

22 The term is first used by a boy with epilepsy describing his bodily state before the seizure, saying to experience a breeze (*Krankheit* 23); this description is later coined by Galen (400 A.D.) as a medical term (Temkin 37ff.).

23 See the ILAE classification by Gastaut from 1989 and the revised version by Anne T. Berg and Ingrid E. Scheffer in "New Concepts in Classification of the Epilepsies: Entering the 21st Century" (2011).

24 Naturally, these attributions greatly vary due to a still very broad understanding of epilepsy (Bladin "Vertigo" 444).

metaphysical alignment do not contradict one another,[25] but form a unified force to attack and resolve the conundrum epilepsy evokes. *Religiousness* as a revelation, prophecy, ecstasy and imposition can now be verified, in a sense, through digital EEG.

THE FIVE LEVELS OF STIGMA PERSISTENCE

In sum, although epilepsy still challenges researchers today, what can definetly be stated is that a defined set of motifs continues to assert itself and upholds its various stigmata. To put the findings of this motif-oriented history in a nutshell, *sleep* precedes the notion of nightly terrors and initiates a correlation with epilepsy. In this manner it combines horror with life, thereby inducing fear. Its stigmatizing power thus operates on Coleman Brown's "affective" as well as an on the "emotional level." *Falling* produces the effect of discrimination and stereotyping on the "linguistic level," since it is in the nomenclature of epilepsy that the motif of the (be-)*fallen* is manifested.

Danger fortifies its influence in the cultural implementation of discriminatory conduct toward and stereotyping of persons with epilepsy: humiliation, exclusion, social declination and pity result in the image of the unclean, contagious, poor and stupid "epileptic." Incarceration, epilepsy colonies, segregation, home schooling, criminal law enforcement and sterilization evoke the image of the morally and intellectually degenerated "epileptic," a ploy and a fraud and a threat to the health of the human species. *Danger* thereby defines the level of "social conduct." Its transformative nature describes another factor strengthening its position: First, *danger* is ascribed to the condition itself, followed by the individuals' actions and sight and, finally, to their genes. With increasing invisibility *danger* remains dynamic in its ability to adapt common beliefs and stable in its discriminatory aims.

Intelligence emphasizes the binary-coded construct of epilepsy represented in the dichotomous dispositions of "genius" and "imbecile." With this introduction of intellectual dis/ability, the "cognitive level" joins the multilayered ensemble. *Religiousness* partakes in the "epileptic" concept

25 This, in fact, resembles the approach of Paracelsus, who tried to combine his understanding of epilepsy with religion and science (*Krankheit* 100ff.).

and conforms itself to this psychiatric model. It is further validated by contemporary neurology, adding the fusion of the *spiritual* and *rational* to Coleman Brown's established levels of affect, emotion, linguistics, social conduct, and cognition. In serving these areas of human existence and social interaction, the persistence of epilepsy as social stigma is safeguarded.

I.B American Literature: From Stigma to Metaphor?

The outlined history of epilepsy points to a rich corpus of literary manifestations and corresponding critical analyses of epilepsy motifs. In the American literary corpus[1] epilepsy motifs link prominent authors throughout the centuries, such as Edgar Allan Poe (1809-1849), Walt Whitman (1819-1892), Raymond Chandler (1888-1959), Thornton Wilder (1897-1975), Walker Percy (1916-1990), Ken Kesey (1935-2001), Thomas Pynchon (1937*), Stephen King (1947*), and Siri Hustvedt (1955*). A tentative approach for understanding the scant critical reception of epilepsy in literature could be its scarce psychoanalytic portrayal in history. Psychoanalysis in the nineteenth and twentieth century was much more inclined to study 'hysteria,' while neuroscience focused on epilepsy. Indeed, the rise in interest in

1 For a general overview of epilepsy in literature, see Hubertus Tellenbach's *Schwermut, Wahn und Fallsucht in der Abendländischen Dichtung* (1992), Anna Vanzan Paladin's "Epilepsy in Twentieth Century Literature" (1995), Friederike Waller's, Hans Dierk Waller's and Georg Marckmann's *Gesichter der 'Heiligen Krankheit'. Die Epilepsie in der Literatur* (2005), as well as Peter Wolf's "Descriptions of Clinical Semiology of Seizures in Literature" (2006), "Epilepsy and Catalepsy in Anglo-American Literature between Romanticism and Realism: Tennyson, Poe, Eliot and Collins" (2000), "The Epileptic Aura in Literature: Aesthetic and Philosophical Dimensions. An Essay" (2013), and "Erfahrung und Vorurteil in literarischen Epilepsiedarstellungen" (1996). Also consider the list of epilepsy motifs provided by the *Deutsches Epilepsiemuseum Kork*: <http://www.epilepsiemuseum.de/> consulted: 02/09/13, 2:15 p.m.

epilepsy parallels the rise of neuroscience in social popularity. What is even more interesting is the limited cultural disability studies' approach, since such a perspective would be most effective in grasping the underlying tensions between metaphor as literary trope and lived disability. Steffi Ehlebracht pleads for such a reading in her analysis of twentieth century German literature on epilepsy, which accounts for the capability of literary metaphor to capture human experiences in a genuine poetics (33).

To begin with, it is save to say that the state of American literature dealing with epilepsy echoes its historical motifs. Its engagement with a fragmented scientific discourse mirrors the (im)patience each explanatory model has revealed in the attempt to disentangle the Gordian knot of modern neuroscience. The analysis of epilepsy in American literature highlights the decisive role disabilities play in disguising malleable demarcations within science, literature and society alike. Both the academic reception and the actual literary corpus call for a systematization in these terms. The academic reception of literature on epilepsy requires attention in terms of identifying the various scientific fields which converge in this topic. The literary corpus mirrors in this respect the history of epilepsy and adheres to its stigmatizing motifs; it is also productive of novel literary forms yet to be systematized which can function as a foundation for theorizing epilepsy as a metaphor.

To do so, I will examine the critical reception of American epilepsy literature in terms of three primary elements: literature, medicine, and cultural (disability) studies. Literary studies' analysis concentrates on the 'epileptic' and the motif of *falling* and formulates epilepsy as metaphorical trope, while medicine presents its diagnostic features as well as rehabilitation exercises in terms of normalization practices.[2] These two areas are challenged by a cultural disability studies' perspective on life narratives and the resulting abandonment of metaphors on the one hand, and critical readings of medical and cultural narratives in cultural studies, on the other hand. The literary corpus of this thesis develops in accordance to this receptions' systematization.

2 See Chapter II.B of this book.

1. THE LITERARY RECEPTION OF EPILEPSY IN THOMAS PYNCHON AND WALKER PERCY

> "But then she wondered if the gemlike 'clues' were only some kind of compensation. To make up for her having lost the direct epileptic Word, the cry that might abolish the night."
> THOMAS PYNCHON, *THE CRYING OF LOT 49*

Douglas Fowler, Ulrich Polednischek-Veit and Peter Wolf ascertain the metaphorical potential of epilepsy in Thomas Pynchon's *The Crying of Lot 49* (1965) in the ambiguity of consciousness that marks the "epileptic"[3] moment and the motif of *falling*.[4] Fowler's two page essay sketches the idea alongside the notion of 'possessions,' which he equates with the deconstructive force of Pynchon's work (10ff.) and thereby reduces epilepsy to the historic motif disguised in a poststructuralist framework. What Fowler calls a 'possession' falls under this thesis' motif of *falling*. The doomed fate of both Oedipa Maas' task to execute the will of her former lover Pierce Inverariety and the reader's mission to detect the hidden truth hinted at throughout the text, is linked to the notion of epilepsy as in the motifs of *falling* and *danger*. The quest for truth is presented as a possession of demonic force, ill-fated from the outset. Polednischek-Veit elaborates further on this search for truth, relying on the epileptic aura as a metaphor orbiting the consciousness of *The Crying of Lot 49*'s characters on five different levels (226): The aura stands, first, for clues and insights into Oedipa Maas' stream of thought. It secondly points to her intuition, before it, thirdly, explains her search for truth which, fourthly, like the "epileptic" moment itself is fugitive (228ff.). Finally it is expressed as revelation through "the epileptic Word" (Pynchon 95).

3 See Chapter I.A of this book.

4 On the motif of *falling* as a metaphor in poetry, see Hans-Jürgen Gerigk "Der Sturz als Metapher. Über Epilepsie im Gedicht" (2000).

Wolf adds to this interpretation of Oedipa Maas' aura-revelation the notion of demise, which echoes the common presentation of the aura, within critical reception, as a precious moment of *jouissance* that resides in the revelation of truth: "In this highly complex metaphor the part of the seizure for which consciousness is lost stands for an unobtainable truth, and the aura, for the presentiment of this truth's revelation" ("Aura" 420). Both of these interpretative streams draw their inspiration, if not solely, then primarily, from Pynchon's formulation of the "epileptic Word." Polednischek-Veit also suggests that the epileptic "cry" is echoed in the title of the novel, *The Crying of Lot 49*, in order to secure the epileptic metaphor on a formal level (228ff.). While Fowler seems to have initiated this reading in calling epilepsy the "master metaphor" (10) of Pynchon's novel, the two succeeding analyses convincingly develop his assertion (Polednischek-Veit 228; "Aura" 420). Polednischek-Veit meticulous exploration of this epilepsy metaphor, as the search for an unobtainable truth, presents epilepsy as "epileptic" and thus dangerous rather than experienced, while Wolf's analysis offers, as far as possible, a biographical reading of Pynchon's work, searching for clues of the author's supposed own epilepsy ("Descriptions" 7). These readings ultimately stabilize the stigma of epilepsy instead of embracing the liminal space Pynchon opens up with the "epileptic Word."

Moving over to Robert Detweiler's "diagnostic-epistemological" analysis of Walker Percy's *The Second Coming*, it centers on the notion of *falling* and its adherent symbolism in theological, phenomenological and linguistic contexts. This novel portrays two psychologically deranged characters: Will Barrett and Allison Huger. While Will Barrett, intelligent and healthy, tries to escape from his traumatizing past, Allison Huger flees from an asylum incapable of remembering her past due to electroshock therapy. Both are prone to falling: Will falls, unexpectedly, on the golf course, while Allison seems to have a form of epilepsy. But they also 'fall in love' with each others' misfit natures. For Detweiler the characters' psychological and medical conditions makes them prone to religious experiences.[5] He argues for *falling* as the "master metaphor," to borrow Fowler's term here, since both the actual and the symbolic fall define the characters' relationships

5 Robert Detweiler is referring, in particular, to Walker Percy's essay "The Diagnostic Novel. On the Uses of Modern Fiction" (1986), where the latter analyzes his own work according to the binary of normalcy and deviance (67ff.).

with each other and with themselves. Percy, thus, transforms a formerly essentially "epileptic" moment into a *human moment* and, likewise, into a destigmatizing metaphor. However promising Detweiler's reading of Percy's novel first appears, he leaves this liminal space of interpretation and relies on the stability of the historical motif. It is the loss of control, inherent in any form of social interaction, bodily or mental alteration that persuades Detweiler to conclude that this 'human moment' makes a person prone to religious experience.

This means that the new contextualization of a former motif, *falling*, is subsumed by the manifestation of another one: *religiousness*. Leaving religion as an explanatory frame aside, what one is confronted with, in Detweiler's discussion of Percy's novel, are the experienced cracks, the felt "apocalypses," of each individuals' daily encounter with themselves and others. These encounters, their tension and resolution "precede the new self" (80) because they impress themselves upon the characters, mark them and force them to re-evaluate their conduct. Detweiler additionally endows the individuals' milieu with imbalances and stresses the necessity of shifts in life; the personally experienced apocalypse and "re-birth" of the individual takes place in every social context through communication and "reciprocal relationships" (81).

2. THE MEDICAL RECEPTION OF EMILY DICKINSON AND EDGAR ALLAN POE

> "The eyes were lifeless, and lusterless, and seemingly pupilless, and I shrank involuntarily from their glassy stare to the contemplation of the thin and shrunken lips."
> EDGAR ALLAN POE, "BERENICE"

From the perspective of the medical and rehabilitation lens, analyses range from posthumous diagnoses of canonical writers to normalization practices of epilepsy while alternating between three categories identified by Dietrich von Engelhardt as the "literary function of medicine . . . , the medical function of literature . . . , [and] the literary-formed medicine" (13)[6]. The interplay of these three categories show the mutual dependence of literature and medicine and their impact on society. The first category elicits the importance of medical history displayed in a literary text; the second relies on the gained medical insights from literary texts[7] into certain conditions; and the last takes the social resonances into consideration. The influence "medical function of literature" can be seen in the posthumous diagnoses of Emily Dickinson and Edgar Allan Poe. The physician's curiosity is triggered by these two authors' leading literary themes and their ostensibly straightforward biographies which are labeled as either "hermit"—Dickinson—or "addict"—Poe. Disguised within these diagnoses is the acknowledgment of Dickinson's and Poe's genius and, thus, the motif of *intelligence.* It is manifested in the authors' verbalization of alleged experiences of distant spiritual spheres of self-awareness, unreachable for ordinary humans: the verbalization of "extra-ordinary" spheres. This aligns with those literary analyses of Pynchon and Percy, whose readings rely on the tropes of the 'possessive,' 'auratic,' and 'destined' and center on the notion of *falling* and *danger* triggered by the desire for an unreachable truth.

When it comes to epilepsy in Dickinson, her biography leads the research. Her "many references to brain disfunction" (13), her supposedly biographical "clues" (23) as well as her constant medication and social exclusion, lead Carla S. Sonntag to equate Dickinson's elaboration of death-like states to experienced epilepsy (26). In Sonntag's words, they bear "considerable evidence that she [Dickinson] did have seizures during sleep" (25). Sonntag's hybrid posthumous diagnosis, which bears elements of a literary

6 The translations in this chapter of German texts are provided by the author of this book.

7 Dostoyevsky is the most prominent example to be named in this category (Trimble 140f.), since his work on ecstatic epilepsy has served a significant function in medical science and continues to play a central role in investigations of the threshold between spirituality, self-awareness, and medicine, attesting to William James' medical materialism (158). For the ongoing relevance of this discourse in neuroscience, see Fabienne Picard and Florian Kurth on the "Ictal Alterations of Consciousness during Ecstatic Seizures" (2014), as well as Markus Gschwind's and Fabienne Picard's "Ecstatic Epileptic Seizures: A Glimpse into the Multiple Roles of the Insula" (2016).

alignment, is replaced by Norbert Hirschhorn and Polly Longsworth's strict medical diagnosis. Their aim is to oppose Lyndall Gordon's Dickinson biography which argues, in line with Sonntag, for the poetess' epilepsy (371). As the following quote evidences, for Hirschhorn and Longsworth the ascription of a condition such as epilepsy to Dickinson is stigmatizing: "We have gone to lengths to counter yet another startling diagnosis, this time Emily Dickinson, not as a literary exercise but in effort to correct a fallacy about an iconic American poet, whose poetry and persona resist such a reductive explanation" (384).

Carl W. Bazil works in line with Sonntag by diagnosing another author-patient, another "truly American icon" (743): Edgar Allan Poe. For Bazil, both Poe's oeuvre and biography, similarly to Sonntag's Dickinson reading, represents expressed symptomatology. Bazil, however, stresses, in contrast to Sonntag, the physician's view, narrowing the readership down to a selected group of specialists capable of understanding his analysis. This hybrid approach oscillates between literary analysis, on the one hand, and the patronization of the reader ignorant to medical knowledge on the other hand:

> "These episodes are difficult to diagnose. Their gradual onset, long duration and absence of movement argue against epilepsy. Paralysis is seen in cataplexy, but attacks are usually brief and consciousness is preserved. Psychiatric diseases such as schizophrenia with catatonia or episodic intermittent explosive disorder would not be paroxysmal. Idiopathic recurring stupor is a recently described, unusual condition in which recurring periods of confusion and ataxia, lasting up to 24 hours, may be due to an excess of endogenous benzodiazepinelike substance known as endozepine." (Bazil 740)

This analysis' aesthetics resembles an anamnesis and transforms the readers into groups of patients, their affected relatives, or colleagues. Bazil assigns Poe this expertise through the author's personal experience (742).

Along with Bazil, Wolf reads in Poe a proliferation and refinement of medical knowledge. For Wolf, Poe displays an expertise in the field when he replaces epilepsy in "Berenice" (1835) with catalepsy in "The Fall of the House of Usher" (1839) and "The Premature Burial" (1844) ("Catalepsy" 288ff.). Despite Wolf's own knowledge of the field, it remains questionable as to whether Poe's stories serve as a certificate of medical knowledge rather than the coining of a literary epoch operating on the edge of the individual's psyche as anxiety inducing force, which ipso facto relies on the abolition of the superiority of a supposed ratio and thereby glimpses into the ostensibly experienced abyss of human existence. Considering, however, for a moment, that Wolf is right, and that Poe's *Tales of Imagination* reflect the author's interest and expertise in medical knowledge and, for that matter, psychological fields, we find evidence of the influence of epilepsy motifs, which were certainly perpetuated by these two disciplines in the nineteenth century. Posthumous diagnoses of authors, epilepsy being only one of many psychological conditions which attracted curiosity, tend to either reduce the literary talent to the condition, thus contributing indirectly to the motif of *intelligence*, or feel the obligation to redeem the authority of the author as a healthy artist which bears the overtone of the condition as stigma.

Poe's expertise in the medical field lures Wolf to solve unresolved cases of medical interest. Poe's literary legacy tickles the scientist's curiosity and promises insightful information into a condition still presenting one of the most prominent conundrums in neuroscience. His compositions capture in words what others merely experience and thereby appears to be a source of great value for readers of his work and physicians alike. It links Wolf's interest with the second intersection between literature and medicine which Engelhardt's identifies as: "medical function of literature" (13).[8] The medical approach appears repetitive since it invigorates the general alignment of the history of epilepsy in strictly pathological terms—as abnormal—and re-

8 The identified "literary function of medicine" works alongside the pathogenesis of an illness and equips the respective work with motifs and folkloristic portrayals; these resonate with counter-movements which also give insight into the experienced condition, depending on the work's fictional or non-fictional character. In this category American authors such as Edgar Allan Poe, Thornton Wilder, Raymond Chandler, Ken Kesey, Stephen King, and Lauren Slater can be placed, although only Slater transforms epilepsy into a literary trope. An analysis of each short story, novel, drama, or piece of poetry where epilepsy has either been used as a source of mystification (Engelhardt 13), exceeds the scope of this book, since the analysis of epilepsy in American literature would require a socio-political, philosophical, and literary framework that begins with the onset of American literature and ends in the ongoing twenty-first century.

fuses to elicit a novel approach for the formulation of epilepsy in non-conceptual terms. Moreover, it introduces the akin social perspective, Engelhardt's third category, as rehabilitation and normalization, which leads me to redefine this category from "literary-formed medicine" to a *disguised medical function of literature*.

3. NORMALIZATION AND REHABILITATION IN MICHAEL CHRICHTON AND RICHARD POLLAK

> "That was what he always said to his patients: 'We can fix you up.'"
> MICHAEL CRICHTON, *THE TERMINAL MAN*

This *disguised medical function of literature* is foremost present in Irma J. Ozer's analysis and denotes the normalization practices in the works of Michael Crichton and Richard Pollak. Ozer identifies a shift in the representation of people with epilepsy in literature and television between the 1970s to the 1990s. Her analysis examines text-immanent motifs of epilepsy which she categorizes as "evil," "genius," "saintliness," "suicidal" and "normality." They overlap with three of the motifs identified in the previous chapter as *danger, intelligence* and *religiousness*.[9] By integrating "normality" into this formation and presenting it as the desired aim of literature and society, Ozer appeals for further inclusion of the individual with epilepsy. The American author she sees as contributing to this category in particular is Michael Crichton with his novel *Terminal Man* (1972). In *Terminal Man*, the main character Harry Benson injures his head, becomes inflicted with epilepsy and transforms, thereby, into an 'evil' person. This mutation of his character is successfully reversed in a complicated surgery. The novel promotes the prime example for the motif of *danger*.[10] In spite of great outrage within the community of people with epilepsy and physicians likewise (Jones 1172; Ozer 804; Wolf "Erfahrung" 152), *Terminal Man* evoked the interest of Richard Pollak, who, having epilepsy himself, released *The Episode* in 1986 in order to counter the discrimination and stereotyping of peo-

9 See Chapter I.A of this book.

10 For further information on this matter, see Friederike Waller's notion of the "symptomatological" (34).

ple with epilepsy present in such depictions. His main character Daniel Cooper, who has epilepsy, turns from the prime suspect of a murder case into the hero that solves it.

Ozer's "genius" category includes *The Miniature Man* (1987) by Richard Muir. Muir's work strengthens Wolf's argument on the aura as a source of inspiration with the lethal allure of addiction for the main character ("Aura" 419f.). The novels of Rona Jaffe and Terry McMillan frame Ozer's analysis by integrating the person with epilepsy into the 'normal' (806) which, according to her, allows the viewer and reader to empathize with the person being portrayed since the distance between them and "the other" is diminished:

> "Prior to the 1970s, several novels or television programs portrayed individuals with epilepsy in a 'realistic' manner (e.g., the 1944 Philip Wylie novel *Night unto Night*). However, these instances represented exceptions to the rule. The new way of presenting characters with epilepsy is part of a total shift in perception of persons with both physical and mental disabilities." (Ozer 805f.)

Central to her argument are thus three U.S. American authors who capture the zeitgeist of this 'normalization': Pollak, whose personally- and politically-motivated novel equals a literary civil rights initiative, and Jaffe and McMillan, whose novels address the problems of people with epilepsy as socially excluded. Ozer's essay is a plea for the rehabilitation of the people with epilepsy and their integration into society and underscores what Jeffrey Jones delineates as the successful trajectory of epilepsy in literature as banishing the possessed to favor its medical and, thus, treatable image (1169). As physicians, Ozer and Jones experience the impact of social discrimination people with epilepsy endure on a daily basis which might explain the stress they place on normalization, integration and social aspects in their analyses.

4. THE CULTURAL (DISABILITY) STUDIES' RECEPTION OF LAUREN SLATER'S *LYING*[11]

> "You couldn't act as if you weren't having a seizure; sometimes your body told the truth, unalterable, essential, clenched."
> LAUREN SLATER, *LYING*

Among the scholars in cultural (disability) studies dealing with the literary representation and literary function of disabilities, G. Thomas Couser and Jeannette Stirling offer a starting point for tackling the preceding receptions. While Couser concentrates on the interfaces of disability and illness in literature—particularly in memoir, diary, illness and (full) life narratives[12]—Stirling dedicates an entire book to the analysis of the medical and cultural discourses on epilepsy narratives that manifest the "epileptic." Couser positions his argument from within the genre's kernel of disability as life narrative, while Stirling scrutinizes the hegemonic power of the "epileptic" that plays out Western literature. Couser's exploration concentrates on the ethical responsibility of a life narrative implied by the author to his readership. Stirling focuses on the representation of master narratives of epilepsy which stratify our cultural knowledge, the ruling and evolution of the "clinical gaze" (Foucault *Birth* 132) as well as the identification of multitudinous forms that account for a broader view on this condition.

With *Representing Epilepsy: Myth and Matter* (2010) Jeannette Stirling presents a book long awaited by scholars interested in shaking the perpetuation of epilepsy motifs and their manifestation in cultural and medical heritage. Considering that the history of epilepsy had, up until that point, been predominantly formulated by physicians, Stirling's book addresses elements of history in a new and enlightening manner which detects and retraces the concept of the "epileptic" in the medical history itself. She works to articulate the responsibility of medical science in the formation of the "epileptic," examining medical treatises as well as exceptionally prominent

11 See Chapter III.A.1 of this book.

12 G. Thomas Couser has defined these terms in his books *Memoir: An Introduction* (2012), *Recovering Bodies. Illness, Disability, and Life Narrative* (1997), and *Signifying Bodies: Disability in Contemporary Life Writing* (2009).

case studies in history. In doing so, she exposes the discourse that legitimized epilepsy treatment practices.

Turning over to the fictional work that initiated a viral discussion, Lauren Slater's mockautobiography *Lying. A Metaphorical Memoir* (2000), functions as the prime example of cultural (disability) studies' literary misrepresentation of epilepsy. Couser's[13] inner conflict while reading the novel results from his acknowledgement of the author's poetic language on the one hand, "she deploys epilepsy as a metaphor in highly creative and inventive ways" (*Signifying* 125) and her exploitation of epilepsy as a stylistic device on the other hand. For him, Slater resides in the "remystification" (113) of this condition and the reiteration of its dominant motif which disregards the implicit ethical responsibility to prevent epilepsy's stigmatization. Grounding his dismissal of the work as a life narrative on two observations, Couser supposes that "[Slater's] impulse to protect the privacy and reputation of those closest to her may have backfired in *Lying*, which fails to respect the porous boundaries between individuals—in this case, between her and the community of people with epilepsy" (120). This delicate topic concerning the ethical responsibility of an author of a life narrative toward his readership is further intensified through Slater's misguidance about her own condition. The author claims to present to the reader an overall life narrative while simultaneously questioning her own credibility and thus depriving the literary form she has chosen of its main characteristic: honesty and reliability (122).

Stirling reacts fiercely to Slater's exploitation of her readers' trust as well. For her, Slater does not qualify as an author of life narratives but, rather, as an author of "medical narrative" (221) which, in Stirling's view, resonates with a series of discriminatory practices:

"She [Slater] jerks: in literary, if not literal, spasm. She jerks us – the reader – around, playing promiscuously with our understanding of her meaning. In travelling the borderlands demarcated by the signifiers of epilepsy, she repeatedly transgresses the boundaries. Her epilepsy is simultaneously over-determined and leached of defining stability. It cannot be 'fixed.'" (226)

---

13 Special attention is given here to Couser's work since his chapter under consideration is the only cultural disability studies analysis of epilepsy in American literature that addresses the issue of epilepsy as a metaphor.

This response by Stirling echoes vividly how Couser expects the community of people with epilepsy to react to Slater's *Lying*.

Since Stirling has epilepsy herself, the reader gets the rare opportunity to dive into the epilepsy community's authentic reaction. In mirroring Slater's "epileptic" metaphor, Stirling evaluates Slater's work according to the same scientific and, thus, obsolete definition of epilepsy, anchoring voyeuristically on the fascination of the "freak."[14] The ambiguity of "jerk," "literary spams" and "promiscuous playing" thrives on the sexually-layered significations attributed to the "epileptic" of the eighteenth, nineteenth and twentieth century, which led, among other practices, toward clitoridectomy and sterilization (Chaudhary, Duncan, and Lemieux 111, Friedlander 263). The ostensibly obsessive drive to masturbate, to "jerk off" for "spasms of joy," along with the label of "promiscuous" distill the image of the "epileptic" in these centuries as indulgent and lustful.

With an expertise in neuroscience as we know it today, the birth of which took place in this very era, Stirling's critique of Slater demonstrates how easily writers can degrade their own work and how vulnerable one's work becomes in the engagement of myths. While her critique of Slater's novel is ultimately polemic, this tone is a natural consequence of the very rhetoric Stirling imitates in Slater. Her polemic reaction affirms Couser's statement on the outraged epilepsy community, given its singularity with regard to the rest of Stirling's book, which presents the cautious work of a well-researched scholar, remaining objective and confronting established systems in medical research in order to strengthen her argument. Even the theorization of irritable case studies such as those of M. P. (a pseudonym given to protect the patient's privacy) in the eighteenth century do not disturb in Stirling's scientific rationale, despite tackling sensitive topics such as over-medicalization and the experimental research of deliberately inducing seizures in patients (170ff.).

14 For more readings on the notion of the 'freak' from a disability studies perspective, see Tom Shakespeare's *Disability Wrights and Wrongs Revisited* (2014), Margrit Shildrick's *Dangerous Discourses of Disability, Subjectivity and Sexuality* (2012), as well as Rosemary Garland-Thomson's *Staring. How We Look* (2009).

In his second observation Couser deploys the literary craftsmanship of Slater's "epileptic" metaphor. He and Stirling conclude that in her deployment of epilepsy as trope, Slater actually fails to defamiliarize epilepsy and thus advocates the stable beliefs that continue to stigmatize this condition. The conflation of both researchers' argumentation at this juncture is striking. Stirling highlights the sexual deprivation innate in the "epileptic" metaphor, since in Slater's *Lying* "epilepsy functions . . . as a figurative representation of psychic fragmentation; a metaphor for maternal ambivalence; a pathologised mimesis of coitus" (233), while Couser delineates Slater's embrace of the "epileptic personality" (*Signifying* 126). Ultimately, each argue that "[Slater] can be faulted for ignoring the rights and interests of people with epilepsy, who suffer from her remystification of a condition still in the process of being demystified" (127).

In placing the person with epilepsy at the center of attention, Couser and Stirling try to disenchant this cultural tradition of *danger*. Despite its various transformations throughout the centuries, *danger* has been continuously used to either mark the condition of epilepsy, objectify the person with it, or, if in subject position be identified with it.[15] Today the cultural and medical traditions and their practices are under scrutiny, and *their* legislation and continuous influence on the social life of people with epilepsy has been identified as the *danger* from which this community suffers. Stirling's whole book redefines the question of what it is like to be an individual with epilepsy by engaging the experience of an individual with epilepsy in a society constituted by medical and cultural narratives. In the terminology of this book then, this is spelled out as: a society permeated with repetitive motifs alongside the theme of *falling asleep* symbolically define the individual as prone to any stigmata attached to the historical motifs of *falling*, *sleep*, *danger*, *religiousness*, and *intelligence*. Stirling therefore asks:

15 See Chapter I.A of this book.

"... how do we exorcise 'the epileptic' still haunting medical-cultural systems of representation? How do we show this figure the exit from the cultural circuit once and for all and begin developing narratives that engage differently with how we conceptualise, think about, understand, respond to, experience the epilepsies? It seems to me that at least some forward momentum can be achieved by ongoing robust and engaged conversations across disciplinary borders: by thoughtfully transgressing long-accepted boundaries, in the spirit of widening the terms of engagement and opening up new terrains of theory and practice." (235f.)

The claim for novel cultural narratives implies the redefinition of a culture's stigmata and its metaphors. Stirling identifies two cornerstones vital for this task: "conceptualization" and the communication of "lived individual experience": On the one hand, literature participates in what Edward Said coins as the "circuit of culture" and thereby perpetuates and hardens rigid, or stable concepts. On the other hand, it disguises possibilities for exiting or reflecting upon it (134). Metaphors comprise concepts and therefore have power to redefine rigid beliefs established in language. To engage a cultural disability studies perspective on this task means to introduce a moment of individual experience deemed pathological and/or deviant into the medical circuit in order to challenge it. To challenge it in its absolute status and to allow maturity to work on all parties involved—physicians, individuals and their milieu.[16] The literary form of disability and life narratives claims experience as its identity, avoiding metaphors exactly because of their role in perpetuating particular beliefs. An innovative literature embarks however on the opportunity to develop a new form of metaphor, enriching literature and culture reciprocally. The consensus of names urges us to focus on the conditions sustaining epilepsy metaphors outside of the objectification of a claimed medical truth and the individual as socially and culturally embedded and accepted.

In sum, the varied reception on epilepsy in American literature follows an overall medical and cultural outline which can be seen in the interplay of the three categories Engelhardt defines as the "literary function of medicine," the "medical function of literature" and the "literary-formed medicine." This focus on medicine is further underscored by the deployment of literary analysis. Medical discourse characterizes epilepsy with mystical

16 See Chapter II.B and Chapter II.C of this book.

qualities, equating it with consciousness' alleged ability to disclose truth, be it the revelation of a non-existing truth in Pynchon or the reassurance of an afterlife that allows for the apocalyptic moment to be experienced in a cathartic reciprocity between individuals in Percy. Both analyses depend on the metaphor of *falling* into and out of consciousness and thereby perpetuate harmful cultural beliefs and stigma. In medical outlines, posthumous diagnoses work alongside the motif of *intelligence*, since the extraordinary ability of certain writers, such as Poe and Dickinson, invite the medically-interested researcher to either search for a symbiotic relationship between condition, biography and talent or to vehemently erase it. In both of these cases it is the authors' text that fails to form the center of the respective analysis.

The nexus between literature and medicine accounts for a variety of features ranging from hybrid textual forms to the certification of medical knowledge and the inclusion of characters into "normalcy." Although the motifs of interest and the perspective of literary reception and medical analyses are diverse in nature, for Pynchon and Percy the analysis captures the "epileptic" and thereby stresses *danger*; with Percy it also points toward *falling* before it dives into the motif of *religiousness*. Dickinson's and Poe's posthumous diagnosis is triggered by *intelligence*. Pynchon and Percy are scrutinized from a literary perspective while Dickinson and Poe are medically stratified, each predicated on the same interpretative source: the other as extraordinary. The codependence of literature and medicine for representation urges the question of breaking this cycle that Stirling so aptly unfolds. From disability and life narratives the discussion finally tackles the importance of distinguishing between those metaphors relying on motifs that are perceived as elements intrinsically connected to epilepsy and those metaphors which include the individual. They bear the potential to "defamiliarize" (*Enforcing* 4), in Lennard J. Davis' term, or to "denaturalize" (*Extraordinary* 14), as Rosemarie Garland-Thomson puts it, and thus initiate new narratives in the medical and cultural sphere through a literary analysis of epilepsy in the age of neuroscience and disability studies alike.

I.C Ableist Metaphors: Historical Motifs and Normalcy

In the course of its history and literary reception, the analysis of epilepsy entails, on each level, common conceptual and methodological denominators which mark central aspects of disability studies. By focusing on concepts such as dis/ability, ableism, normalcy, diversity, extraordinariness, embodiment, corporeality and freak, disability studies' theories disentangle the genesis and power-relations of ideologies circumscribing and defining the body. By diving into their cultural construction and literary manifestation, this interdisciplinary field of research positions itself within the humanities and forces the rethinking of stable categories of bodily differences as dynamic, focusing on the liminal space that arises between them. Disability studies scrutinizes, thereby, the coming into being and the persistence of stigmatization and discrimination practices in our societies. But before entering this discussion, a short detour into the central outline of this academic field will be provided. By introducing its leading models—the disability-impairment distinction and the concept of normalcy—one can see the various roles disabilities, including epilepsy, play in literature. An understanding of these central issues is necessary for understanding the theorization of epilepsy metaphors in the chapter that follows.

Similar to likeminded academic fields theorizing minorities such as gender, ethnic and queer studies, disability studies develops as an academic counterpart to the earlier transnational social movements that began in San Francisco at the end of the 1950s. The most prominent one sparked off in the 1960s and 1970s and is known under the umbrella term of "Independent Living." Lennard J. Davis describes the formation of this civil rights movement in terms of two decisive identity-conceptions. The first concerns the establishment of a medically-classified diversity which leads to a separated identity-conception while the second establishes a common political lead of "People with Disabilities . . . finding diversity within the group" (*Bending* 11). This identity transformation successfully influences law at the beginning of the 1990s with the landmark decision "Americans with Disabilities Act of 1990" (ADA), which acknowledges disability as a basic human condition;

"While each of the act's five titles covers specific spheres such as employment, public services, and communications technology, the conceptual reach of the ADA goes beyond these aspects of policy to impact the most fundamental concepts in American citizenship, including independence, individualism, and public responsibility to citizens. Crucial to the passage of the ADA was the insistence that disabled Americans were not seeking so-called special treatment, but demanding foundational civil rights." (Russel 1)

The respective disability studies' academic model substantiates this political agenda through different conceptualizations and even negations of the impairment-disability distinction. Starting with the formation of the "Union of the Physically Impaired Against Segregation" (UPIAS) in 1976, the "social model of disability" is introduced next to the ruling "medical model," known also as "deficit model," or as "individual model." The medical model equates the impaired body with the disabled body, thus treating and classifying it as deviant from a bodily norm. This "social model," also referred to as the "British social model," is rooted in the clear demarcation of a physical lack, referred to as 'impairment,' and the resulting social discrimination called 'disability.'

With this shift in perspective, the role of the state and its institutions are put at stake, putting disability on the political agenda and activating civil rights initiatives. This model embodies a highly political point of view which results in better life conditions for people with disabilities. It does, however, participate in what should be challenged in the first place. Despite numerous critiques triggered by this model within disability studies, Shelly Tremain in particular rejects the model's implied affirmation of the ableist ideal of the body, since what remains crucially unchallenged and in need of further theorization is the notion of an impairment per se (618).[1] The expression "ableist" conjoins 'able' with the suffix '-ism,' thereby sensitizing the ruling socio-cultural image of the healthy, fit and productive. The impaired body is considered and treated as a given in this model without returning to the conditions underlying its ableist definition.

The "US social model" describes a similar approach. It comes to terms with the social perception of the disabled body as an impaired body that fails to fulfill the norm. Set by a statistical average applied to the human body, Davis explores how the idea of a norm entered Western society in the eighteenth century, established itself through industrialization and enforced a paradigm considered normal. The transformation of his theory on normalcy highlights the adaptability of this concept. First, the "average becomes the ideal" (*Enforcing* 32) until the ideal shifts toward the frontiers of the average again, becoming a desirable form of "edgy" (*The End* 40) or liminality. Davis describes the desire of people to achieve an exotic aesthetics that distinguishes itself from the mass, the average, the mainstream. This ideal, however, loses its power in its need to be close enough to the familiar in order to avoid signifying it as, rather than exotic, 'freakish.' It, furthermore, stresses the rule of ableism and the constant oscillation between exclusion and inclusion of un/desired deviances. Rosemary Garland-Thomsoncoins this ability-based excluding force by introducing the nomenclature of the "normate" (*Extraordinary* 8), conjoining her analysis, even more strongly than Davis does his, to Erving Goffman's stigma theory. It unravels the blurred, culturally specific ideals setting these norms and disguises the paradox of the normal as such by introducing the "normal deviant" which speaks for the general inability to satisfy the normal's tenets.

In contrast to the "US Social Model," the "realistic turn," pushed forward by Tom Shakespeare, Carol Thomas and Tobin Siebers, focuses on the notion of embodiment and argues that if the notion of impairment is negated, the fulfilling of the individual's needs becomes jeopardized:

1 See Chapter II.B of this book.

"If late twentieth-century disability studies was associated with establishing the factors that led structural, economic and cultural exclusion of people with sensory, physical and cognitive impairments, then disability studies in the current century could be seen as a time developing nuanced theoretical responses to these factors. The politicization is at the heart of these developments." (Goodley 631)

Along these lines, philosophies of embodiment, psychological considerations and social constructionist's theories enter the stage. They disclose the immanent force that the disabled body executes on central ideologies of Westernized culture, such as the body-mind dualism and the notion of normalcy. Beside the body politic, it is the notion of embodiment, in particular, that promises to mediate between political models of disability, on the one hand, and the consideration of the individual's needs, on the other (Mladenov 65; Turner 160). From this phenomenological embodiment, the focus switches to highlight the psychological reactions of vulnerability[2] and anxiety connected to and evoked by the disabled body. The disabled body's status is also explored from a "transhistorical" (Shildrick "Disabled" 757) perspective, situating the human condition outside a historic, socially-constructed norm-ideal.

With respect to the previous models, Tremain's radical constructionist approach elucidates finally the impairment-disability binary. She theorizes the seemingly unproblematic notion of impairments, represented by the "British Social Model." She also discusses the social discriminating practices comprising the "U.S. Social Model," which are based on the normal ideal that produces 'disability' and promotes 'ability.' Her argument transcends this binary by shifting social construction from the disabled body to the preceding stage, the impairment, and thereby accounting to the "realist turn" as well. Through this act she calls into question what researchers of all models claimed to have achieved so far: the denaturalization of disability. Founded on a Foucauldian analysis of bio-power and governmentality, Tremain retraces the objectification of the body to the eighteenth century and unveils the naturalization of impairment as the social construction of power and knowledge. She thereby eradicates any binary-based model of impairment/disability, normal/abnormal, healthy/pathological and presents a culturally-specific account of the discrimination of a certain group of

2 See Chapter III.C.1 of this book.

people whose bodily and mental traits were instrumentalized to satisfy power regulations:

> "As *effects* of a historically specific political discourse (namely, bio-power), impairments are materialized as universal attributes (properties) of subjects through the interaction and reiteration of rather culturally specific regulatory norms and ideals about (for example) human function and structure, competency, intelligence, and ability. As universalized attributes of subjects, furthermore, impairments are naturalized as an interior identity or essence *on which* culture acts in order to camouflage the historically contingent power relations that materialized them *as* natural... impairment has been disability all along." (original emphasis 632)

The Westernized world's acceptance of this medical objectification defines the source of discrimination against people with disabilities.[3] This medical-cultural model conceptualizes the notion of how people with disabilities are seen and, for that matter, how they are presented in literature—or, rather, how their condition functions as a platform from which to perpetuate this stable view. For this reason, metaphors play a decisive role in this literary formation.

The social construction of disability thus evokes the question of its literary correlate, gaining a first insightful theoretical twist by Heinz Ickstadt's analysis of "the creation of normalcy." Ickstadt tries to unfold the American identity and its continuous renegotiation through the concept of ordinariness that for him defines the notion of normal. In contrast to the preceding theories of normalcy, Ickstadt argues that it is in a state of continuous reinvention rather than something static and enforced (16ff.). Here, Ickstadt relies on George Canguilhem's and Jürgen Link's work, where the former relies on an individualized understanding of bodily norms and the latter emphasizes the flexibility and permeability of a society's perceived normalcy which expands in parallelism to the population's variety. Both concepts allow Ickstadt to formulate the pluralistic character and integrative function of the normal. How this creation is transformed into a creative moment can be explored by way of literature and disability studies' textualization of the corporeal.

---

3 See also Simi Linton's *Claiming Disability* (1998).

Amy Vidali, Vivian M. May and Beth A. Ferri as well as Sami Schalk strengthen this bond between literature and disability through the concept of the "ableist metaphor," i.e. these metaphors rely on the above-mentioned assumption of a universalized experience of the body as healthy, functioning, and, thus, normal. They perpetuate negative views on bodily and mental diversities and naturalize the undesirability of disability through language. Such an objectified experience of the body's pathological state remains in contrast to what these cultural disability studies scholars wish to be integrated into the metaphorical notion of disability: "experience" (Dolmage 108; May and Ferri 123; Schalk 7; Vidali 50).

This notion of this experience-based approach evolves around Susan Sontag's analysis of the destructive and controlling power of illness metaphors, such as those concerning tuberculosis and cancer in the nineteenth and twentieth century and AIDS in the twenty-first century, where an abundance of illness metaphors is supposed to make up for the lack of medical knowledge. The turn to metaphors stems from the fear of the unknown and is identified by Sontag as surrogates for this uncertainty. Metaphors stress the role of medicine in this discourse, since it is the medically-unknown and non-classifiable state which accumulates stereotypes. Tuberculosis and cancer attracted a range of contradictory stereotypes, such as "sloth, idleness, and death" (18) for cancer, and "poverty, beauty, and angelic" (35) for tuberculosis. Epilepsy not only signals a variety of metaphors, such as the historically derived motifs of *falling, sleeping, danger, intelligence* and *religiousness*, but also describes a characteristic device, namely that of being "epileptic." Sontag's theory provides an explanation for the abundance of epilepsy motifs. This cultural view on metaphors about people with epilepsy underlines the argument within disability studies about the perpetration of medical discourse against this group in order to empower the ideal of normal. With this outline in mind I shift the focus to literature and disability studies, where this power relation becomes open for new discussion.

In analyzing the functions of disability metaphors, then, we see that these metaphors indeed outreach the literary world and enter into the political dimension of normalcy. Relevant positions in this area are represented by the works of Davis, Garland-Thomson as well as Sharon Snyder and David Mitchell (Murray 247). Dealing with the normal-abnormal binary, Davis and Garland-Thomson highlight the mechanisms of the normal, while Snyder and Mitchell introduce the literary capacity of the abnormal. Both perspectives need to be seen in symbiotic relation with each other, since, in presenting the normal as a favorable identification plateau for the reader, it is simultaneously the abnormal that awakens their excitement. The coinciding elements of both perspectives initiate the investigation of a novel theoretical approach to this discussion.

Davis and Garland-Thomson highlight and criticize the ruling dominance of prejudicial representations that have been attached to disabilities in literature, while Snyder and Mitchell deploy the interrogation of a stable belief system through staging the disabled body as deviant and thus interesting (223f.). When Davis calls for a "defamiliarization" (*Enforcing* 4) of disability, he appeals to everyone to subvert the legislation of the nineteenth century novel that at its heart promotes the ruling image of the bourgeois. The disabled body is presented here as the static-other and is thus approached from a distance. Outside this particular genre, other scholars consent to approaching disability from a normal perspective which allows the reader to pity the character's fate or admire their overcoming it. Garland-Thomson commences the "gap between the representation and reality" (*Extraordinary* 12) that arises when so-called 'normate' ideas paint the picture of the disabled experience instead of concentrating on the "actual lived experience." For her

> ". . . representation often obscures these complexities [disability as fluid and diverse category] in favor of the rhetorical or symbolic potential of the prototypical disabled figure, who often functions as a lightning rod for the pity, fear, discomfort, guilt, or sense of normalcy of the reader or a more significant other." (13)

Conclusively, a representation true to the fluidity and the diversity of disability might bridge the two worlds Garland-Thomson identifies as normate and disabled.

In the rhetoric of language and literature, however, the task of transferring meaning is captured etymologically and per definition in the concept of the metaphor.[4] Snyder and Mitchell, too, interrogate stable beliefs about the body, however, by introducing the concept of the "narrative prosthesis." They discuss the respective counterpart on the disabled body in literature.

4 ". . . the Greek root of the word, *metapherein*, means 'to carry across.'" (original emphasis Dolmage 109).

The narrative prosthesis' strength lies exactly in the perceived deviant nature which challenges any era's respective norm affiliation and thereby fulfills the task of literature by attracting the reader who indulges in the extraordinary (228). In different cultural aspects the extraordinary appears as this symbol of attraction; it is the visible deformity that is staged as a 'monster' in antiquity, a 'freak' in nineteenth and twentieth-century and the congenitally, pathologically 'disabled' of today (*Extraordinary* 70; *Staring* 45; Lewiecki-Wilson and Wilson 14ff.). I thus argue that the visible applies in as much to epilepsy as the seizure fascinates and scares the beholder likewise.

Snyder's and Mitchell's theory of the "narrative prosthesis" provides the first measure outside of stigmatization to display the material strength idiosyncratic to the disabled body (222f.). Here, the disabled—and, for that matter, also epileptic—body, provides indispensable 'ruptures' to literature's ability to generate new forms. This argument elicits a crucial view of literature as such. Since, as the argument goes, literature has always been in need of a disabled body, even if it is only marginally presented, to provoke the interest of a readership, literature has always been in need of a prosthesis. By implicating literature as disabled and as a productive force, disability, in turn, turns into a productive force. This theorization of epilepsy metaphors will serve in the analysis of the literary corpus I engage in this dissertation. As Snyder and Mitchell point out, the function of narrative relies on the exceptional: "The disabled body occupies a crossroads in the age-old literary debate about the relationship of form and content" (229).

This relationship between form and content is why for Jay Dolmage poetry appears to be the most obvious genre of literature to incorporate disability metaphors, since it is through the ruptures of content and form complementing each other that poetry reaffirms and constantly reinvents its identity (109). The quintessential shift from non-stereotypical, disruptive expressions of feelings and thoughts can thus lead to a first formulation for tackling the established way of conduct from an uninformed outsider's perspective to the depiction of disability as it is experienced. The new genre of disability poetry concentrates on the materiality of "somatic experiences" (Scheuer 156) and builds up metaphors around it. It is a connection of physical perception and affection that forms poetic language captured in metaphors. Through the disclosure of the individual's felt disability it counteracts stereotypes (156ff.). Disability poetry transgresses actively metrical norms and standards (Popp 38), mimicking the impaired body that challenges "somatonormativity" (Caeton 73) and posing a central question with regard to metaphors in a cultural disability studies context: "Are we dealing with metaphors or medicine?" (ibid.). If we are dealing with both, as Caeton suggests in his elaboration on Denis Diderot, or if, as this thesis cautiously tries to propose, "[w]e are dealing with metaphors and the individual" (ibid.), then how stable or liminal, how dynamic, flexible or relational are the biological norms defining the body—as either healthy or sick, abnormal or normal—in a society?

Since the discourse evolves around somatonormativity, it is useful to focus on the individual's state in order to display the reciprocity between body and society. Poetry, although in a privileged position for introducing transgressions in form and content, does not exclusively bear this task. To understand to what extent this transgression can equally be achieved in prose, we must begin with the discussion of the power of conceptual metaphors, as formulated in George Lakoff's and Mark Johnson's cognitive linguistics.[5] At this point, the debate in disability studies becomes heated. Amy Vidali promises new approaches toward disability metaphors that disenchant the underlying "abled-bodiness" (37) that accompanies daily metaphors (Couser *Signifying* 150). Therefore,

> "[a] disability studies' approach to metaphor must engage the full range of disability; resist the desire to simply 'police' or remove disability metaphors; actively transgress disability metaphors by employing a diverse vocabulary; artistically create and historically reinterpret metaphors of disability." (Vidali 42)

Vidali and Couser receive support not only from Stuart Murray who recognizes "within such thinking that we can rework the idea of disability and writing, especially the use of metaphor" (249) but they also can be placed next to Jay Dolmage who concludes his essay by stating that "new metaphors of disability can table a new algebra of possibility. The result might be an exponentially expansive view of humanity. At the foot of this infinitive multiplication, the *author's words are just the opening stanza…*" (emphasis added, 117). Taking these quotations as a starting point, they de-

5 See Chapter II.C of this book.

mand a new approach toward disability metaphors that positions itself between mere aesthetics and political agenda.

The gist of Vidali's first claim hinges on "the full range of disability." The full range of disability alludes to the notion of disability as the embodiment of and platform for ableist power relations; it also serves as a social construct that displays, beside intrinsic power relations, the potentiality to transform. In reaction to the ongoing discrimination transferred into culture through language and vice versa, the impulse emerges to "remove" disability metaphors once and for all. May and Ferri describe this reflex as the need for a "cure" (134) of language, highlighting the arbitrariness of value signification implicit in the norm-affirming metaphors of healthy bodily states. Here, the dominant language becomes the disease in need of treatment and adjustment.

In their essay, the focus lies on the impositions of "ableist metaphors" that enforce stereotypes and accentuate "the need for more nuanced uses of language and metaphor that do not characterize people with disabilities stereotypical, and in one-dimensional ways" (May and Ferri 134). The question, nevertheless, of how "the full range of disability" and the "nuanced uses of language" can be formulated, continues to elude an answer. Dolmage highlights the reciprocity implied in a new approach toward metaphors of disability for language, prose and the individual, and argues in line with Kathrine Hayes for an enriched utilization of metaphors as tools to mediate knowledge by integrating the experience of disability into language (116). This idea is further explicated by Sami Schalk who introduces the concept of the "creative disability metaphor" (12). She argues for the oppressive power of disability metaphors in feminist writings, where the inferior party within the gender inequality debate is marked with 'disabled' features. Relying on Vidali, who discusses the denaturalization of disability metaphors through the exchange of perceptive embodiment, she acknowledges a way of introducing disability metaphors. They all however stop their elaborations at this jucture, giving thereby rise for a theorization of disability metaphors yet to come.

In sum, the preceding history of epilepsy and its literary reception allow us to see epilepsy as a disability. Epilepsy, thereby, challenges the notion of the impairment-disability binary and normalcy, alike, and bears the potential to question stable belief systems about the body and mind that circulate in society under the heading: ability as ableism. Examining literature and daily language alike, what appears crucial is the echo of this ableism in the form of metaphors. In order to challenge these stable concepts, that, with respect to epilepsy, rely on historical motifs, a new theorization of these metaphors is needed for capturing "the full range of disability." Such a theorization would provide the opportunity for the destigmatization of people with disability and, hence, epilepsy. This is where this thesis gains the motivation to formulate epilepsy metaphors that pay tribute to the complexity of metaphors as literary trope as well as to their inclination to conceptualize according to stable belief systems. Metaphors are, thus, prone to stigmatization, but looking into American literature from 1990-2015, one can see that they are capable of capturing the individual and of challenging the very binary of healthy/sick, able/disable or normal/abnormal by representing the liminal space that arises between them. In order to understand the mechanisms of these new metaphors, the following chapter will examine the spheres that have been critical to stigmatization: society, the body and everyday language.

II. Liminal Spaces of Individuation

II.A Jürgen Link and Michel Foucault: Symptomatic Signification of Proto- and Flexmetaphors

This chapter presents the first of three theoretical means for accounting for the innovative power of epilepsy metaphors. Metaphors of this first category are premised on the nexus of the clinical and the normal, pushing forward the question of 'who is normal?'. This is due to the fact that epilepsy, as a disorder, triggers the clinical, becomes visible, requires treatment, and thereby deviates from the normal. Thus, an analysis of the clinical and the normal seems inevitable when it comes to understanding the (de)stigmatizing mechanisms of epilepsy metaphors. This is even more apparent in light of the fact that clinical definitions of epilepsy proliferate as metaphors in fiction. This chapter will examine how these metaphors function, and if the clinical enforces the inference of the stigmatizing. The clinical and the normal define two concepts that, paradoxically, strengthen each other's stability. The clinical markers of epilepsy, or 'symptoms,' initiate a correlation with the normal insofar as the increase of epilepsy symptoms corresponds to its deviation from the statistical average. This normal reflects a social consciousness of the statistically-average body and mind and, thus, by means of the clinical, shields its borders from the sick and verifies itself as healthy.

The clinical perspective of epilepsy shapes society's understanding of it and is therefore pivotal to this project's theorization of epilepsy metaphors. The reciprocity between the clinical and the normal is decisive because it fathoms the demarcations of exclusion and inclusion. Epilepsy metaphors position themselves in the liminal space that arises between these two. To account for this liminal space and further specify the clinical perspective of epilepsy, I will look first to Michel Foucault's conception of symptoms and signs. I will then turn to Jürgen Link's concepts of protonormalism and flexible normalism. Protonormalism designates an impervious society that omits aberrations from its mean. It also strengthens the inner core of a society and hardens its borders. Flexible normalism, on the other hand thrives on the variety of people it can include. The combination of Foucault's physiological sign and pathological symptom with Link's two notions of normalism will set the stage for this first theorization of epilepsy metaphors. Protonormalism will refer to epilepsy as a symptom, whereas flexible normalism will underscore the innovative power of the sign. The chapter will culminate in the contrasting juxtaposition of what I come to define as *protometaphors* and *flexmetaphors.*

For Foucault, the emergence of the clinic at the beginning of the nineteenth century heralds the medical field's self-conception as positivistic and leads to a new understanding of the individual through clinical language and statistical probability. To encounter the individual through medical positivism means to analyze the individual against the most stable factor inherent to all living beings: death (*Birth* 243; *Sexuality* 20). Death and its precursory states of disorders or diseases thus become the objects of knowledge. This objectification of disorder starts with the annihilation of the sign-symptom differentiation. Before the era of the clinic, the sign accounts for the moment of recognizing an alteration in the individual. These alterations do not allude to anything other than the mere recognition of a disturbance. They remain at this level, which means for epilepsy that the cramp remains simply a cramp. The sign, however, could serve as the impetus for further diagnosis. Being open for interpretation, it defines the liminal space between disease and health, at once embodying each of these states and denying a strict affiliation with either. The symptom, nevertheless, claims to signify a disease; in this sense, the symptom accounts for knowledge. The symptom is not open for interpretation but contributes to a specific form of knowledge. It announces a new means for knowing and talking about the individual.

For Foucault, the clinic is, per se, a space of knowledge. It expresses this knowledge through language and secures its scientific value through probabilistic measures. Everything in the clinic is observed and described. The formerly liminal space of recognition disappears in favor of a simultaneity of "seeing and knowing" (*Birth* 131); the plain recognition of alteration is no longer possible. This simultaneity further manifests in the very architecture of the clinic and in the orchestration of staff and patients as through the requirements of a positivist medicine: "comparing organisms . . . , normal functioning . . . , frequency of simultaneity or succession, . . . autopsy" (114). Every perceived alteration of the individual in the clinic designates new insights into the mechanisms of disorder and death. There is no way of looking at the individual without claiming knowledge about it. This scrutinizing "clinical gaze" turns the symptom into a linguistic sign and introduces a language about individuals that explains their being in terms of their condition. These two parameters of the clinic, the dissolving distinction between open sign and closed symptom and the transformation of the closed symptom into a linguistic sign, lead to Foucault's notion of the "descriptive act":

> "It is no longer a question of giving that *by which* the disease can be recognized, but of restoring, at the level of words, a history that covers its total being. To the exhaustive presence of the disease in its symptoms corresponds the unobstructed transparency of the pathological being with the syntax of a descriptive language: a fundamental isomorphism of the structure of the disease and of the verbal form that circumscribes it. The descriptive act is, by right, a 'seizure of being' (une prise d'être), and, inversely being does not appear in symptomatic and therefore essential manifestations without offering itself to the mastery of a language that is the very speech of things." (original emphasis 116)

The difficulty of the clinic is how to avoid this "descriptive act" to turn into a wild archive of singular, unforeseeable "uncertainties" (ibid.). The term uncertainty is used by Foucault because the descriptive act captures one's personal illness history and does not provide any knowledge outside of its own being. The structure of the clinic, however, circumvents this individuality through the notion of "case." The case captures all of the *symptoms* of the individual but not the individual itself. Through a focus on the case, the clinic can accumulate different possible combinations and degrees of symptoms; it can measure the frequency of their occurrence and it can put them in relation to one another (117ff.). The fact that a case has a scientific validity because it is said to display an objective, statistical certainty is illustrated in the clinical definition of epilepsy in the year 2014:

"Conceptually, epilepsy exists after at least one unprovoked seizure, when there is high risk for another, although the actual required risk is subject to debate. After a single unprovoked seizure, risk for another one is 40-52%. With two unprovoked nonfebril seizures, the chance by 4 years of having another one is 73%, with a 95% confidence interval (CI) of 59-87%, subsequently herein portrayed as 60-90%." (Fisher 475)

This modern account of epilepsy is rooted in a statistical outline of its symptomology, characterizing epilepsy, through the probability of its occurrence, as either normal or abnormal, leading me, thus, to the second criterion for qualifying stability: normal.

In order to understand the sense of something or someone being 'normal,' Link disentangles the notions of norm, normativity, and normality from each other.[1] This etymological clarification is required to appropriately refer to the mundane usage of the word normal, which sustains Link's models of "protonormalism" and "flexible normalism." Link addresses the misconceptions that arise from the word normal, since it resonates etymologically with 'the norm' and therefore triggers the idea of a standardized means all too quickly. He wants to sensitize the reader to the misleading semantic conflation of norm with normal in order to get to the core of the latter's idiomatic usage. He states that both terms, normal and norm, "developed in two completely different directions" ("Power" 17) which led to partially blurred usages of these words, especially in the context of disability ("Flexible" 130). He identifies three semantic fields where this conflation of the normal and the norm has taken place: the rule, the demarcation of a field, and normality. The first is jurisdictive; the second specifies groups sharing a statistical threshold-value, e.g. IQ tests; and the third can be traced back to the twentieth century, where the reference to a statistical norm designates normality. The second and the third modes highlight two perspectives of the same approach—that of statistics—while the first mode is strictly distinguished from these two, since it refers, in an anthropological

1 All translations in this chapter of Jürgen Link's German texts are provided by the author of this book. In order to distinguish semantically between Lennard Davis' socio-cultural construction of "normalcy" from Jürgen Link's sociological research, the German term "Normalität" is translated as "normalism."

sense, to the means employed by a society or group for obtaining a code of law or ethical rules by which to guide life (ibid).

Link continues with a categorical distinction between 'normativity' and 'normality.' Normativity, as norm-oriented social conduct, includes laws and ethical rules. Although laws and rules are obligatory for the regulation of social life, they do not ground our understanding of the word 'normal' in its everyday sense. Norms are rules, explicit or implicit, "therefore, [they] always pre-exist (social) action" ("Power" 17). In contrast to that, normality is a Westernized concept found only in data- processing societies. Normality can only be described as "postexistent to action." This difference is crucial since normativity regulates conduct in advance while normality values it afterwards. In his account of an ahistorical notion of normality, Link identifies normal as "everydayness" ("Power" 19).[2]

What is referred to when people characterize themselves as 'normal' is the idea of such an everydayness understood as a statistical average—something that, according to Link and similar to Davis' analysis, entered the European and North American systems in the eighteenth century ("Flexible" 133; *Enforcing* 25). Link coins this specific, data-based understanding of normality "Normalismus [normalism]" ("Flexible" 133). This normalism depicts the bell-curve distribution which classifies results according to three main parameters: under average, as average, and above average. For Link, normalism influences normativity. For example, what is considered to fit into the average inclination of sexuality is mirrored in those social norms that label variance as perverse or forbidden or, in terms of mental or bodily aberration, as disabled.[3] This resulting normal-abnormal distinction is ongoing because it follows what J.V.F. Broussais introduces as the "continuity principle" in 1808 (Rolleston 405), which was

2 This notion existed prior to the data-based concept of Westernized societies but is now connected to it. Jürgen Link's theory merges ("Power" 19) with Lennard J. Davis' research, as both subscribe to an idea of normality (Link), or normalcy (Davis), in that sense. Davis sees normalcy entering society through industrialization (*Enforcing* 40), while Link distinguishes the industrial norm from both normativity and normality ("Power" 21).

3 This influence of Link's normalism is parallel with Michel Foucault's and George Canguilhem's notion of normalization, which is further explicated in the juxtaposition of social and vital norms in Chapter II.B of this book.

later on taken up by August Comte in 1828 (Canguilhem *Normal* 47). Based on this model, abnormal and normal are not two opposing extremes, but describe a possible continuity from one state to the other; they are in fluid transition. This inherent continuity between the abnormal and the normal can either be counteracted or nourished in its flexibility (Link *Crises* 106). Link formulates his two kinds of normalism in this manner as "Protonormalismus [protonormalism]" and "flexibler Normalismus [flexible normalism]" ("Flexible" 134, 135).

Link coins the term protonormalism in order to define the "first [Greek: proteron] one and half centuries of our notion of normalism" (*Crises* 106), which he traces from the beginning of the eighteenth century until the beginning of the twentieth century. What is considered normal is a narrow range of people.[4] In accordance with this first narrow group of 'normal people' or "normates" (Garland-Thomson *Extraordinary* 12), the second group encompasses everyone, who does not fit into this scheme. This group is considerably large and encompasses the majority of people. Taking the first and second characteristic of protonormalism together, the third aspect asserts rigid, non-fluid demarcations between these two groups. The narrow, small group of normal people protects itself against any variation or tendency toward the abnormal and "builds up real and massive walls against it (ranging from prisons to psychiatric facilities)" ("Flexible" 135). Considering the underlying "principle of continuity," it seems appropriate to counteract a natural smooth movement from one state to the other through actual, material walls. Grounded in the assumption that biology defines one's inclination toward criminality, this form of normalism forbids, per definition, a switching from one area to the other: success or failure in life are inevitably linked to one's body or mind.[5] One is either in- or outside of what is considered (ab)normal. Rigid borders, as in actual prisons or institutions, evoke and promote fear of the abnormal, since walls and exclusion are erected visually and actually before the eyes of the normal beholder. They create the abnormal, stigmatizing the people within this spectrum, controlling them through the illusion of normality, and requiring authority

4 What is pushed forward here is what Everett C. Hughes and later on Howard S. Becker as well as Erving Goffman identify as the ". . . upper middle class, white, male, and Protestant" (Hughes referred to in Becker 32).

5 See Chapter I.A of this book.

for their security (*Crises* 106ff.). In visual means, this distribution curve is best represented by a thin, vertically-high-rising bell-curve that almost duplicates the y-axis, ridiculing the term 'curve' and triggering the image of a singular robust skyscraper.

The opposed concept is flexible normalism. While protonormalism actively creates the abnormal and stigmatizes instantaneously, flexible normalism seeks to expand the notion of the normal according to the varieties of a society's population. In line with the principle of continuity, the demarcations between the abnormal and normal are "porös [porous]" (*Crises* 107) allowing for a transition between these two modes. To stretch the meaning of porous a bit further, one could say that the demarcation strives to dissolve itself. Link states, however, that the dissolution cannot be achieved. Two groups, in particular, continue to be treated as abnormal without any prospect of being included within the idiomatic usage normal—that is, pedophilia along with all of those prenatally-diagnosable disabilities that legitimize abortion ("Flexible" 136f.). Hence, the group of abnormal is, accordingly, small, while the group of normal is large. The normal is not understood as that which seeks to shield itself from the abnormal but, on the contrary, as that which seeks to integrate and broaden its own notion through it (*Crises* 106ff.). There is no authoritarian regime to secure the borders; instead flexible normalism follows a "hedonistic" impulse to encounter the manifold variety of individual forms of life. Flexible normalism maintains a certain stability that actively broadens the normal through its porous borders. It thereby redefines its center without abandoning it. In visual terms this distribution curve is illustrated by Link as a flat, smooth, wide curve that converges to the x-axis and resembles a horizontal line.

I will now consider the outline of Link's protonormalism and his flexible normalism alongside Foucault's observations of the clinic. Both theories can be thought together because their general outlines consider the effects of statistics on the individual from the beginning of the eighteenth century until the beginning of the twentieth century. While Foucault focuses on one specific institution of a society, Link provides a more comprehensive perspective. Foucault's lens on the clinic scrutinizes the renegotiation of the individual through death and disorder (*Birth* 243). On the one hand, by working through the descriptive act, the clinic helps to theorize the epilepsy-specific feature of the following metaphors. On the other hand, the clinic accounts for epilepsy's recognizable, stable moment. I thereby claim that Link's theory mirrors the social ability for inclusion or exclusion according to bodily variances and can thereby capture the (ab)normal moment of epilepsy. The overall analytic outline for this task is to systematize epilepsy metaphors in relation to their history, their (de)stigmatizing power, and the quality of their stability. As both Foucault and Link stress, first and foremost, the historical, rigid and stigmatizing moment, I introduce two theories of epilepsy metaphors. The concept of *protometaphors* functions as the stigmatizing, highly stable concept against which liminal space metaphors, *flexmetaphors*, can be formulated.

Protometaphors of epilepsy exert their stigmatizing power by relying on the notion of the symptom as a "linguistic sign" and as a "descriptive act." With the emergence of the clinic, the symptom as a closed system of knowledge turned into a linguistic sign. Before this shift, the symptom merely designated knowledge about a disorder. It had been stated that, in contrast to the sign, the symptom signified the disorder; it was the first marker for identification. This notion of the symptom is, per se, neither stigmatizing nor destigmatizing; it is a stable factor without any characterization of this stability. It describes, for example, the diagnosis of epilepsy through the observation of multiple seizures. This neutral quality of the symptom changes, however, with the turn of the symptom into a linguistic sign. Analogous to epilepsy, this means that, by turning into a linguistic sign, epilepsy symptoms come to form the signifier and its history comes to function as the signified. This transcription of epilepsy captures the moment when epilepsy metaphors transmit stigmatization—the moment when the symptom signifies history and restrains epilepsy to this limited notion of itself, incapable of expressing anything other than itself. And it is this isolation that characterizes the stability in terms of rigidity. The motifs of epilepsy—*sleep, falling, danger, intelligence, religiousness*—are triggered through epilepsy symptoms such as cramps and seizures. Metaphors that rely on imbecile nature, genius abilities, possessions, or foresight through the reference of cramps, seizures, or tremors are stigmatizing, resemble the clinical gaze in as much as a 'seeing' of these metaphors calls for a 'knowing.' They reinvent the mechanisms of the clinic in the text. By these means they also strengthen the perception of epilepsy in protonormalistic terms, because they engage an authoritative reading.

The symptom as "descriptive act" redefines the individual as text and designates epilepsy metaphors as ontological impetuses for what I coin the *epileptic* text. In the clinic, the individual's being is the compilation of its symptoms. This allows for two inferences. First, since everything that the individual displays or doesn't display is treated as a symptom, the individual cannot escape its disorder; it is reduced to it and transformed into a "pathological being" (*Birth* 116). Second, this pathological being becomes omniscient in its textual form. The "seeing and knowing" of the clinic is captured in the text that describes it: the case. In the case, the individual is no longer a human being, but the structured compilation of symptoms. There is no outside of this *textualized* pathological being once the individual has entered the clinic. Autopsies and cases allow for the endurance of the pathological being long after its physical death. *Protometaphors* of epilepsy that function through the symptom as a "descriptive act" transform the text into a *textualized* pathological being. These texts need to follow a certain syntax as well as a chronology that mirrors the clinical observation of epilepsy. They need to secure their ontological status through explicit clinical definitions of epilepsy but, also, through implicit ones, since everything turns into a symptom in the clinic. They, furthermore, define this ontological status as a priori through the formal superiority that positions them, although texts themselves, *before* the text. Throughout the text, this a priori position is continuously reaffirmed. The protonormalistic moment of these metaphors rests upon this ontological view of the *textualized* pathological being which does not allow for any other reading of the text than the clinical concept of epilepsy. These *protometaphors* transform the text into an *epileptic* text.

In contradistinction to *protometaphors*, *flexmetaphors* are destigmatizing through the liminal space of the open sign. Before the emergence of the clinic, the medical point-of-view distinguished between the physiological sign and pathological symptom. While the first designates a mere state of recognition, or irritation, the second expresses knowledge about a disease or disorder. As the sign is, thus, the intermediate step between health and sickness, it can refer to any noticeable alteration of the body or mind, e.g. a lesion, a cramp, a headache. What is experienced as a sign is, hence, highly distinct and varies from one individual to the other. The sign yields individual experience and allows for individuation. Through this individually-experienced body and mind, the sign marks a sphere of imprecision, indecision and uncertainty. It does not designate a scientific onset for further diagnosis, but, rather, marks a being in-between states. It is a stable moment in as much as it abides in this transitory state; it rests in the liminal space. This sign, with respect to epilepsy metaphors, allows for interpretations of epilepsy beyond the historical or the clinical. It actively outsources these moments because the historical motifs as well as the clinic rely on a specific knowledge. The sign, however, requires uncertainty, favoring the noticeable without giving in to the urge to assert or confirm a truth. The sign is stable in its uncertainty and is strenuous to sustain.

Flexmetaphors of epilepsy require the exercise of this uncertainty. Epilepsy, itself, can be said to function as an open sign on the 'everydayness' of the person, because the individual never knows if or when a seizure will occur. In order to sustain the uncertainty of everydayness, these metaphors indulge in that moment of epilepsy that is at the edge of common experience. The difficulty of recollecting one's own history in a precise linear timeline is not an exclusively epileptic experience. Shifts, blank spots and memorable encounters merge with noticeable gaps which, taken as singular incidents, appear normal but, viewed in their successive compilation, uphold the uneasiness of noticeable uncertainty. It is this everydayness of the epileptic experience that accounts for the flexible normalism of these metaphors. The liminal space of the open signs allows for epileptic experiences to exist as normal experiences and vice versa.

In sum, my first socio-historic theorization of epilepsy metaphors results in the two distinct concepts of *protometaphors* and *flexmetaphors*. While the first accounts for those metaphors that are stigmatizing and highly stable, the second denotes an innovative, destigmatizing rhetorical device that thrives on liminality. The stigmatizing and destigmatizing tendencies of these metaphors results from the overall socio-historic perspective. This perspective was chosen to account for the most common view of epilepsy and its relation to the normal as perceived everydayness. This everydayness is mirrored in the statistical tendency of a society to either include or exclude bodily and mental varieties. The notion of normal is either narrow or broad; in terms of stability, it is either rigid or flexible. A society's protonormalistic profile is often echoed in those novels that follow a clinical concept of epilepsy.

The clinical outline uses the symptoms of epilepsy to formulate metaphors which then function as a "linguistic sign" or as a "descriptive act." The linguistic sign reiterates the historical motifs and displays a hermetic knowledge of epilepsy. The descriptive act transforms the whole text into an *epileptic text*. *Protometaphors* are rigidly stable because they constantly reaffirm knowledge about epilepsy (in the linguistic sign) or reduce the individual to its symptoms (in the descriptive act). *Flexmetaphors* highlight the liminal space between the normal and abnormal because they emphasize those moments of everyday experience that are common for people with epilepsy but are also experienced by everyone else. These metaphors perform a balancing act that resonates with the sign's feature of recognition. These metaphors help to renegotiate the person with epilepsy as neither epileptic nor normal but, instead, liminal.

II.B George Canguilhem: Vital Materiality and Relational Metaphors

The previous chapter focused on epilepsy metaphors displaying a statistical stability or liminality. The underlying concept accounting for this stability or liminality is the notion of the normal as 'everydayness.' It sought to understand under what conditions or terms people consider themselves 'normal.' In this chapter, however, instead of asking 'who is normal?' George Canguilhem's theory of the normal and the pathological will allow us to focus on the question of 'what is the normal?'. In direct opposition, these two questions mark a radical shift concerning the theorization of epilepsy metaphors because they restate the perspectives on the central concepts of stability and liminal space. While Link's question relies on a social view that constitutes a notion of a shared 'everydayness,' Canguilhem's inquiry describes a principle that actively transgresses comparison because it emphasizes the individuality of each body. With this theory, the notion of the normal becomes a principle of life, which expresses itself in each body, manifesting individuality through the body's own specific materiality. The central issues of stability and liminality correlate with this shift insofar as they no longer describe the rigidity or flexibility of a group's exclusive or inclusive practices but, rather, emphasize the individuals' relations to themselves and their surroundings, becoming *relational* in that sense.

Stability, thus, changes from a parameter that organizes a society's predisposition to a means that describes individuals—stabilizing, however, from within one's own body, arguing for alterity (Ingold and Pállson). In line with this shift in stability, the character of liminal space changes. Liminal space as transitional space between abnormal and normal people is absent in Link's protonormalism[1] and strengthens, therefore, stability's firmness; it pushes forward discrimination practices. This means that people are bound to be either inside or outside of the normal spectrum. With Canguilhem, however, the focus switches to the single organism and reformulates the stable and the liminal accordingly. I argue that while epilepsy would remain a disorder in this theory, it gains new meaning with each novel metaphor that is formed. The stable, the recognizable, is linked to epilepsy and becomes *relational* insofar as it simultaneously cuts off its historical and clinical heritage. It is in this break with tradition that the liminal develops between the individual and its surrounding and initiates novel epilepsy metaphors. Each body highlights the uniqueness of the individual and, thus, the uniqueness of the metaphor.

In order to theorize *relational metaphors* of epilepsy, this chapter derives the notion of the individual through the concepts of norm, normativity, pain, and patient as introduced by French philosopher and physician George Canguilhem (1904-1955). Seen as a principle of vital materiality, Canguilhem's notion of the individual is echoed in recent explications of brain plasticity and the immune system.[2] In order to understand what *relational* epilepsy metaphors are, and how they differ from *flexmetaphors*, one needs to answer the previously posed question as to what constitutes 'normal.' To do so, we will concentrate on Canguilhem's understanding of vital norms. The notion of norms lies at the heart of Canguilhem's theory and is key for the identification of epilepsy metaphors. I argue that the identification of norms goes along with 'the stable,' the recognizable feature of epilepsy metaphors. Their *relational,* non-discriminating feature becomes apparent and graspable through the dynamic force in Canguilhem's theory, which describes the alternating process of these norms: normativity. The

1 See Chapter II.A of this book.

2 On how George Canguilhem's notion of normativity enters current medical discourses, see Claude Debru's "The Concept of Normativity from Philosophy to Medicine" (2011) and Amin T. Turki's "On the Normativity of the Immune System" (2011). For Canguilhem's resonances with (neurological) plasticity, see Sebastian Rand on "Organism, Normativity, Plasticity: Canguilhem, Kant, Malabou" (2011). For Canguilhem's impact on current anthropological and ethnological debates, see Tim Ingold's and Gísli Pállson's *Biosocial Becoming* (2013).

importance, too, of theorizing the two concepts of pain and patient lies in Canguilhem's acknowledgement of the individual's experience with a disorder or disease.

To understand Canghuilhem's concept of norms one needs to keep the question of 'what is the normal?' in mind. First and foremost, norms are, for Canguilhem, temporarily stable conditions in an alternating, successive process. They are, in this sense, the organism in homeostasis and display its exposition and relation to its milieu. These homeostases are not stable in relation to a statistical average or an ideal outside of the organism but, rather, stable in and of themselves and capable of incorporating as well as influencing the variations imposed on them by their milieu. Put differently, norms emphasize the relational materiality of the body to itself and its milieu through its ability to sufficiently stabilize itself. Biological, vital norms explain and justify the variety of the living and contribute, therefore, to a new understanding of the normal as original. In contrast to Link's consideration of the normal as average or everydayness, the guiding question of this chapter—what is the normal?—considered via Canguilhem, begins with this concept of vital norms:

> ". . . we think that the concepts of norm and average must be considered as two different concepts: it seems vain to try to reduce them to one by wiping out the originality of the first. It seems to us that physiology has better to do than to search for an objective definition of the normal, and that is to recognize the original normative character of life. The true role of physiology, of sufficient importance and difficulty, would then be to determine exactly the content of the norms to which life has succeeded in fixing itself without prejudicing the possibility or impossibility of eventually correcting these norms." (*Normal* 177f.)

For Canguilhem each living organism has its own norm and acquires norms throughout life through aging, diseases, accidents, social relations, geographical position and psychosomatic effects. All of these define those states of an organism as before, in, and after crisis, each describing a norm for itself different from the one preceding and the one following. With relation to our topic at hand, a person with epilepsy exposes visibly, to a certain degree, these different norms, since a person walking is obviously different from one convulsing or recovering. This process of obtaining norms precludes a reversal to a former state. Each attack, be it major or minor, initiates a new norm for this particular organism: an alteration has taken place. The terms "cure" and "rehabilitation" are, hence, concepts Canguilhem actively tackles and discloses as medical Gordian knots. This contributes to his critique of medicine as a science of health since medicine strives toward an outcome which is not, in itself, obtainable: complete recovery to a healthy state. For Canguilhem, the exchange of one norm for another leads to a novel norm, never the recourse to a previous one; "biological innocence" can therefore never be restored (228). For Canguilhem no/body is biologically innocent.

How does this strictly material view of the body relate to society then? Canguilhem draws, at the end of his research, a sharp line between "vital" and "social norms" (Muhle 1ff.). Firstly, the apposition of both terms, emphasizing their antonymic relationship, assists us in understanding the innovative meaning of the concept of 'normal' that Canguilhem introduces with his biological, vital norms. Secondly, it pays tribute to the materiality of a body as well as to its social construction. A person with epilepsy convulses and might suffer pain in the aftermath of the event including social exclusion. For Canguilhem, a convulsing body as well as a society's regulatory mechanisms for dealing with it, describe two moments worthy of separate analysis. While vital norms are immanent, not deliberate or calculated, in an organism and, therefore, refer only to a particular individual organism, social norms are applied, learned, and enforced—from the outside—by society (*New Reflections* 238ff.). Vital norms generate new modes of the living while social norms naturalize politically dictated conduct. Accordingly, social norms unify, whereas biological norms imply multiplicities. It is the juxtaposition of a generalization and a regulation according to a statistical mean against individuality and quality that is of importance here. Biological, or vital norms do not display any sort of political agenda but describe the organism's relations to its surroundings and itself.[3] This means, they refer to the organism's holistic function, where organs and cells are in a constant communication with each other and stabilize themselves after crisis. Contrary to that, social organizations are not content with their given

3 In contrast to a Darwinist position based on either duration or selection, Canguilhem focuses on the moment of mutation which anchors in the normativity of the body that introduces novel forms of itself through the relational materiality toward its environment (*New Reflections* 263).

amount of 'state-organs' but reinvent new modes to sustain normalization (*New Reflections* 247ff.).

Canguilhem thus implies a new concept of ability and disability through individually stable conditions where neither the labeled abled nor disabled body is marked as healthy, impaired or sufficient, insufficient but rather displays a vital norm. It is this momentum toward self-stabilization, that vital norms account for the variety and singularity of each body, placing each next to the other without comparison. Each body differs in regard to the variety of milieus in which it can stabilize itself. This is where all socially-labeled disabilities—vital norms for Canguilhem—are juxtaposed with the so-called abled/normal. It is here that a society, in shaping the milieu through e.g. architecture, prefers some vital norms over others, depending on the discourses of a time. Within their very structure, vital norms do not embody a "judgment of value," but they all serve as a platform to mirror "our image of the world" (*Normal* 179). The impact of social norms on vital norms suggests a natural hierarchy of bodies, making social and vital norms indistinguishable. This hierarchy is not, however, immanent in vital norms per se and a disentanglement of both social and norms is pivotal for my argument. From the concept of vital norms Canguilhem manages to derive a notion of the normal that includes everyone and simultaneously accounts for the individual in pain or distress.

Hence, vital and social norms meet at the level of bio-power, where social norms are explicitly set to regulate vital norms. This is where the nexus of teacher's and student's research, George Canguilhem and Michel Foucault, becomes visible. Canguilhem retraces the normalization practices of language through grammar and health through sanitation, as they evolved in France as "normalization" practices at the beginning of the seventeenth century (*New Reflections* 244f.). Foucault aligns with this thinking, as shown in his treatises on the construction and resulting incarceration of madness (*Madness*), in the establishment of a clinical diagnosis (*Birth*) and in the discourses that prevailed on sexuality in the nineteenth century (*Sexuality*). Social norms, both Foucault and Canguilhem agree, regulate according to economic and juridical state interest (*New Reflections* 246) and manifest and distribute power based on an orchestration of "economy, pedagogy, medicine, and justice" (*Sexuality* 33). In a nutshell, social norms cause normalization practices whereas vital norms lead to normativity.

Normativity, or rather biological normativity, the force of the living to move from one vital norm to the other, describes a principle of life. In the terminology of this thesis, normativity defines the liminal space between two norms. Biological normativity defines a principle of the living that relies on the concept of "life [as a] dynamic polarity" (*Normal* 205), oscillating between the two states of physical health and sickness. In this conception,

> "[normativity] would not express a specific stable equilibrium but rather the unstable equilibrium of nearly equal norms and forms of life temporarily brought together. Instead of considering a specific type as being really stable because it presents characteristics devoid of any incompatibility, it could be considered as being apparently stable because it has temporarily succeeded in reconciling opposing demands by means of a set of compensation." (162)

Although "biological innocence," total recovery or cure, is not possible during sickness, surgery, or any other significantly incisive alteration of the body, normativity endures as a principle of the living within the organism. This means that the organism can still obtain future norms. For people with epilepsy, the aftermath of a severe seizure establishes a new norm (capable of preventing them from again exposing themselves to epilepsy-triggering situations), a severe seizure might, nevertheless, also have everlasting physiological or psychological effects. For Canguilhem, however, this does not mean that the person is vitally incapable or impaired from pursuing his or her life. For Canguilhem even the term 'impairment,' for this describes the physical difference without the social label of disability, is obsolete. Bodies are not impaired but rather individually-normative, alive. It is in adaptation to manifold milieus that differentiation in the sustainability of a body can be detected. This notion of 'absolute health,' measured alongside the resistance and adaptability of the body to all influences, is a chimera because the restriction to certain milieus is common to every organism.

It is through pain, however, that the notion of the pathological enters the normal and simultaneously differentiates it from the physiological and tackles the validity of the clinic in its positivistic outline.[4] First of all, Canguilhem restates and defines the role of the pathological and the physiological in relation to pain by way of René Leriche and Immanuel Kant (*New Reflections* 233f.). As Canguilhem puts it, Leriche's investigations are a "theory of pain" (*Normal* 97) that unfold according to four parameters. First, while in pain, the body's individual parts gain attention because they hurt. Secondly, through this pain, the role of the physician undergoes a slight but important shift: the purpose of the physician is now to sooth pain and not, as the word "physician" implies, to serve as a scientist of health. Thirdly, the individual in pain gains a voice in its initiation and/or termination of the treatment. Finally, the notion of the normal is enriched because it implies pain. Physiology, as the science of the healthy working body, the silent body, relies on the body's disturbances in order to understand its mechanisms.

A silent body is, thus, not a body of scientific interest, because no knowledge can be extracted from it. The body in pain speaks, which logically deprives physiology of its raison d'être and establishes pathology as intrinsically linked to the individual which experiences pain and distress. It legitimizes and reinforces the physician's proficiency in accordance with the specific pain and patient—that is to say, not in accordance with a statistical means descriptive of the physiological average. The pathological is located within the patients who consider themselves sick and thereby do not serve a clinical definition. The normal is thus subjective through its normativity which describes the continuous reestablishment of relational stability—that is, new norms—between individual organism and its milieu. This means that no one can be dismissed objectively based on either statistical standards or empirical data. It is the patient's voice, rather than their reduction to visible symptoms, that secures their integrity, regardless of whether or not their pain adheres to a particular schema or is professionally expressible.[5]

4 See Chapter II.A of this book.

5 The "*over-all structure of the expressible*" (original emphasis *Birth* 140) denotes the operating, dissecting mode of the clinical gaze that scans the body for symptoms which it thereby invents through naming. It is a reduction to the visible and

Canguilhem thereby emphasizes the power of the patient. The patient initiates and terminates the doctor-patient relationship, not the doctor (*Normal* 226). The patient is not in the position of a supplicant but affirms the position of the doctor, if not to say of medicine as such. To put it in the terminology of Canguilhem, it is the pathological that sets the parameters for the physiological entrance into science. Finally, the notion of the normal is enriched through a deconstruction of health. Health manifests itself in the absence of pain, which means it cannot be actively felt through the body but can, only in hindsight, if in pain, be remembered in its past perceptive silence. Furthermore, while health refers to the ability of the body to recover from sickness, the experience of sickness precludes an identification with health. The alteration of pathological states and new norms thus defines the scope of the normal, whereas health is considered a privilege:

> "What characterizes health is the possibility of transcending the norm, which defines the momentary normal, the possibility of infractions of the habitual norm and instituting new norms in new situations . . . . To be in good health means being able to fall sick and recover, it is a biological luxury." (196, 199)

Taking these findings into account, one can formulate *relational metaphors* on behalf of Canguilhem's concepts. It is through the notion of vital norms that epilepsy metaphors—or any disability—can work on the ground of a conceptual moment, which is defined by stability. Vital norms also have the possibility of attributing new meaning to epilepsy, since the stability is of momentary and not permanent character, taking on individual meaning through the liminal as *relational*. They open up the space to "artistically create" (Vidali 42)[6] new means of approach to epilepsy through their strict demarcation between and active transgression of social norms. Epilepsy metaphors which do not reiterate social normalization processes but capture novel moments of life—since vital norms are the essence of the living and therefore carry with them a multiplicity of readings—function as the basis

an exclusion of the invisible, elevating the medically-scientific reading over the patient's individual experience through specialized terminology which demarcates the space of the physician in contrast to that of the patient. During this process the patients lose their sovereignty and integrity.

6 See Chapter I.C of this book.

for a renegotiation of epilepsy metaphors that neither reiterate history nor enforce the clinic. They can do that because what accounts for historical and social influence is not part of the concept of vital norms. Furthermore, to view epilepsy as a basis for metaphors through the principle of normativity repudiates the idea of a restriction that is innate to the notion of impairments or limitation. Rather, epilepsy metaphors of this type describe the modes of living as coining their own "perspective and pragmatic experience"[7] (*Knowledge* 112). This "pragmatic experience" captures all modes of the living, be they in pain or in delight. In this sense, epilepsy metaphors, or any other disability metaphors, are simply metaphors of life that express a temporary stability that can focus on, but do not have to restrict themselves to the notion of pain. Alongside the concepts of norm, normativity, *silent* and *speaking organs* and the patient, epilepsy metaphors find a theoretical corpus that strengthen individuation through liminal spaces.

The fact that Canguilhem believes that vital norms incorporate "originality" secures, on the one hand, the feature of stability and, on the other hand, as I argue, allows for the introduction of creativity and multiplicity into epilepsy metaphors. One can say that Canguilhem's vital norms display stability since they mark a homeostasis, however temporary this stable organic situation might be, and thereby also mark the necessary, recognizable moment for the theorization of epilepsy metaphors. Vital norms thus emphasize the origin of the metaphor's topic, which is here epilepsy. Alongside the concept of vital norms epilepsy metaphors emerge. They can only be formed if epilepsy is explicitly spelled out and is additionally incorporated by the main character—as the main organism. It requires the main character[8]—and not any other minor one—because of the vital norm's

7 Canguilhem's notion of the "milieu" is preceded by Maurice Merleau-Ponty's phenomenology and the active participation one exercises in extracting and shaping it (Günzel and Windgätter 590f.). This focus on and reading of the milieu is later echoed in Gilles Deleuze's reference while describing the tick (Bardin 2 Footnote 8) as well as in Gilbert Simondon's *On the Mode of Existence of Techinical Objects* (1958). It responds to the question of the active participation of humans in shaping their direct surroundings in so far as they are living beings with needs among others and participate in their environment (*Knowledge* 112ff.).

8 See Chapter I.C of this book.

feature of relational reciprocity between the organism and its surrounding. Only if a constant exchange between the organism and the surrounding is taken into account, one can one identify an acquired bodily norm. In narratological terms, this continuity of relationality is a characteristic of protagonists, for they are the ones whose relational exchange with their milieu leads to action. Only if epilepsy is present and linked to the main character can it mark the character's vital norm and thus serve as a basis for a *relational metaphor*.

How, then, can this explicitly-articulated and foregrounded disorder work on destigmatizing terms? The answer lies again at the heart of what Canguilhem understands vital norms to be: original. They stress a personal, immediate, unique experience of one's body, thus introducing an individual notion of a material normal that is not objectively described or, for that matter, articulated through adaptations or deviations from a statistical or perceived average. The term 'original' highlights both the stable as well as the creative reading. It is within the organism itself that both meanings of 'originality,' the source/invariant and the creative/variant appear.[9] In that manner, main characters with epilepsy who actively own epilepsy as an experience to relate to their surroundings and allow these surroundings to shape themselves, in turn, transgress any historical characterization and thus categorization. They establish an original account of the world through their individual bodily experience of it.

With this link to the main character, multiplicity enters this theorization of *relational metaphors*. With every new experience of epilepsy a main character has, without relying on a historical set of features, the multiplicity of vital norms and, thus, the very argument of an individuality of bodies, becomes evident. The multiplicity thrives with the increase of epileptic protagonists. For each individually, non-historic metaphor of epilepsy the destigmatization strengthens. Furthermore, epilepsy turns into a metaphor for life through these protagonists as it serves as the material grid that filters their experience and guides their actions. From this perspective, epilepsy remains a sudden uncontrollable outburst of electrical discharge, though its meaning for the individuals is not prescribed or imprinted in their biology through history but affects their surroundings as much as it affects them-

9 For the notion of "(in)variant" see Hanjo Berressem's *Eigenvalue [Eigenwert]. A Philological History* (forthcoming).

selves. It initiates an orientation toward the world that is *epilepsy*, and as such, individual life. The three novels I will examine, which set the ground for this theorization, denote epilepsy as a form of compassion,[10] archive[11] or communication[12]—three moments that clearly counteract the historical and help the characters in question to individuate through epilepsy. Epilepsy metaphors denote, in this first feature of vital norms, stability through the disorder by being the recognizable feature. They also display relationality which unfolds alongside the protagonist's development, thus securing creativity through multiplicity.

Since vital norms put stress on stability, normativity denotes the vital movement that explains how these homeostases are achieved. In Canguilhem's words, it is the necessary principle that makes the organisms "unstable . . . [or] apparently stable" (*Normal* 162). In addition to this formulation, the explanation that this principle captures the in-between state that emerges between health and sickness, or "life [as] dynamic polarity" (205), makes parallel the notion of normativity to that of liminality. The two poles of health and sickness mark the negotiating range. Normativity, within my theorization of epilepsy metaphors, explains how the stable factor of a disorder gains new meaning for the individual and thus transcends a reductive reading. It describes the progress from epilepsy, as a disorder, to epilepsy as the individual character's own life experience. While in each of the three texts epilepsy is first presented as a disorder of social exclusion, it successively enters the individual character's mindset as a particular, unique form of being oneself without any glorification or euphemism. Through the notion of normativity, epilepsy metaphors, although initiated by the protagonist's physical condition, persist throughout the narrative. The narrative becomes *relational* because it helps to retrace and detect those moments in the novel that are of importance for the individuation of the character.

Epilepsy becomes even more evident as a *relational metaphor* when considering the 'epileptic cry' and what was referred to as the *organ in sound.* In this formulation these two concept describe "[d]iseases [as] new ways of life" (100). Canguilhem's notion of disease radically emphasizes the individuality of one's own bodily experience, as there is no overall no-

10 See Chapter III.B.1 of this book.

11 See Chapter III.B.2 of this book.

12 See Chapter III.B.3 of this book.

tion of health but only individual physical judgment. This is even more so true since it refers to the individual's unique inner materiality, its organs. Pain, thus, becomes a way of communication, of organic language. One's own organic language of pain is highly individual. This sound is, however, silent for others and only audible for oneself—another factor that stresses individuality. In addition to that, the notion of ability again becomes obsolete from the perspective of this theory, since the notion of an impairment is not at stake with the silence of the organs and vice versa. *Organs in sound* do not automatically imply impairment; it is, rather, a focus on pain that can be seen as a moment of individuation. Pain turns into the vital moment as it denotes the sounding, speaking organ. For epilepsy metaphors the *organ in sound* thus denotes a shift in perspective.

While the individual is still in communication with its body during the preliminary stages of auras, vertigos or any other private language, it loses this ability at the beginning of the seizure, when the body turns into sound. The 'epileptic cry' is the moment where the individual's inner, material language with itself turns outward, toward the surrounding, when the body as a body takes over to communicate with its milieu. The mere body becomes hearable for others. After the seizure the sound is again turned inward, defining the painful aftermath of the recovery stage. The fact that with epilepsy the intensity of electrical brain activity causes this *organ language* with the world, it elevates electricity from a physical phenomenon into a social conduct. *Relational metaphors* describe, due to the 'epileptic cry,' a vital materiality and rely on this *organ in sound* in order to introduce a new, *electric way of life*. And in this same manner "[d]iseases are new ways of life." It is not a euphemism on disease. It merely brings disease and pain into the spectrum of the normal, which, at its core, works upon the normativity of a body that searches to restore a temporary stability in relation to the milieu which, eventually, can include pain.

This theory of pain offers another aspect worthy of consideration with regard to epilepsy metaphors—that is, the redistribution of power in the doctor-patient relationship which incites a challenge of social norms on bodily alteration. It is an alteration that condenses the theorization of epilepsy metaphors as it has thus far been explicated because of the implied importance of the individual. As patients initiate and terminate the relationship with their physician, they turn into the owner of their pathological and physiological state, suggesting that they are the ones who ultimately identify and articulate their degree of physical well-being. A physician works in an assisting manner to meet the patient's needs. This assistance does not mean that it restores a former state of health or 'cures' the patient, but, rather, that it supports the patient's normativity. Thus, it is the individual that serves as the nexus of all four concepts—norm, normativity, pain, patient. Main characters with epilepsy who experience their relation to their surrounding through epilepsy become mature; they liberate themselves from an enforced ideal of the normal, since they express themselves through their normativity, and abandon the historical and clinical burden.

With respect to epilepsy metaphors and the multiplicity of its new possible readings, the maturity of the main character is pivotal for individuation. It describes an individuation that neither excludes pain or suffering nor prefers it over well-being, but incorporates it as a new orientation toward the world that favors experience over objective validity and accepts the progress of normativity. It is in this sense that *relational metaphors* of epilepsy demarcate individuation between health and pathology—describing the liminal space between norms—as they are experienced through the body and as a social being. The redirection of objective physiology, embodied by the physician, and individual pathology coupled to the *patient* lies at the heart of this new emphasis on the main character.

In sum, Canguilhem provides a theoretical means for introducing the individual as in normal relation to itself. The notion of vital norm is to be strictly distinguished from its social counterpart since they are epistemologically distinct. While social norms are sociologically and politically allied, vital norms reveal an ontogenetic principle of life that becomes visible through biology. For Canguilhem, the conflation of social and vital norms results in the given domination of the social over the vital and allows for the emergence of normalization practices that lead to discriminations and stigmatizations. Through this clear epistemological demarcation, Canguilhem never enters the impairment-dis/ability distinction but discusses the normal as the general alterity of bodies. In doing so, Canguilhem's concept of 'normal' encompasses the notion of pain, deconstructs the concept of health, and reestablishes the doctor-patient relationship. His principle of life, of normativity, stabilizes itself in successive homeostases. Life is an "unstable equilibrium" that is made in and out of balance through the individual's experience and relation to the world. This relational normativity reinterprets the individual's milieu not in terms of its restrictions and limitations but in terms of the influence it exercises on, as well as in its receptivity to, its milieu.

With respect to epilepsy metaphors, the theorization of *relational metaphors* put forward in this chapter defines stability and liminal space through the vital materiality of the body. The concept of norm, which is an original if not creative force for Canguilhem, denotes singular, acquired, stable conditions that bodies acquire by living in the world. Monitoring an epileptic main character and delineating his stable conditions as well as his alterations demarcates the process of individuation in epilepsy, because it is the main character whose homodiegetic narrative leads the level of action. The multiplicity of protagonists with epilepsy who individuate according to their own normative disposition, always asserting the body as a mediator between the individuals and their milieu, counteracts discrimination because the *relational* is individual. This individuality is echoed in the doctor-patient relationship which, in narrative terms, helps to explain how epilepsy can be experienced. At this level of mediation 'the epileptic cry' turns into a decisive moment for capturing how the materiality of the body prompts consideration of how *organs in sound* trigger an *electric way of life* that enters the narrative. The leading question of 'who is normal?' in *proto-* and *flexmetaphors* pinned the normal down to a common 'everydayness' of experience, while Cangiulhem's underlying question of 'what is the normal?' requires to focus on the organic life principle and thereby argues for an elevation of individuals who establish their own way of normal through their uniqueness.

II.C Gilbert Simondon: Transindividual Metastability and Conceptual Metaphors

This chapter forms the last of three approaches for theorizing epilepsy as a metaphor. The preceding two methodologies employ different angles for addressing the question of the normal, and this chapter, likewise, introduces another methodological point-of-view. Considering Link's examination of the (normal) *flexible* society and Canguilhem's scrutiny of the (normal) *relational* body, a fresh look on the area of daily, idiomatic (normal) language is now of interest. It promises to further survey the vast field opened up by Vidali when she called for metaphors to embrace the "full range of disability."[1] Examining the field of daily language, it bears a cultural value of displaying belief systems that form the decisive moments for the following theorization: stability and liminality. Since stability defines the critical moment of a possible naturalization of discrimination, a closer look into George Lakoff's and Mark Johnson's theory will aid in the analysis of the ostensible rigidity of "conceptual metaphors." The ongoing dispute within cultural disability studies concerning these conceptual metaphors lies at the very heart of this thesis and calls for a short description of the problem as well as a tentatively proposed solution.

After this short detour and in line with this theoretical foundation of cognitive linguistics, French philosopher Gilbert Simondon's notion of "metastability" and "transindividuality" will serve to theorize the quality of stability as well as its required liminal space. These concepts will help to anchor individuation within daily communication. On this basis, epilepsy

1 See Chapter I.C of this book.

metaphors appear to be as much a vital part of daily communication as they reflect and partake in the coming-into-being of the individual. The core of this cognitive-linguistic approach, together with metastability as ontogenetic principle of individuation, will lead to the proposal for thinking epilepsy as a conceptual metaphor because both share common ground in the "event structure." That means looking at those words of daily communication and their respective implications that range outside of the explicitly spelled-out epileptic[2] and, instead, shifting toward those moments and words of 'tremble, spasm, buckling, dimming, awakening etc.' that correspond to epilepsy as well as to other forms of experiences, thus creating a bond of mutual experience through being in the world. In that sense, epilepsy functions as a conceptual metaphor of daily communication that will be referred to as: EPILEPSY IS METASTABILITY[3].

The general statement of Lakoff's and Johnson's theory stresses that we think metaphorically and never outside of metaphors. Metaphors cannot, thereby, be reduced to a stylistic means with persuasive power, as the tradition starting from Aristotle does (Johnson "Philosophy" 310).[4] Considering

---

2 The explicitly spelled out epileptic condition is central to the theorization and formation of epilepsy metaphors in Chapter II.B of this book.

3 This capitalization follows George Lakoff's and Mark Johnson's style in identifying conceptual metaphors.

4 This first formulation of metaphors within Western thinking establishes one of the general modes of metaphors to be identified with the "correspondence theory of truth" which states that "the truth bearing capacity of language corresponds to valid a perception and cognition of the external world. The theory assumes that these sets of correspondences allow for the consistent and reliable relation of references between words, images, and objects" (Cazeaux 1f.). This forms the basis for philosophers such as Paul Ricoeur, Jacques Derrida, and Martin Heidegger to dispute over the respective ontological status of metaphors (Theodorou n. pag.). From a pathological linguistics' point of view, however, it is Roman Jakobson, for example, who is interested in the distinction between metonym and metaphor. Metaphors have ever since Aristotle's first theorization been at the core of philosophical and linguistic traditions. A historization of this journey would form a book of its own. For further information, the research laboratory in Amsterdam dedicates conferences and dissertations to the current

epilepsy metaphors, one needs to understand that for Lakoff and Johnson the term "concept" refers to a structural set of "ontological correspondences" (Lakoff "Contemporary" 208). This means that concepts circumscribe the body of knowledge about a certain domain of thought—for example, love. This body of knowledge takes on an ontological position, for it serves as the basis for pragmatically expressing and thinking about love in all its variety of emotional, physical, hypothetical or affective appearances. This domain of thought, love, then, is linked to another domain that helps to further structure it. This mapping of domains explains why domains are "correspondences" rather than separated entities. In the case of love, the domain of journey joins in. The concept of love is then articulated in the conceptual metaphor of LOVE IS A JOURNEY which "map[s] the ontology of travel onto the ontology of love" (210). This means that "the lovers correspond to travelers. The love relationship corresponds to the vehicle. The lovers' common goals correspond to their common destination on the journey" (207). This mapping of ontological correspondence explains, on the one hand, how idioms such as "their love has been a dead-end" evolve, but, on the other hand, reveals a structural hierarchy between these two concepts that already alludes to the overarching effect of the meaning of metaphors for thought.

This structural hierarchy of concepts, or their "inheritance hierarchy," implies that one can pin down a certain set of concepts that function on a regular basis as "source domain" (207) and are thus said to structure thought per se. First of all, this inheritance hierarchy implies that the source domain, the ontological correspondence of the journey, structures the "target domain" (ibid.), love. Each concept helps to elucidate the other, which elevates metaphorical mapping to a cognitive device. Throughout their research years, Lakoff and Johnson derive an enormous corpus of conceptual metaphors that mirror our perception of the world. For example, we perceive time in a linear movement, or we connect the concept of knowledge with the ability to see. These mappings, of e.g. time and movement, or understanding and seeing, reveal a structural hierarchy that defines one concept as target domain and the other as source domain. It is therefore interesting, for the task at hand, to see that there is a certain set of concepts that

state of metaphors in various disciplines <http://metaphorlab.org/> consulted: 07/17/17, 7:30 a.m. of the Metaphor Lab, Amsterdam.

are often used as source domain, because they delineate in their specific ontological outline the structure of an event: "time, state, change, causation, action, purpose and means" ("Contemporary" 222). This proposed "event structure" encompasses, structurally, the way in which the world unfolds to us and articulates itself in daily expressions. Though it is rooted in a cognitive-linguistic perspective, it ultimately formulates an ontological principle which refers, in its aim to express a process, to an ontogenetic principle, or to *being as it happens*. If the variety of conceptual metaphors can be traced back to an overall structure that promotes the event—setting the potentiality of change in relation to time and space as epistemological a priori—then these source domains are reaching out to ontologically validate life.

This process-oriented "event structure" does not, however, describe a principle outside of daily action, but the very notion of experience, thus leading us to the aforementioned detour. They underline the validity of their "event structure" using a phenomenologist framework arguing thereby for embodiment. Within this notion of conceptual metaphors, Lakoff and Johnson find a means for thinking in line with Baruch Spinoza and in harmony with American pragmatists William James and John Dewey, reaching their scholarly peak with French phenomenologist Maurice Merleau-Ponty ("Contemporary" 207; Johnson"Mind" 51ff.). The traces of these theories echo in current neurological research, beginning with the 1990s and Antonio Damasio's groundbreaking work on the plasticity and individuality of the brain's mapping ("Mind" 48f.). Recent philosophical discussions in this area also adhere to this delineation of thought: Clive Cazeaux confirms to Lakoff and Johnson by starting, however, from the senses and their epistemological value as introduced by Locke's empiricism. Cazeaux sees this as a movement against the ratio-centered philosophy of Descartes and Leibnitz and proceeds from Kant's idealism to Merleau-Ponty's phenomenology over to Lakoff's and Johnson's cognitivism. In doing so, Cazeaux formulates his notion of metaphors as well as he defines "the structure of experience" (60).

This philosophical delineation of embodiment that both metaphor theories by Lakoff and Johnson as well as by Cazeaux define, starts with the critique on Descartes' body-mind dualism and results in an elevated positioning of experience for cognition. It is in this understanding of experience, of embodiment, that the dispute between a cultural disabilities studies' approach to conceptual metaphors roots in. Although the notion of embodiment finds its place in both theoretical streams, counteracting on both sides the body-mind dualism, they each value, nevertheless, a different aspect that sets them ostensibly far apart from each other. While for a cognitive-linguistics' reading the structural functioning of the brain, its mapping character, is the one worthwhile for research, asking how basic concepts of knowledge evolve in relation to experience, it is the cultural de/evaluative aspect inherent in conceptual metaphors such as "UNDERSTANDING IS SEEING" (Johnson "Cognition" 410) that suppose a healthy body at its base that is tackled by the cultural disability studies' scheme. Embodiment is thus viewed as a conceptual means for Lakoff, Johnson and Cazeaux whereas it serves as a means through which individualization and alterity should be grasped for cultural disability studies scholars such as Jay Dolmage, Vivian M. May, Beth A. Ferri, Sami Schalk, and Amy Vidali,[5] to name only a few.

Taking the following formulation by Lakoff as a paradigm, it serves to harden the positions between both disciplines since it promotes an identity of bodies, presupposing a general, universal set of equal experiences, cross-culturally:

> "Gary called such metaphors 'primary metaphors' and observed that they are learned by the hundreds the same way all over the world because people have the same bodies and basically the same environments. Therefore, we will very much have the same experiences in childhood in which two domains are simultaneously active, and so we will learn neuronal metaphorical mappings linking those domains naturally, just by functioning in the world. Just living an everyday life gives you the experience and suitable brain activations to give rise to a huge system of the same primary metaphorical mappings that are learned around the world without any awareness." (original emphasis "Neuronal" 26)

This universalizing implication of experience juxtaposes a cultural disability studies' perspective of an alterity of bodies and an individual experience with a universalizing one. "[L]iving an everyday life" triggers the question as to what this everyday life is characterized by. But even if the everyday life question could be characterized in terms of a loving family, man and woman, and white etc., triggering Goffman's characteristic of the normal

5 See Chapter I.C of this book.

ideal which led Garland-Thomson to designate her notion of the normate,[6] thus favoring Westernized cultural ideals, most people on earth are not living it. The expression "functioning in the world" highlights, furthermore, an ability-oriented body, excluding sickness and age. This "functioning" confronts Davis' "living in the world" (*Bending* 11) by which disability, naturally, is acquired.

Looking closer at Lakoff's and Johnson's theory, common ground between their outline and disability studies scholars can, nevertheless, be found on three levels. First, in the notion of creative metaphors:

> "The metaphors we have discussed so far are *conventional* metaphors, that is, metaphors that structure the ordinary conceptual system of our culture, which is reflected in our everyday language. We would now like to turn to metaphors that are outside our conventional conceptual system, metaphors that are imaginative and creative. Such metaphors are capable of giving us a new understanding of our experience. Thus, they can give new meaning to our pasts, to our daily activity, and to what we know and believe." (original emphasis 128)

Secondly, the emphasis on embodiment creates a momentum for changing and challenging rigid belief systems:

> "New metaphors have the power to create a new reality. This can begin to happen when we start to comprehend our experience in terms of a metaphor, and it becomes a deeper reality when we begin to act in terms of it. If a new metaphor enters the conceptual system that we base our actions on, it will alter that conceptual system and the perceptions and actions that the system gives rise to. Much of cultural change arises from the introduction of new metaphorical concepts and the loss of old ones." (131)

And finally, accepting that daily communication conduct denotes this stable belief system in the first place and can thus be a tool of either oppression or liberation:

6 See Chapter I.C of this book.

> "We need not be slaves operating blindly under the harsh influence of our metaphors. We can learn what our founding metaphors are and how they work. We can analyze the metaphors underlying other cultures and philosophical systems, too. Our ability to do this type of analysis is, admittedly, always itself shaped by metaphorical conceptions of which we are hardly ever aware. However, we can become aware of those metaphors, we can subject them to critical evaluation, and we can creatively elaborate them in developing *new philosophies* to help us deal with the problems that confront us in our daily lives." (emphasis added, 128).

These remarks on creating new metaphors which emphasize the role of experience and the valuing of language—metaphors in particular—for the revelation of intrinsic belief systems, are constant factors in Lakoff's and Johnson's work. They help us to understand that metaphors are not only means of stigmatization, but are capable of shifting cultural values. It resides in this creative elaboration of the above mentioned "new philosophies" that a theorization of epilepsy metaphors can be formulated. Given the power of conceptual metaphors on the belief system of a culture, they form the theoretical starting point from which to examine the "event structure" of epilepsy and develop its new mapping as part of a conceptual metaphor. This means that the stable factor in this approach signifies the ontological correspondence of the conceptual metaphors in daily language.

This new mapping will connect epilepsy to the notion of *metastability* and, henceforth, account for the notion of individuation. Epilepsy will thus be ontologically correspondent to metastability. This means that, instead of characterizing and conceptualizing epilepsy with its cultural and medical heritage, epilepsy can be understood, through the notion of metastability, as displaying a principle of individuation. This ontological correspondence between epilepsy and metastability rests in the source domain of metastability. This means that through the "event structure" that metastability describes, on a higher level of abstraction, it can subsume how epilepsy processes and, simultaneously, how these processes can be linked back to experience as mirrored in new idiomatic expression and thus "help us to deal with the problems that confront us in our daily lives" (Johnson "Philosophy" 51). The ontological correspondence works, however, both ways. Epilepsy as target domain defines a process which is known through the stages of aura, rigid state, convulsion and regeneration. Starting from this specific target domain, epilepsy, one can understand how metastability proceeds.

Through their ontological mapping both form a principle of daily communication and life and integrate this new form of an "event structure" as just another concept standing alongside: "time, state, change, causation, action, purpose and means" ("Contemporary" 222). The way epilepsy proceeds, mirrors how metastability can take place and vice versa; EPILEPSY IS METASTABILITY.

Simondon's notion of metastability describes how the process of individuation ensues. In order to understand metastability, therefore, one first needs to gain a theoretical grasp on the notion of individuation. Individuation, for Simondon, refers to "haecceity" and "life" and encompasses all entities from a physico-chemical, vital and psycho-social standpoint—that is, from the crystal, to the fauna and flora, and finally to the subject, all of which he terms 'individuals.' In order to get a grip on this notion of individuation, one is asked to leave aside classic approaches toward ontogenesis such as atomism or hylemorphism and to even resist the temptation to place Simondon next to his vitalist precursors who, unlike him, approach individuation from the position of the individual, trying to explain the individual, instead of focusing on the process that led to its constitution ("Individual" 297f.). He emphasizes that, although both principles take on a different explanatory approach, they nevertheless display theories that derive a principle by looking at the already given individual. It, therefore, does not matter if they posit the principle of individuation as anterior or posterior to the individual, because their explanation is initiated by the concept of the already-given-individual rather than the notion of the process. Thus, Simondon argues that "[w]e would try to grasp the entire unfolding of ontogenesis in all its variety, and *to understand the individual from the perspective of the process of individuation rather than the process of individuation by means of the individual*" (original emphasis 298).

What he thus pushes forward is the process[7] or the "event structure." This elevated position of "[t]he process of individuation must be considered primordial," Simondon writes, "for it is this process that at once brings the individual into being and determines all the distinguishing characteristics of the *development, organization* and *modalities*" (emphasis added, "Individual" 300). It is crucial to envision how this primordial process works for it stresses what Simondon understands when he talks about "being as it becomes." For him, the process is thought of as part of the being which means that being incorporates its "non-identity" and is thus always, as Muriel Combes puts it so eloquently, "more-than-identity" (3). Being needs to be itself, because being as such stresses identity and unity, but also more than itself in order to continue the process; to keep itself going. Consequently, identity and unity become obsolete terms through the incorporation of their non-identity. In thinking being as becoming, the process turns into a mode for thinking and understanding individuation, for embracing the "haecceity," which stresses the aspect of being at the very moment it becomes alive and thereby acts out life. Looking further into the quote, it is worthwhile to highlight the nuances of this process that Simondon introduces when he states that the process of individuation—being as itself and as becoming—"determines all the distinguishing characteristics of the *development, organization* and *modalities*" (emphasis added, "Individual" 300). What he refers to is how the process of individuation is echoed in the physical, vital and the psycho-social domain, differentiating even further that with sub-

---

7 The emphasis on the process mirrors Simondon's general philosophical thinking, for it also dominates his philosophy of technology. Both his ontogenesis, as well as his technological thinking, bear an epistemological argument which can only be understood if the "process" constitutes the onset of thought. Regarding his philosophy of technology, it explains the coming into being of technical objects—concretization—which offers an anthropological, ethical, social and epistemological account of how humans understand themselves 'as humans' through technology and simultaneously characterizes the pure utilization of technical objects in today's society as alienation. In an epistemological sense, he advocates the term "*a praesenti*" (original emphasis "Ontogenesis" Footnote 18) in contrast to a apriori or a posteriori, leaving classical notions of intellectualism and empiricism aside to join in the ranks of thinkers such as Alfred Northon Withehead and Maurice Merleau-Ponty, setting the ground for Gilles Deleuze.

jects one enters the psychic as well the collective, that is, the single human and the group.

Simondon sees the process of individuation as acting out itself, its history, and bearing the potential of its future through a participation in what he understands as the preindividual being. The differences in the above emphasized "development" include, for example, from a spatiotemporal and topological perspective, that while crystals individuate in a continuous, repetitive mode of "quantum leaps," living beings, and among them, the subject in particular, individuate more slowly and in a rather discontinuous manner due to their mediating actions upon themselves and other individuals. The second concept to grasp the process of individuation refers to his mentioned "organization[s]" in which the processes of individuation materialize or signify the respective individual; this organization is, for example, the lattice of the crystal, or the coral reef, or the subject's psyche and its social behavior. Next to the development and the organization of the process of individuation Simondon points toward the "modalities." These modalities refer to the corresponding individual-milieu dyad, which means for the crystal seed that it requires the supersaturated solution, as the coral animal requires the rock, and then for subjects, other subjects as well as their surrounding nature and technology.

Since the "process of individuation" defines the modes of existence of individual beings, one can step further into Simondon's thinking and behold how the being unfolds itself through becoming:

> "Now, these notions [unity and identity] are useless in helping us to discover the actual process of individuation itself. They are not valid for understanding ontogenesis in the full sense of the term, that is, for the becoming of the being insofar as it doubles itself and falls out of step with itself [*se déphaser*] in the process of individuation." (original emphasis "Individual" 300)

It is important to see, here, that being proceeds through "doubl[ing]," which does not connote duplication as in the creation of another, exchangeable entity, but rather implies the gradual realization of an individual. The individual is, in its "haecceity," already itself, which includes its past but also its future being. An individual being can, therefore, only become what is already potentially inherent to it. This is what "double" implies; it is an unfolding of the being while it becomes, always denoting its own being in the process. Therefore, the term double requires the rethinking of identity together with the non-identity as "more-than-identity."

In accordance with that, Simondon envision as exemplary the image of the individual as "fall[ing] out of step with itself." In a way, it merely visualizes doubling as non-duplication, but we can better grasp it through the image of a walking person. From a spatiotemporal perspective, "steps" imply a meter, rhythm or continuity and, thus, characteristics of a somehow controlled movement toward an aim or destination. A walking person sets one foot before the other and by means of this continuity (of steps) accepts the implication of a potential discontinuous momentum (fall). Walking contains the potential to fall, sometimes even as the result of the slightest disturbance. It is the newly attained movement after the fall, which is essential in order to understand Simondon's notion of metastability. Contrary to understanding the fall as stopping the movement, the fall characterizes it. The reflexive pronoun "itself," furthermore emphasizes, that a continuation of the same person (being as it becomes) is secured after the fall. This individual, in whatever altered form she might appear, is still herself, on the one hand, identical to the person she was before the fall; on the other hand, she has been altered, carrying with her the past experience of the fall as well as a future potential to fall again.

This inherent potentiality is metastability. Via the establishment of this specific equilibrium which, in physics, with regard to a system's potential, "is said to be in metastable equilibrium (or false equilibrium) when the least modification to the parameters of the system (pressure, temperature, etc.) suffices to break its equlibrium" (Combes 3), the liminal space between stability and instability finds its place for individuation. In its time, this expression was a philosophical novelty since rest and movement, or stability and instability, are not treated as ontological categories in dialectic relation to each other. Rather, the metastable is introduced as a distinct ontological category capable, for Simondon, of truly capturing ontogenesis without resolving the one (being) in the other (becoming). His explanation for this is that metastability, as a physical phenomenon, was simply not known or scientifically explainable and could thus not serve as a basis for deriving ethical conduct from ontological categories.[8]

Metastability can be said to mark the not-yet-actualized potential that resides in a system, ready to be released. It is, thus, a sensitive equilibrium, an equilibrium, however, with the decisive feature of being able to be thrown of balance, or, so to speak, out of itself; maintaining its state at the highest possible energy, it is always ready to spontaneously de-phase. Thinking back to the crystal in the supersaturated solution, metastability bears the potential for crystallization. On a larger scale, we can consider the snow-covered mountain, whose energy is capable of triggering the avalanche. Metastability occurs, thus, on several levels in our physical, vital and psycho-social life. Simondon sees in this state of metastability, this inherent potentiality within a system, an ethical principle and thus calls for a rethinking of the individual and his psychological and social systems as inherently dynamic, affected, as they are, by the constant mediation of others. For Simondon, the individual is in a continuous process of mediating tensions, some of which constitute crises while others are willingly embraced. Both of which, however, bear the potential to throw the individual out of balance. This acknowledgment of one's own and another's sensitive equilibrium—that is, the power to affect and be affected—calls for an ethics of responsibility, compassion, and dependency. Or as Simondon puts it:

> "To say that the living being is problematic is to consider becoming as a dimension of the living: the living is according to its becoming, which operates a mediation. The living is both agent and theater of individuation; its becoming is a permanent individuation, or rather, a series of outbreaks of individuation advancing from one metastability to another." ("Ontogenesis" 8)

Simondon thinks the individual as it lives in a moment, together with its past and potential future. The individual is a distinct unit. It is in resonance with itself, and in that manner stable and with identity while simultaneously allowing its actualized past, its experience, as well as its potential future to reside in the present moment and, thus, be more than itself. It is in this

8 It is, nevertheless, not the aim of this book to position Simondon against the backdrop of continental dialectics in order to prove his claim as either right or wrong, but rather to pay respect to his positioning outside of this methodology.

sense that the individual is both agent and theater of individuation; it individuates at the same time as it serves as the platform for future individuation to take place. And in order to become, to live, individuals advance from one metastable moment to the other by mediating between forces working within and upon them. With the living individual, and more specifically with us humans, the metastable is found as what can be described as "psychic tension" (9f.). In living in this world with problems that we need to solve by mediating between ourselves and others, we shift, according to the degree of problem at hand, into our next phase. And with each new phase, the encounter begins afresh, making life the advancement from one metastability to another.

To put it differently, metastability means the upholding of a certain tension, but also the ability to be able to give in to the tension. In order to do that, one needs to *expose* oneself to other people—to form a bond with them by mediating between the expectations posed by them and the willingness to fulfill these expectations. The metastable serves as the paradigm of Simondon's philosophy which aims at the mediation of any forms of extremes. With regard to stability and instability, metastability is the "event structure" as mediating moment. One needs to think metastability as a continuous liminality, as a process that affects and is affected by one's surroundings—objects as well as living beings—and hence describes life. Metastability accounts for identity and change, for continuity and discontinuity, for values and norms, for young and old, healthy and sick, the independent and the dependent, always placing the individual in a mediating, middle position, describing thereby as David Scott puts it a characteristic of "values" rather than of "norms" (185).

Thinking metastability as this mediating position—mediating between two forces—invites us to consider Simondon's philosophy as a problem-oriented ontology, or, put differently, as defining the individual as that which becomes through anxiety[9]. This stands, nonetheless, far from his interests. In lieu of anxiety, Simondon's stance is quite sound considering its hindering effect on the process of individuation:

9 See also Arne de Boever et al. *Gilbert Simondon. Being and Technology* (2012).

> "If the individual being puts itself, but nothing else, into question, then it will not be able to move beyond the limits of anxiety, for anxiety is a process without action, a permanent emotion that does not succeed in resolving affectivity, a challenge in which the individuated being explores the dimensions of its being without being able to progress beyond them. To the collective understood as an axiomatic that resolves the psychic problematic corresponds the notion of the transindividual." ("Individual" 310)

This passage illustrates how a state of pure being without the potential of becoming, opposes Simondon's notion of the individuation process. With the expression "anxiety is a process without action" Simondon confirms the experience of anxiety as an emotion. However, while it is an isolating emotion, it does not conceal individuation because it does not open up the individual to be part of its community, on the contrary, it keeps the individual to itself. In this context, it is important to note that Simondon stresses the role of the community in relation to the individual's coming into being and vice versa, thereby creating the notion of the transindividual. This, in turn, rests in the collective. The collective already denotes any kind of social structure or network that brings individuals of a community together. If we apply Simondon's concept of the transindividual to the psycho-social dimension, the transindividual can be used to describe the internet or even language as such. Both are means of open, social organization systems and connectivity that display processes of individuation. The transindividual signifies an open system in which individuals partake as part of their shared reality.

Viewing language as a possible transindividual in a Simondonian sense, metastability enters the picture and it does so on three levels: linguistics, social interaction, and conceptual mapping. Regarding grammar, daily language functions as a supposedly stable medium of communication, whose nevertheless sensitive equilibrium exposes itself through shifts, it explains and retraces the stability of rules and contains the potential for change. The same can be said for morphology, semantics, phonology or phonetics. Even looking at the subdisciplines of sociolinguistics, psycholinguistics, (historical) pragmatics, or semiotics, one deals with a given state of art that displays the history of its being and its future becoming. On the level of social interaction, metastability also illustrates how any kind of language, seen as a transindividual, serves as the means for resolving an inner conflict through an exchange with others. And finally, when integrating the notion of metastability even further into language, we enter the level of conceptual mapping.

Given metastability's ability to describe how processes of individuation succeed, we can see a parallel between it and Lakoff's and Johnson's conceptual metaphors stressing the "event structure" of certain source domains. Given that metastability denotes an ontogenetic principle which, in its abstract formation, leads to the consideration of movement within rest, it operates smoothly along the "event structure" domains Lakoff identifies as "time, state, change, causation, action, purpose and means" ("Contemporary" 222). Metastability occurs in a spatiotemporal framework, carrying with it its own causation, that of potentiality. In addressing the parallel between metastability and source domains, I want to show that, among those concepts of ontological privilege, metastability can also be seen as a source domains. Given its characterization, namely as a sensitive equilibrium which contains its own being thrown out of balance and the corresponding potential to reestablish itself in a new manner, metastability, once it has entered daily language, bears the potential to counteract the discrimination of stereotypes in forcing us to think in liminal, mediating terms. To function as part of a conceptual metaphor, though, metastability requires mapping with a target domain.

In light of this chapter which seeks to theorize epilepsy metaphors in order to tentatively proclaim a tool that sensitizes for already existing destigmatizing metaphors, epilepsy is set as target domain. It is with epilepsy in particular, that the mapping with metastability finds great resonance. This mapping is destigmatizing because it requires a view of epilepsy from the perspective of metastability. EPILEPSY IS METASTABILITY denotes a sensitive equilibrium. A state whose vulnerability[10] is constantly present without showing itself. Metastability exposes itself to the viewer the moment it is lost; before that it appears as stability. The avalanche is the lost metastability of the snow-covered mountain. And that is how epilepsy is experienced for the person with it. Epilepsy cannot be reduced to the grand mal that becomes obvious to the viewer but rather describes a constant factor structuring daily life. A person with epilepsy falls out of step with herself through the seizures, despite their intensity. The 'falls' can vary from

10 See Chapter III.C.2 of this book.

stumbles to actual falls, as do epileptic forms vary in intensity from daydream-like absences to grand mal seizures.

People with epilepsy are, in this sense, more aware of their individuation than others because they experience the sensitivity and fragility[11] of (daily) life, knowing evermore so consciously that they are in an equilibrium that can be broken: they "fall out of step with [them]self." This leads to another opportunity for mapping epilepsy with metastability: reacquisition. In the same way that the process of individuation succeeds from one metastable equilibrium to another, epilepsy persists in the individual through its repetition. One seizure does not make a person epileptic, in the same way as breaking the metastable equilibrium once, without regaining another form of it, does not display the process of individuation. In both cases the repetition denotes the process, the development. This means that although one part of the experience of a person with epilepsy is the actual break, which appears frightening, another part of the experience is this actual awareness of individuation as reestablishing this equilibrium.

In lieu of this conceptual metaphor then, the question arises as to how it enters daily (normal) language. I argue that within the scope of Siri Hustvedt's oeuvre the conceptual metaphor of EPILEPSY IS METASTABILITY forms a constant, subtle rhetoric which designates her poetics and thereby displays a new mode for approaching the sensitive equilibrium of life that everyone is exposed to. The beauty of her rhetoric lies exactly in the cautious reorganization of idiomatic phrases which include words that bear the potential to directly address epilepsy, such as 'drop, fall, collapse, shiver, tremble, quiver, spasm,' without the necessity to give in to it. Hustvedt rather upholds metastability, thus being true to both terms and establishing them through a repetition that takes on a different meaning of sensitivity each time. Hustvedt's new mapping of these idiomatic expression leads to a reconsideration of the meanings of fragility, vulnerability, and endurance and thus verifies what Cazeaux writes of Lakoff's and Johnson's conceptual metaphors:

11 See Chapter III.C.1 of this book.

"An original, freshly minted trope . . . is an instance of creative, subjective language yet, far from producing nonsense, [this] new metaphor offers insight on its subject and, as such, could be said to be objective or to contain an objective component. If the world is in some sense determined by the order and distribution of human concepts, then metaphor, as the creation of new combinations of concepts, would appear to be a mode of thinking in which human creativity constructs an objective world." (1)

In sum, conceptual metaphors structure daily (normal) language and serve as powerful tools for exposing and reinforcing rigid belief systems as well as for challenging them. In the ontological correspondence between epilepsy and metastability, that is, through an understanding of epilepsy as a metastable event, we find the new conceptual metaphor for epilepsy: EPILEPSY IS METASTABILITY. This metaphor, which introduces a means for thinking the liminal within the stable, can be located most definitively in Siri Hustvedt's use of everyday language.

III. Epilepsy Metaphors in American Literature (1990-2015)

III.A Metaphor and Society: Proto- and Flexmetaphors and Calculated Individuation

III.A.1 Lauren Slater's *Lying*: The *Epileptic* Text I (Ellipse & Ellipsis)

"You couldn't act as if you weren't having a seizure; . . . . My Memoirs, please. Sell it as nonfiction, please."
LAUREN SLATER, *LYING*

This chapter reads epilepsy in Lauren Slater's *Lying. A Metaphorical Memoir* (2000) as a master metaphor defining the *epileptic* text. *Lying* confirms *protometaphors*[1] as highly rigid and stable, erasing any liminal space for the individual to develop. They confirm to the notion of the symptom as a linguistic sign[2] and to the symptom as descriptive act[3] which denotes the *epileptic* text.[4] From this first perspective, *Lying* appears highly discriminatory and, hence, falls under the concept of *protometaphors*. However, a second reading of this text introduces a new meaning of *protometaphors* that allows for an understanding of 'proteron,' not as Jürgen Link suggests, designating the first historical epoch of normalization practices,[1] but in its very notion of a 'first.' This seems approachable since the narrator's main fea-

1 See Chapter II.A of this book.

2 See Chapter II.A of this book.

3 See Chapter II.A of this book.

4 See Chapter II.A of this book.

ture of unreliability tackles the very essence of the genre of life narratives and thereby reverses the roles of stability and liminality, elevating the liminal, and pushing forward the author's unique genre of metaphorical memoir.

To lay the groundwork for the two parts of the analysis, I will begin with a summary of the book and an analysis of its structure.[5] In order to argue for epilepsy as master metaphor of the text, the historical motifs that permeate it will lead the analysis. They will confirm the notion of the *epileptic* text and affirm the already existing cultural disability studies reception of this text's epilepsy metaphor as stigmatizing.[6] This chapter then argues for another reading of the novel and its epilepsy metaphor that will derive the logic[7] of the *epileptic* text in the form of their respective mathematical graph (ellipse) and rhetorical figure (ellipsis).

Starting off, then, with a short summary, the plot of *Lying* centers on the main character Lauren and her childhood memories as well as her teenage years, concluding with a retrospective evaluation of her (university) life from a middle aged Lauren, who pursues, like the author herself, the profession of a psychiatrist. Throughout her life, Lauren seems to be prone to lying, leaving the reader with doubts about her credibility. Decisive for this notorious lying seems to be her relationship with her mother which is torn between longing for approval, admiration, and loathing. Linked to her mother, Lauren develops, at least supposedly, epilepsy during her childhood years where she experiences her auras as moments of overflowing creativity and her seizures as social discrimination. During her teenage years, she manifests a passion for writing, and falls in love, first with her imaginative neurosurgeon, and then with a famous married author. These two loves of hers are analogous to the two leading themes of this novel: epilepsy and fiction. It is during her first years at college that the extent of Lauren's compulsion to lie reveals its magnitude, cutting off the diegesis and leaping forward twenty years in time.

---

5 Given that Lauren Slater's *Lying. A Metaphorical Memoir* (2000) formed the main novel for scholars in cultural (disability) studies to consider epilepsy as a metaphor, the reception, which unanimously declared the work to be stigmatizing, was already addressed in Chapter I.B of this book.

6 See Chapter II.B of this book.

7 See Chapter I.A of this book.

That epilepsy serves as the master metaphor of this book is evident since the four stages of an epileptic seizure not only precede the novel in terms of a clinical definition, but function as means for structuring the chapters according to Lauren's life stages. Her childhood years are thus defined as the "the onset" of her life, while the second, "the rigid stage," denotes the transition between childhood and puberty. Going over then to "the convulsive stage," late puberty, where Lauren exploits the years of sexual encounters, until she ends her memoir's timeline with "the stage of recovery" which glimpse into her first academic experience. One cannot say that the recovery marks a cure since the "afterword" stresses clearly that medicine shall be deprived of any objective validity: "Illness, medicine itself, is the ultimate narrative; there is no truth there, as diagnoses come in and out of vogue as fast as yearly fashions" (Slater 220). Lauren, thus, stresses the metaphorical aspect of illnesses per se. Besides this structural metaphorization of epilepsy with life, the main character immerses herself in epilepsy metaphors, so much so that one could argue she herself serves as the history of epilepsy, all her experiences are continuously relayed by way of the motifs *sleep,*[8] *falling,*[9] *danger,*[10] *intelligence,*[11] *religiousness.*[12]

In line with the accumulation and proliferation of the historical motifs with epilepsy, the symptom as linguistic sign manifests itself at the level of content. In this sense epilepsy is captured in a confined notion of itself incapable of expressing anything other than itself. This means that those moments in the novel that signify epilepsy—for the symptom turns into the signifier—the history assists as signified. Considering first the motif of *sleep,* the history correlates it with prophecy, due to its resemblance with death and the dream-state. When Lauren equates her auratic feeling to "the huge hand of God reaching down from the sky" (111), it comes as no surprise to the reader, not only because "[p]eople called me 'dreamy' and 'space cadet,' and my father chuckled when he saw me staring out the window and said 'This girl of ours is a guru'" (ibid.), but because "I became dreamy, sometimes hours and hours passing, and afterward, although I

8 See Chapter I.A of this book.

9 See Chapter I.A of this book.

10 See Chapter I.A of this book.

11 See Chapter I.A of this book.

12 See Chapter I.A of this book.

hadn't been asleep, I would feel like I was waking, and my head hurt. This is how epilepsy begins" (9). Lauren's onset stage of life and epilepsy build up to these allegedly prophetic experiences through the constant reiteration of different dreamy-states throughout the novel that are, in one way or another, related to divination or spirituality (9, 48, 80, 82, 111, 188).

In this appreciation of the historical, *falling* as the "cardinal symptom"[13] of epilepsy enters this memoir as manifold as the nomenclature it initiates. One metaphor, however, stands out because it tackles the core of this "cardinal symptom." *Falling* defines, from early on, the moment of Lauren's godly devotion. When Slater dedicates the entirety of "Chapter 3: Learning to Fall" to this very aspect of epilepsy, she stays true to the impact of this symptom. There, Lauren is put into a "school for falling children" (45), Saint Christopher, funded by the Epilepsy Society. Already at this point the historical-as-metaphorical abounds in analogous matches, considering that epilepsy colonies were established at the beginning of the nineteenth century.[14] Although Jewish herself, Lauren feels a strong connection to the nuns at this school, who teach her how to fall, erasing thus any institutionalized differences between religions in favor of an overall devotion to God. And indeed, the motif of *falling*,[15] permeates in religious contexts such as, the Bible, the Talmud or in receptions of the Muslim world. Similar to the Three Wise Men,[16] King Saul and Mohammed,[17] Lauren learns to literally and metaphorically fall into her belief. In this sense, she embraces epilepsy as the "falling sickness,"[18] and by consecutively learning how to actually fall without harming herself, she metaphorically learns to give in to the loss of control.

Falling learned through the devotion to God becomes an act of liberation from her mother and serves as a metaphor for Lauren's life—for the cardinal symptom of life. Back home from the epilepsy school, Lauren shows her new ability of falling to everyone who wants to see it by continuously "crashing onto the floor and standing seconds later, unharmed" (55).

13 See Chapter I.A of this book.

14 See Chapter I.A of this book.

15 See Chapter I.A of this book.

16 See Chapter I.A of this book.

17 See Chapter I.A of this book.

18 See Chapter I.A of this book.

This marks the decisive break between her and her controlling mother "in her Christian Dior nightgown" (56) who cannot even allow herself to fall asleep. This ability of letting go, of falling, becomes crucial for Lauren to perceive the world and understand life:

"Two weeks into our training the physical therapists [the nuns] moved us onto land. Now, years later, I can see the sense in all this, how evolutionarily correct it all was, how they were teaching us much more than falling; they were teaching us living. From fish to amphibian, from flippers to feet, we walked onto mats and the therapists said, 'Take a deep breath and let yourself go.'" (49)

"I think secretly each and every one of us longs to fall, and knows in a deep wise place in our brains that surrender is the means by which we gain, not lose, our lives. We know this, and that is why we have bad backs and pulled necks and throbbing pain between our shoulder blades. We want to go down, and it hurts to fight the force of gravity." (51)

Similar to a religious missionary outreach, Slater encompasses, with the cardinal symptom of epilepsy, humanity, linking epilepsy through *falling* to devotion and life: "We create all sorts of lies, all sorts of stories and metaphors, to avoid the final truth, which is the fact of falling. Our stories are seizures. They clutch us up, they are spastic grasps, they are losses of consciousness. Epileptics, every one of us; I am not alone" (196f.).

The motifs of *sleep*—connecting epilepsy to prophecy—and *falling*, linking epilepsy with devotion, encourage a reading of epilepsy's historical motif of *religiousness*. The continuity in which Lauren's personal experiences of prophecy, devotion and personal divination are relayed throughout the text further enforce the stigma of epilepsy (12, 46, 57, 61, 72, 111, 169f., 177f., 183f., 201). Taking up three whole chapters in addition to that, it is safe to say that *religiousness* as a metaphor for epilepsy penetrates the text. Chapter 2, "Three Blind Mice," embeds divination into the flamboyant language triggered by Lauren's synesthetic auras. Chapter 3, "Learning How to Fall," focuses on Lauren and her Catholic upbringing in the "school for falling children," and Chapter 8, "Amazing Grace," problematizes her sneaking into an AA group which meets up at the local church. Highlighting, thus, one out of many examples in the text, the "cardinal singing" (57) is as suitable as any other example, since it resonates quite nicely with the "cardinal symptom" of *falling*.

This "cardinal singing" describes a sound that only Lauren can hear while she is standing in front of her recently deceased neighbor's empty grave, waiting with the community for the coffin to arrive. This inner music of Lauren's releases itself to the community through the epileptic fall: "[She] fell for centuries, and as [she] went down, [she] opened [her] mouth, and the cardinal flew out, and was free" (58). The inner voice which Lauren attributes to a higher power, speaks to her due to her *falling*, or her epilepsy. By now she has learned to experience her epilepsy as devotion, prophecy and divination. Moreover, epilepsy appears to become a moment of liberation. This time Lauren turns into God's mouthpiece and her body into his medium for speaking freely to the crowd. The experienced duration of this fall—centuries-long—underlines even more so the unearthly timelessness of a higher entity. Lauren gives in to the divine sound distorted by the thorax as it presses out the remaining air. Be it as it may, this fall into the grave is unveiled as a deception later on in the text. Lauren never fell into the grave in front of her community; she merely imagined doing it. A confession which leads us to question Lauren's honesty.

Following this, Lauren appears to have a compulsory urge to lie—as the title of the novel already suggest—grounding the motif of *danger*. It is almost impossible to retrace all of the lies hidden in the text, but the following two paragraphs will present an outline of them. The persistence and depth with which Slater/Lauren explores moments of lying, tricking, and manipulation covers only one aspect of the "epileptic character."[19] This, however, Slater/Lauren addresses in all of its facets and mentions the "unclean" and "filthy" (10, 11)[20] the "compulsory sexual drive," the "irritability" (10, 23, 128f., 131),[21] as well as the "traumatic experience induced in the observer" (157).[22] Slater/Lauren secures thus the motif of *danger* in many of its historical dimensions stabilizing its position of master metaphor as *protometaphor*. Lying stands out, however, because "I [Lauren] told myself I could not help my lies, (a) because I was a genius, and (b) because I

19 See Chapter I.A of this book.

20 See Chapter I.A of this book.

21 See Chapter I.A of this book.

22 See Chapter I.A of this book.

had the epileptic personality style, my brain more myth than matter" (133). Her brain is more myth than matter, a myth, a story told for make believe; and in that sense a lie of great power.

With the same force of a myth, the lie overpowers main character, Lauren, until she finally seems to dissolve into it. Epilepsy, as the root of her lying, thus explains her urge to steal from her neighbors' houses, her trickery at schoolmates' parties where she claims to have cancer, not epilepsy, in order to gain pity, her self-induced seizures where she stages her epilepsy as spectacle;[23] like an actress she accumulates different personas with each new ER that she is brought to. She lies about her age in order to get accepted into a writer's conference. She plagiarizes other people's texts. She lies herself into an AA meeting at a church, and she even applies the lie to epilepsy, stating that she might as well have Munchausen syndrome after all.

To lie about the condition that is supposedly the trigger of this very compulsion, is a logical conundrum that leads to its very annihilation. The lying does not only trick on the level of fiction, though, but reaches out to manipulate the reader on the non-fictional level as well. Her reliability displays severe fissures, as the reader, once acquainted, over the course of two chapters, with Lauren's surgery, is faced with her neurosurgeon and the exercised corpus callostomy as a chimera (175). Even the introductory words of a certain, cited Howard Kriegel, Professor of Philosophy, who praises Lauren Slater's literary craftsmanship, turns out to be a lie. Lauren turns into her own lie, not graspable to the reader as anything other than a repeated lie that even confession cannot mitigate the effects of.

Considering the final historical motif of *intelligence*, it seems at first as if Slater/Lauren breaks with the historical heritage for the first time, only to then later fortify its legacy. The affiliation of epilepsy with either one of the cognitive extremes, genius or stupidity, makes an entrance when Lauren's narcissistic mother takes up the historical motif's features: "Once, she had thought I might do it for her, be a skating star or a genius. Now, however, I was just a person with a disease" (62). Later on, however, this position of mediocrity is superseded by herself elevating her artistic skill to that of a genius. As Lauren pursues her writing career, linking her auras and her epilepsy to her creativity, she draws on the genius of Dostoyevsky's, van

23 See Chapter I.A of this book.

Gogh's and even Shakespeare's as inspirational and exemplarily for her own writing (81, 112, 73).

These examples visualize how epilepsy can turn into the signifier of its own history, and thus stress the symptomatic signification. Lauren, having epilepsy, experiences everything in parallel with the stigmata revealed in epilepsy's social history: prophecy, divination, devotion, character flaws and genius affiliation. To read about Lauren's epilepsy is to verify what is already known about epilepsy. In that sense, one can say that epilepsy as symptom signifies its own history and is thus bound to refer to nothing other than itself: it is confined.[24] In this way, the act of the "clinical gaze" that knows the moment it sees[25] is literarily exemplified in these epilepsy metaphors, and reading them stabilizes their force. Therefore, these epilepsy metaphors push forward an authoritative reading of epilepsy, tightening the borders between abnormal and normal since, with the increase of symptoms, the increase of epilepsy metaphors initiates the clinical that distances the individual from the normal spectrum.

Similarly to protonormalism, where the borders between abnormal and normal people are visually erect before the eyes of the beholder,[26] these metaphors function as borders. They diminish the amount of liminal space available for the individual, Lauren, to develop and thus confine it to the abnormal realm. The resemblance between protonormalism and these epilepsy metaphors peaks here, considering that protonormalism designates the same historical epoch, the beginning of the nineteenth century, as the proliferation of the "epileptic character." Through the stability of the metaphors and the concluding annihilation of liminal space, the symptomatic signification of Lauren in this work prohibits individuation and relegates Lauren to the history of epilepsy.

The timeline of protonormalism also conforms to the clinical definition of epilepsy, from 1854, that Lauren Slater uses as a prelude to the first chapter. Given the importance of the clinical definition for my reading of *Lying* as an *epileptic* text, I have provided it here in its full length:

---

24 See Chapter II.A of this book.

25 See Chapter II.A of this book.

26 See Chapter II.A of this book.

"The classic grand mal attack, such as this youth suffers, may be divided into four distinct stages. One, the onset. Two, the rigid state. Three, the convulsive stage. Four, the stage of recovery. During stages two and three, the main treatment must be to prevent the convulsion from injuring the patient. There is no fear at this stage of him injuring other people, though the relaxing of the sphincter and the contracture of the abdominal musculature may cause incontinence. A wooden gag should be placed between the teeth before they become clenched, to prevent the patient from either biting himself or those who are assisting him. During stage two, and before stage three has been reached, the clothing should be loosened and the head, the arms, and the legs laid firmly on the ground with pressure continued for the duration.
FROM *The Text Book of Grand and Petite Mal Seizures in Childhood*, 1854."
(Epigraph)

This epigraph transforms the memoir, at the outset, into an *epileptic* text,[27] which works, I argue, to validate the definition. Indeed, every reading of the memoir can be traced back to this definition. This memoir, thus, does not portray, as suggested by its genre, the individual's life, but transforms the individual into a text, into the written compilation of its symptoms, a *textualized* pathological being.[28] The content as well as the form of the text can always be explained through this definition. There is no margin, no liminal space left for escaping this symptomology through individuation. And since this epigraph addresses "the epileptic," the *textualized* pathological being is the *epileptic* text. Even without any explicit epilepsy metaphor in the text, these memoirs would be read as *epileptic* because they automatically follow the logic, the chronology and syntax[29] of this *epilepsy*.

27 See Chapter II.A of this book.

28 See Chapter II.A of this book.

29 See Chapter II.A of this book.

THE *EPILEPTIC* TEXT I

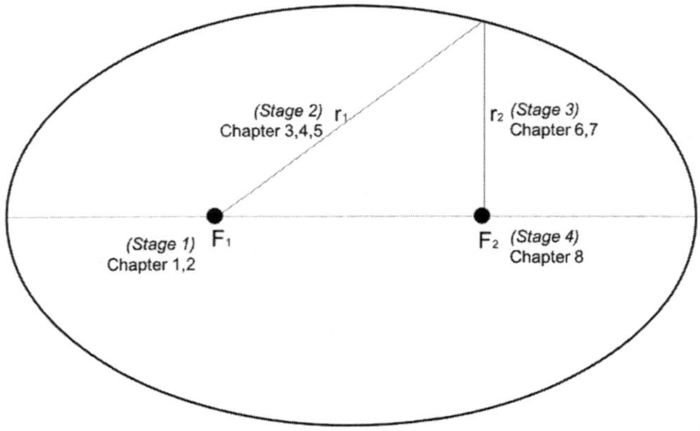

E.V.

The clinical chronology and syntax of this *epileptic* text follow the logic of the ellipse and the ellipsis. Considering the chronology, the novel's structure defines a closed curve since it describes one epileptic attack from beginning to end, nothing more or less. An ellipse is defined as "a curve that is the locus of all points in the plane the sum of whose distances r_1 and r_2 from two fixed points F_1 and F_2 (the foci) separated by a distance of 2_c is a given positive constant 2a . . . ."[30] In the context of this discussion I argue it is of particular significance that, in contrast to a circle, an ellipse relies on two distances and foci. Syntactically, an ellipsis indicates the grammatical notion of omission. Both, ellipse and ellipsis, define the logic of this *epileptic* text.

To do so, one can identify four explicitly-named stages of the grand mal definition quoted by Slater in her epigraph—"One, the onset. Two, the rigid state. Three, the convulsive stage. Four, the stage of recovery." This definition captures the novel's ellipse/ellipsis logic. Considering their implied chronology, these four sentences seem to trigger a steadiness, since the quotation displays in each sentence the structure of 'number, definite article and subject.' This gives reason to assume a linear unfolding of these four

30 <http://mathworld.wolfram.com/Ellipse.html> consulted: 04/20/16, 5:12 p.m.

stages in the upcoming passage of the definition. However, looking at the definition, stage one and stage four are not explained at all. This can be understood by looking at the logic of the ellipse. Stage one and stage four can be equated as behaving like the two focal points, F_1 and F_2, of the ellipse, while stage two and three as the distances r_1 and r_2. I argue, that given that stage one and four are not further elaborated in the definition, we can see them as a given, as points, defining those two moments and foci without which an attack could not begin (stage one/F_1) or end (stage four/F_2). Their determinacy for the whole chronology is as crucial as is the position of the F_1 and F_2 to define the "squashed" shape of the ellipse. They do not, however, mark the distance, that is, the time, of the epileptic attack. The actual time is defined by stage two and stage three, thus r_1 and r_2 of the ellipse. It is in this sense that the chronology of this *epileptic* text can be understood as an *ellipse*.

The syntax of this *epileptic* text also follows this logic, which means that stages one and four can be left out as well—following the logic of the ellipsis they have already been mentioned and do not require further elaboration. They are implied in the rest of the definition, it is only because of them that stage two and three can unfold at all. Similar to the visible plane of the ellipse, stages two and three are syntactically nuanced. The definition unfolds in the sentences, giving descriptions and conduct advice. One can thereby see that, in terms of syntax, the ellipsis stresses the *epileptic* logic through a focus on the seizure, leaving the stage of individual auratic experience (stage one), invisible for the observers, as is the recovery (stage four), uninteresting for the observer, literally out of sight. It thereby reduces the individual to the epileptic attack (stage two and stage three).

Taking this *epileptic* text's logic, the four epileptic stages structure the eight chapters of this book as mirroring one ellipse. They, therefore, stress the metaphorical impact of stage/part two and three (r_1 & r_2), while arguing for stage/part one and four (F_1 & F_2) to be the two focal points which stabilize the metaphor of epilepsy as the 'successfully performed lie' by the narrator. Looking thus, at F_1, stage one first encompasses Chapter 1 and 2 is called the "the onset." It is striking that Chapter 1 is the only untitled chapter in the whole book and that it includes only the single sentence, "I exaggerate." "Chapter 2: Three Blind Mice" defines the mother-daughter relationship as the instigator of Lauren's epilepsy. Growing up with a highly narcissistic mother with a drinking problem who views her daughter's worth in the fulfillment of what she lacks in extraordinariness, and a silenced, almost invisible father who leaves hardly any imprint on Lauren's life, a difficult mother-daughter relationship manifests. Before Lauren experiences her first epileptic seizure on a family vacation in Barbados, she experiences synesthetic auras that begin with an exposure to the omnipresent smell of jasmine. Lauren's first seizure is triggered by her mother embarrassing herself in front of a hotel crowd, where she claims to be able to outplay the pianist:

> "And then she [the mother] went forward . . . . She pushed out a seat and sat down to take it. She made a big show of positioning her hands and straightening her shoulders, just like she had practiced all those hours at home. The party waited, waited for the symphony . . . . *Just play it, Mom,* I thought. *Three blind mice, see how they run, just play it and get it over with* . . . . You could've heard a pin drop. You could've heard the petals fall from a flower while we waited, and waited. Her hands posed over the keys. Sobering up. 'I suppose not,' she finally said, and stood, and carefully, carefully walked away." (original emphasis 18f.)

Lauren views her seizure immediately following this scene as her body's attempt to compensate for her mother's lack of shame, for her missed opportunity to perform for the crowd (24).

F_2, part four, which consists of "Chapter 8: Amazing Grace" and defines the recovery stage, restates these moments from the onset stage that include exaggeration, the mother-daughter relationship, epilepsy and alcohol. In this chapter, Lauren finds shelter in an AA group meeting at the local church where she finds, in the recovering addict Elaine, a suitable mother surrogate. Through lies and the relation of her mother's drinking habits and conduct, Lauren integrates successfully into the group, becoming a participating member. Lauren not only exchanges her mother with another person, Elaine, she also transforms into her mother by claiming to be an alcoholic herself. Drawing parallels between alcoholism and her supposed epilepsy, Lauren deduces that both obey to the logic of addiction. In a great performance of staging her ostensible addiction in front of the group, she, in contrast to her mother, does not disappoint the audience (203ff.). Quite the contrary, Lauren feels the excitement rising up in her while lying so convincingly that

"I stopped. Everyone was looking at me. I had them in my hands. I felt this was the best drunk-a-logue anyone had ever done. It wasn't what I was saying, but how I was saying it, my voice so genuine, so painful, so utterly, absolutely authentic, and it was! It was! . . . Everyone clapped like crazy and cried, even the men." (206, 208.)

The novel, then, is framed by two events of lying—Lauren's mother's failure in lying (F_1) and Lauren's success (F_2)—which, in turn, manifest the unreliability of the narrator.

Having the focal points set along the lie and the unreliability of the narrator, "Part Two, the Rigid Stage" (r_1) and "Part Three, the Convulsive Stage" (r_2) assemble, as stated in the first part of this analysis, the accumulation of lies, all linked in one way or another to epilepsy. Especially with respect to the syntax-as-ellipsis, while the first part includes an empty chapter and the fourth part ends abruptly with Lauren leaving college and skipping several years ahead, parts two and three gather the lies. This is the means of this *epileptic* text: unreliability and lying. Both are thought in accordance: the unreliability exposes itself to the reader or the characters—depending on the level of narration—with the failure of the lie, allowing the text to cramp, articulating one big epileptic seizure. This means that "[d]uring stages two and three, the main treatment must be to prevent the convulsion from injuring the patient. There is no fear at this stage of him injuring other people" (Epigraph). The lies told at this stage, or the effect they have, do not really display any threat. In the rigid stage (r_1), which comprises chapters 3, 4, and 5, the unreliability of the narrator has merely been mentioned but has not only severed the genre of memoir with its inherent reliability. At this point, it has not really exposed its overarching effect, which will put the whole genre of memoir writing into question—this will happen toward the end of the novel (r_2).

At the end of this second stage (r_1), so to speak, "[d]uring stage two, and before stage three has been reached, the clothing should be loosened and the head, the arms, and the legs laid firmly on the ground with pressure continued for the duration" (Epigraph), the *epileptic* text as *textualized* pathological being gives in to the cramp, the unreliability. Here, the "Introduction," written by a supposed Hayward Krieger, is revealed to be a lie by Lauren's surgeon, Dr. Neu, who has, supposedly, just performed the incision on Lauren's cerebral hemisphere: "She [Lauren] frequently spoke of a correspondence with a professor of philosophy—a Hayward Krieger—with whom she discussed Ouspenskian ideas. However, we have been unable to locate or confirm the existence of any Hayward Krieger, which is not surprising, and only further underscores her diagnosis" (101). The reader is now confronted with 101 pages of an unmentioned, proliferating lie. At this point the novel seems to lose its only stabilizing momentum, the narrator's reliability, thus turning the reader's attention to its unreliability. Like the body turning rigid and the mind slipping into unconsciousness, the text slowly destabilizes.

This 'cramp' climaxes in the convulsive stage (r_2), in Chapters 6 and 7, where the magnitude of the narrator's unreliability is revealed. Dr. Neu and the surgery expose themselves as lies as well (176) and Lauren's reliability—originally manifest in her meticulous explanation of the rigid stage, which included Chapters 3, 4 and 5, her epilepsy, the sessions with Dr. Neu, the preparation for the open brain surgery, and Dr. Neu's scientific article—has disappeared and with it, it seems, the genre of the memoir. "A wooden gag should be placed between the teeth before they become clenched, to prevent the patient from either biting himself or those who are assisting him" (Epigraph). In Chapter 7, "How to Market this Book," Lauren places a wooden gag between her teeth. Although giving in to her unreliability, she manages to uphold the memoir arguing from a neurological position, that the same part of the brain is both responsible for generating fictional narrative as well as for generating lies (164). In line with this, she thus claims that—because any kind of narration is a lie—her book should be published as nonfiction.

> "I am asking you to enter the confusion with me, to give up the ground with me, because sometimes that frightening floaty place is really the truest of all. Kierkegaard says, 'The greatest lie of all is the feeling of firmness beneath our feet. We are at our most honest when we are lost.' Enter that lostness with me. Live in the place I am, where the view is murky, where the connecting bridges and orienting maps have been surgically stripped away." (163)

Her means of handing out her life to the reader is not only best conveyed through metaphor but through epilepsy as metaphor, strengthening once more the *epileptic* text's ontological a priori.

In sum, epilepsy in this first text verifies the mechanisms of a *protometaphor*. Along with the 'symptomatic signification' that includes the 'symptom as linguistic sign' which yields the historical motifs and the 'symptom as descriptive act' that generates the *epileptic* text, the epilepsy metaphor is highly stigmatizing in this text. While the historical motifs stabilize the stigma of epilepsy on a content level, the *epileptic* text generates the *textualized* pathological being on formal grounds through the unreliability of the narrator. This unreliability displays itself in the chronology and syntax, calculating precisely, thereby, its being. In as much as the truth is stretched and the lies convincingly told, the text verifies its *epileptic* a priori position. The unreliability becomes ontological. This unreliability does not, however, as Couser suggests, diminish the ethical responsibility of the memoir.[31] It is in the exploitation of historical motifs as metaphors that the clinical definition is stigmatizing. Concerning the unreliability, however, the author's epistemological position roots within the very fact that no truth can be conveyed through the text as such; it thus delivers her memoir in the manner in which she experienced her life: unreliably. This could be said to introduce a different understanding of the term *protometaphor* since it denotes the first memoir that, using a literary fictional trope as means of mediation, achieves the status of a nonfictional text.

31 See Chapter I.B of this book.

III.A Metaphor and Society: Proto- and Flexmetaphors and Calculated Individuation

III.A.2 Audrey Niffenegger's *The Time Traveler's Wife*: From Flexmetaphor to Protometaphor

"You've mislocated yourself again . . . . Sometimes you feel euphoric. Everything is sublime and has an aura, and suddenly you are intensely nauseated and then you are gone."
AUDREY NIFFENEGGER, *THE TIME TRAVELER'S WIFE*

In this chapter on Audrey Niffenegger's debut and bestselling novel *The Time Traveler's Wife* (2003),[1] epilepsy appears as one possible metaphor for reading the main character's involuntary time travel. This time travel gives reason enough to see how epilepsy works along the liminal space of the open sign,[2] marking epilepsy as a *flexmetaphor*,[3] before it then gives in to the stability of the linguistic sign[4] and creates a *protometaphor*.[5] From

1 The eponymous motion picture *The Time Traveler's Wife* (2009), directed by Robert Schwenke, starred Rachel McAdams and Eric Bana in the roles of Clare Abshire and Henry DeTamble.

2 See Chapter II.A of this book.

3 See Chapter II.A of this book.

4 See Chapter II.A of this book.

this first point-of-view, *The Time Traveler's Wife* destigmatizes epilepsy as it avoids a clear categorization of the main character as "epileptic,"[6] constantly referring to time travelling instead. Considering, however, that the character contains a history of epilepsy, in his alcoholic, eccentric, promiscuous ways, along with his defective genes, the mechanisms of *protometaphor* overrule the modest beginnings of the *flexmetaphor*. I will begin with an extensive summary of the plot in order to introduce the two main characters and Niffenegger's presentation of epilepsy as time travel, which comprises the focal point of the novel's critical reception. In light of this reception, I will then argue for time travel as epilepsy metaphor. In order to account for the movement from *flexmetaphor* (the open sign) to *protometaphor* (the linguistic sign), that is, from mere recognition to being caught in a hermetic space of self-reference, I will split the analysis accordingly.

The story of the *The Time Traveler's Wife* revolves around the love of the two main characters Clare Abshire, a born-wealthy artist, and the librarian Henry DeTamble. Henry is a time-traveler whose spontaneous involuntary evaporations, his "falling out of time" (Niffenegger 12), challenge the genre of romance, overlapping with a classic theme of science fiction. In spite of the time travelling, the novel's zealous reflections on the politics, technologies and zeitgeist of the 1960s to the early 2000s does not, however, call for a science fiction reading. Keeping this time frame in mind, the novel forwards a realistic setting permeated by time travel. Henry's first time travel experience occurs when he is a child in what appears to be a reaction to a traumatic car accident where his mother, an internationally-acclaimed opera singer, is decapitated. As the reader gets to know further ahead in the novel, Henry tried on several occasions to travel back in time to prevent the accident from happening. Unable to do so, he is bound to one of the time travel logic limitations where cause precedes effect in order to avoid a casual loop (Ryan 151f.). He thereby cannot alter the past, as he explains later, to his wife Clare.

Self-diagnosed with what he calls "chronological displacement" (Niffenegger 63), Henry's time travel leads the plot in terms of its chronology as well as its narratology, evoking incalculable shifts. A general remark on his time travel is his inability to really control the space or the time he will be

5 See Chapter II.A of this book.

6 See Chapter I.A of this book.

travelling to, or even the fact to actively initiate a time travel himself. On top of this, he cannot take anything with him while he travels but wakes up stark-naked, without any indication of his whereabouts or the time he has traveled to. In order to survive, Henry learns from a young age to steal clothes, money and food, as well as to protect himself by fighting effectively. Looking at the plot, the reader is confronted with two timelines, Henry's and Clare's, yet, only Clare's is bound to chronological linearity. To transport these two different perspectives to the reader, Niffenegger establishes two first-person narrators. Clare gets to know Henry in 1968 when she is six years old and Henry, being 36 at that time, is visiting her from the future. From that time on, Clare will prepare clothes and food for Henry for his upcoming visits.

They eventually meet in what is considered their 'mutual real time' and get married. Their marriage, although they are excessively devoted to each other, is star-crossed as Henry's time travel is an identified genetic defect, diagnosed by a Dr. Kendricks who is dedicated to finding a cure for Henry. It stands to reason that this genetic defect is the cause for the several miscarriages Clare had before their daughter Alba was born. Alba, who has inherited Henry's condition, grows up in a society full of people with this genetic condition, known as CPD "Chrono-Displaced-Person[s]" (382). In contrast to Henry, Alba enjoys her time travels as she learns to take a bit more control of them, in spite of the fact that she is incapable of taking anything valuable or helpful along with her. Henry's time travel, however, leads to a series of dramatic events after his daughter is born. He finds himself naked in the cold, leading to the emergency amputation of his feet. Back in real time, without feet, he falls into a depression before he dies at the age of 43, being accidently shot during hunting season by Clare's brother Mark who mistakes him for an animal in the woods. After Henry's death, Clare and Henry will meet one more time when Clare is 82 and Henry 42, being thus truly married until death, having Henry dying with 43 and Clare supposedly with this final visit of Henry's.

With this summary in mind, Audrey Niffenegger's conceptualization of time travelling, as it is linked to the love story of the book, leads the critical reception of the novel. Oscillating between the challenges time travel poses to the logic of a narrative's chronology, genre categorizations, as well as its cultural implications, critics focus on bringing together the two "storyworld chronolog[ies]" (Segal 529) of the text. These two chronologies point to, on the one hand, the present time of the couple in love, Henry and Clare, and, on the other hand, Henry's episodes of time travelling which tend to place him in the past. For Eyal Segal the narratological benefits of a text playing with the chronology of cause and effect and thereby sensitizing its readers to the theme of temporality, outweigh the inherent logical paradox of time travel. Emphasizing this reading, David Beard and Kate Vo Thi-Beard align with Barry Trott and see in Niffenegger's novel a means to challenge classic genre categories. The science fiction element of time travel stands in direct correlation to the love story of the book, making it difficult, if not impossible, to categorize *The Time Traveler's Wife* in accordance to either one of its two dominating motifs (Beard and Vo Thi-Beard 332). Marie-Laurie Ryan, however, pursues exactly what Segal avoids, scrutinizing the issue of time travel from a logical standpoint.

The logics of time travel evoke two strong interpretative streams that, on the one hand, underscore the love between the protagonists and, on the other hand, derive a cultural studies' reading. Ryan hints toward Niffenegger's entering of a paradox with the causal loop in allowing Henry to influence the future while he travels back in time. However, Ryan considers this paradox necessary for enforcing the bond between Henry and Clare; their love becomes inevitable as there is no scenario or universe possible where they would not have fallen in love with each other (Ryan 153). In line with this, Stefanie Caeners regards time travel as a means for emphasizing the strong love between Henry and Clare, equating it with an "locus amoenus" (265). Brian Baker and Sylvia Mieszkowski focus on the cultural implications of time travel. While Baker views the "shift from a mechanical means of time travel (Wells' Time Machine) to a biological, genetic or psychological one [that] is diagnostic of a turn towards a pathologised and traumatized masculinity that is increasingly visible in contemporary culture" (83), Mieszkowski provides a psychoanalytic perspective on time travel considering Freud's, Lacan's and Žižek's notion of phantasma, while also looking into Derrida's notion of "pharmakon." With the first reading she views Henry's stress-initiated time travels as escapes from reality, a materialization of an unconscious wish fulfillment (393ff.). With Derrida's pharmakon, Mieszkowski captures the meaning time travel has for the time traveler: Based on the ambiguous Greek term, entering philosophy with Plato, it defines a cure as well as a poison. Viewing time travel as a mean to escape from as well as to miss out on significant life events, the Derridean "pharmakon" describes, precisely, Henry's approach to social interactions in this novel (397ff.)

Taking these readings into account, time travel defines the central motif of this novel, standing for love (Ryan, Caeners), the deprivation of masculinity (Baker), or wish fulfillment (Mieszkowski). This chapter argues, however, first, for time travel as an epilepsy metaphor before addressing whether or not it allows for the individual to leave behind the history of epilepsy. Time travel as epilepsy can be identified according to four features: stress and trauma, the progression of the time travellings, the corporeality of time travel and daily conduct. Leaving the direct references to epilepsy within the novel aside (4, 80ff., 160), these four characteristics allow for a recognition without giving in to the symptom. Beginning with the first, stress and trauma (112), we see that Henry misses out on what is actually happening to him. Every time he time travels, he leaves his present situation, which is usually a situation of high stress. Stress designates similarities to the experience of an epileptic attack but does not explicitly refer to it. Regardless of the stress' outcome as positive or negative, Henry leaves these situations involuntarily, not able to prevent the travelling, and thereby misses out on his own wedding, where his future older self marries Clare (203ff.), and on his daughter's birth (323). A further consideration of stress links it with Henry's first time travel experience, or epileptic attack, in the brutal car crash that kills his mother, allowing for the affiliation between epilepsy and posttraumatic stress disorder (54).

In addition to stress and trauma, another indication of the relation between epilepsy and time travel are Henry's *actual* time travels and the circumstances he finds himself in, which begin in involuntary evaporations described by spectators as "impressive" (130) or "scary" (167). Such observations are made possible when Henry does not manage to get out of sight beforehand. In line with this, the fact that he feels the urge to hide his time travelling evaporations invites their comparison with epileptic attacks––that is, as something that is stigmatized as incomprehensible. In light of this, Henry finds himself continuously "misplaced" and out of time, with nothing on him, when he arrives at the time travel destinations. This feeling of being exposed after an epileptic attack is represented in his nudity during time travel, and is further underscored by the fact that he is at first disoriented in the respective "spacetime" (85). Additionally, the logical paradox that he, on the one hand, cannot prevent anything from happening in the past but, on the other hand, can influence his future from the time of the past, could relate to Ryan's interpretation of the casual loop, which is explicitly set to underscore the inevitability of Henry's and Clare's love. It could also serve to emphasize the inevitability of Henry's falling out of time, from having epilepsy—that there is, as Ryan puts it, no possible scenario in which Clare and Henry would not have fallen in love.

The third means for approaching the central motif of the story as a metaphor for epilepsy are the corporeal signs that bear similarities to epilepsy. Henry experiences auratic moments while his evaporation, according to bystanders (2), is accompanied by a "noise like all the sound is being sucked out of the world" (125). This sound, which is also only heard by the bystanders but never by Henry himself, echoes the sound produced in an epileptic seizure when the lungs and the larynx contract and thus expel the remaining air from the lungs before it escapes through a cramped larynx. Typical injuries that can occur in an epileptic attack such as the biting of the tongue (40), head injuries or his "right palm and [the] four deep crescent-shaped cuts [that] appear in a row" (91), and vomiting, also appear on a regular basis in the novel and thus further emphasize the relationship Niffenegger develops between time travel and epilepsy. Additionally, the fact that his death is closely related to his time travel, as in the loss of his amputated feet and resulting inability to run from danger thereafter, stress the threatening aspect that lies in extreme cases of epilepsy. And finally, his DNA as well as the traumatic experience of the car accident cover common reasons of the etiology of epilepsy.[7]

The final feature of time travelling as epilepsy is the fact that Henry's life is ruled by the preparation, avoidance and anticipation of situations that could trigger "episodes" (3). In an attempt to be prepared to survive time travel, older Henry teaches his child-self how to steal and fight, and he continuous to perfect these survival skills over the years, so much so that his friend Gomez is left speechless upon witnessing Henry's effortless break into a high-security department store (96). A classic self-protection mechanism for people with epilepsy, Henry's avoidance of situations capable of triggering time travel can be seen in his inability to enter an airplane, since the idea of a confined, moving space in time scares him (162). Airplane police might vary according to the medical clearance of a person with epilep-

7 See Chapter I.A of this book.

sy, but regulations and preparation indicate that flying is still a precarious mode of transportation. Henry also avoids driving cars, as the thought of time travelling while driving and maybe killing another person, scares him as well (85). Finally, although he knows that his time travels are bound to come on in stressful or exciting situations, he also knows that they can appear in states of total relaxation (3). Given, then, his constant exposure to time travel, he researches excessively when it comes to finding a means to control his time travel for important occasions. Similar to people who avoid constant medication for treating epilepsy, Henry takes the occasional and sometimes frequently occurring travels into account. Only for very important situation, such as his wedding, he forces himself to take medication, and what is very striking, is that among these drugs he also takes anticonvulsants. His vasectomy (346), furthermore indicates the parallel to epilepsy; after all, it was common practice to sterilize people with epilepsy up until the 1950s in several states in the US.

We can now see more clearly how the relation between time travel and epilepsy serve as the novel's master metaphor. But it is important to see, too, how the metaphor creates liminal space or presupposes stability for the individual. In the first instance, we can see a destigmatization of epilepsy that goes hand-in-hand with epilepsy's role in the individuation process, while the second case leads to the reiteration of history, prohibiting epilepsy from signifying anything other than itself. My first approach toward this epilepsy metaphor will thus examine how time travel allows for a liminal space which is achieved through the open sign of the *flexmetaphor* and its destigmatizing function. I will then consider the principles of stability and the linguistic sign that designates it as a *protometaphor*.

The reading of epilepsy as a *flexmetaphor* rests on the metaphor of time travelling, which secures Henry's and Clare's love for each other as well as society's acceptance of Alba as a time traveler. Considering the fact that Henry's and Clare's love, a love that persists until both characters die, is inextricably bound to time travelling, it is key to the novel's presentation of epilepsy. Epilepsy serves as an impetus to find love, to keep it, and to live through the challenges posed by life as they appear in the form of Henry's frequent absences and Clare's longing for him. To view epilepsy from this perspective is a remarkable destigmatizing approach, as it is grounded in a universal feeling: love. Being in love can account for a shared yet highly individual everyday experience.[8] Niffenegger manages, through Henry's and Clare's love, to use it as the open sign for epilepsy that signifies it outside of the historical or clinical realm. Henry defines himself through his time travel and he can thereby individuate by changing from a "charming sociopath" (146), as Gomez refers to him, "into the man Clare will marry" (186). The time travel allows for this liminal space because moments of recognition, as in Henry's disappearance, hint toward epilepsy, as metaphor, resisting however identification with both its symptoms and its history; only vague descriptions of "chrono-impairment" (18) or "mislocat[ion]" (1) can be found mixing with the dominant motif of time travel as love.

Another factor that argues for a *flexmetaphorical* reading is the open society Alba, their daughter, grows up in. While Henry learned to hide his condition in order not to scare people, Alba accepts her time travelling as part of her self. One decisive scene exemplifying this is when Alba, aged ten and time travelling herself, meets her deceased father in a museum where she is with her classmates. She introduces him to her teacher as a person like herself, a "Chrono-Displaced-Person" (382). The naturalness with which she embraces her father shows that she is, on the one hand, familiar with a conception of life that includes death and, on the other hand, accepts who she is, even in public. Although she experiences the same exposure to nakedness and confusion as her father after evaporations, she has a different approach to it. Alba sees these moments as an the opportunity to visit her father, to search for him at a time when he was still alive. Her case, thus, shows that genetic disposition is not the exclusive perspective from which to view an individual as 'normal' or 'abnormal.' In Alba's world—New York in 2011—the idea of time travel and, thus, epilepsy, has entered into 'the normal.'

But there are even more reasons for viewing epilepsy-as-time-travel as a *protometaphor*. Although epilepsy is not the official diagnosis of either Henry or Alba, Niffenegger misses out on an important opportunity to destigmatize it. The linguistic sign of epilepsy is still prominent as Niffenegger reiterates the history of epilepsy all over again and furthermore underlines Henry's wish for his daughter to lead a "normal" life by depriving her of this "genetic defect" (350). Against Clare's wish he takes her to Dr. Kendricks in hopes of preempting further episodes of time travel in his

8 See Chapter II.A of this book.

daughter; he wants to secure a cure for her. The history of epilepsy in Clare focuses especially on the motifs of *sleep*[9] and *danger*[10] and reinforces what was known from the beginning of the nineteenth century until the mid-twentieth century as the "epileptic character."[11] Considering the motif of *sleep* that, among many ascriptions, views a person with epilepsy as possessed by a demon, this stigmatization is uttered by Clare's grandmother when she meets Henry for the first time and he disappears. As she cannot see the disappearance but hears the cry, it strikes her as unearthly and the man as possessed (113).

The motifs of *danger* as well as the "epileptic character" are, nevertheless, the most active in transforming epilepsy into a linguistic sign, beginning with Henry's alcoholism[12] at the beginning of the novel, when he almost drinks himself to death (215). The survival skills Henry acquires for his time travels—stealing and fighting—mirror the findings of Samuel Livingston M.D., who, in the 1960s, claimed that behavioral deviance in the conduct of persons with epilepsy appears to be a result of social exclusion (30).[13] We see this 'deviance,' too, in Henry's irritability[14] (135), ruthlessness when it comes to revenge, his alleged "fucking around"[15] (138), and in his father's estimation of him as "unreliable, volatile, and not even especially concerned with anyone else but himself" (232). Except for Clare and his neighbor Mrs. Kim, who functions as his stepmother, Henry appears as a secluded character deprived of any friends. The most significant *protometaphor* is, however, Henry's vasectomy, which he secretly undergoes in order to prevent his genes from being passed on, in order to protect Clare from more pain (343). Though Clare will get pregnant by sleeping with a pre-vasectomy version of Henry, his self-loathing echoes a eugenicist's perspective[16] on epilepsy. When Henry states early on in the novel that "'[o]ne time traveler per family is more than enough. It's dangerous,

9 See Chapter I.A of this book.

10 See Chapter I.A of this book.

11 See Chapter I.A of this book.

12 See Chapter III.A.1 of this book.

13 See Chapter I.A of this book.

14 See Chapter I.A of this book.

15 See Chapter I.A of this book.

16 See Chapter I.A of this book.

Clare'" (71), we see that he has, at the outset, adopted a protonormalistic view on his condition.

Focusing on protonormalism, it works on three levels in the novel: in the form of Clare's wealthy, privileged family; in Henry's and Clare's marriage; and in their stand on the issue of adoption. Considering Clare's family, which, besides living in a mansion with nannies and housekeepers, her father and her brother promote what has been known as the normal minority in protonormalism,[17] or the "normate"[18] in cultural disability studies. Henry comes from a privileged family himself whose downfall is caused not only by the mother's sudden death but also by his father's blaming his wife's death on their son. The symbolism in Henry's death, being shot by Mark Abshire, Clare's brother, allows us to see Henry being killed in a society that has never managed to include what might threaten its superior elite. On this level, protonormalism upholds but is criticized by the author.

Looking at Clare and Henry, their love is presented as predestined, to the level of a Hollywood cliché. Clare will experience her first sexual encounter with Henry, waiting all of her teenage years to achieve the ostensibly appropriate age to do so. Knowing him since childhood, she was never given the opportunity to love someone else. This is why, after his death, she will only sleep once with another man, her friend Gomez, though not without crying out Henry's name (430). Their love, furthermore, mirrors a Christian ideal, pairing religious fanatisms with a near holiness, as both will stay faithful to each other until their respective deaths. Clare experiences and witnesses Henry's death, and due to his time travel, he will accompany her in this final moment of her life. The only other sexual experience that Clare has is with a boy while she was in high school who abuses her physically—an act that is revenged by Clare and Henry, together, in a humiliating and brutal manner, taking jurisdiction and execution into their own hands (104). Furthermore, the fact that Clare does not want to adopt a child because it would undermine their 'holy' love bond, highlights the protonormalistic character of their relationship.

17 See Chapter II.A of this book.

18 See Chapter I.C of this book.

While *The Time Traveler's Wife* introduces a new means—through time travelling and love—for deriving a metaphor for epilepsy, it nevertheless conforms to the discriminatory mechanisms of a society with highly stable stereotypes. Therefore, my initial proposition of a *flexmetaphor* cannot withstand the dominant history of epilepsy; instead of destigmatizing it, it stabilizes its stigma. The very fact that Niffenegger's novel was turned into a Hollywood motion picture of blockbuster-level success, underscores the longing for a romanticized, simplified world that upholds its norms. And the fact that the novel misses out on the opportunity to use the scientific nature of time travel as a means for disrupting this stereotypical portrayal of 'deviance' further confirms its failure to challenge protonormalism. I have shown how the novel's use of time travel is generally perceived as challenging the classical notions of genre and narratology and thus as capable of inspiring change. In the end, however, we see instead, a deviant who, is killed in order to secure and maintain the borders of the protonormalistic society (Garland-Thomson *Extraordinary* 60).

III.A Metaphor and Society: Proto- and Flexmetaphors and Calculated Individuation

III.A.3 Dennis Mahagin's *Grand Mal*: The *Epileptic* Text II (Cosine & Enjambment)

> "Lately, I'd begun to wonder,
> as these Winters run, one into
> another, and another
> and another, if existence
> . . ."
>
> DENNIS MAHAGIN, "PUXATAWNIE IN HIS DUN PERIOD"

The poetry collection *Grand Mal*[1] by Dennis Mahagin portrays how the individual experiences protonormalism through epilepsy as its master metaphor. It results in an analysis of the text of epilepsy as *protometaphor*, yet this time offering insights into the stigmatized individual. To explicate epilepsy as the master metaphor of this *epileptic*[2] collection of 50 poems, each, of course worthy of its own analysis, I will approach the collection as a single text. As the *Grand Mal* portrays the experience of the *textualized* pathological being, it exposes the stability of social exclusion practices and their

1 "Publishers on the frontiers of liminal space. Founded in 2007, Rebel Satori now has over 80 titles in its list" <http://svendavisson.com/?page_id=287> consulted: 08/06/15, 11:40 a.m.

2 See Chapter II.A of this book.

confinement of the individual. Mahagin's poetics, I argue, are also present in his presentation of the *textualized* pathological being, and it is from this perspective that I will read this largely over-looked poet. One could go as far as to say that in giving voice to the pathological being, the poet is shut out of sight.

To 'see' the protonormalism of this text, then, my reading seeks to bring to light the logic of its *epileptic* being in terms of the chronology and syntax which structures the collection, defines Mahagin's poetics, and imprints itself on the book's cover and binding. In contrast to *Lying*,[3] the logic of this text does not expose mathematical ellipse and syntactic ellipsis, but rather, stresses steady continuity. While the subject of *Lying* can be summarized as one big seizure,[4] *Grand Mal* verifies itself as epileptic through its presentation of epilepsy as a series of repeated seizures. This continuity through repetition is achieved primarily through enjambment as predicament for both the clinical chronology and syntax. While we will see that in terms of clinical syntax, enjambment is an appropriate term, it does not describe a chronological concept. To follow the logic of continuity and repetition that denotes the process of 'run on,' however, the cosine curve as mathematical 'run on' functions as a tool for conceptualizing the *epileptic* text's logic. In line with this, the experience of protonormalism from within the clinical conveys itself. To identify Mahagin's style as what I will call *dissecting poetics*, I will examine the epileptic text's logic in the poem, "Dr Dre In Passing Bedside Manor." The experience of being captured in the clinical gaze ultimately reiterates itself on *Grand Mal*'s binding and cover, highlighting the *epileptic* text as *texture*alized pathological being.

In the following passage, I will quote the clinical definition of epilepsy, Mahagin himself quotes, as it structures the whole collection, preceding each of the four sections. Beginning with the logic of continuity and repetition the clinical definition of epilepsy stabilizes this text:

> ...Grand mal or tonic-clonic seizures are characterized by 4 phases. Recognizing these may be important. They are often preceded by an odd feeling strange taste or odor, or headache. These warning signs are known as auras (Phase 1)... (*Grand Mal* 0)

---

3 See Chapter III.A.1 of this book.

4 See Chapter III.A.1 of this book.

> ...Not all grand mal seizures are preceded by an aura. This type of seizure generally begins with a rigid stiffening of the body, and sometimes a tingling in the flesh, lasting a minute or less and followed by loss of consciousness. This is known as tonic (Phase 2)... (31)

> ...The tonic-clonic phase of a grand mal seizure (Phase 3) is generally accompanied by intense muscle contractions and, occasionally, convulsions. Unconsciousness generally follows these vigorous muscle contractions, as well as loss of bladder and/or peristaltic control... (59)

> ...Persistence of tonic-clonic seizure activity is a medical emergency called status epilepticus. Immediately after the seizure is the postictal phase where the patient gradually returns to consciousness from a level of stupor and confusion (Phase 4)... (89)

Considering the mere positioning of the four parts of this definition, the *textualized* pathological being is already established, framing the collection, as it does, according to the single phases of epilepsy. Although it is one single definition it does not only precede or close this poetry collection, but most effectively frames and separates the collection according to the single phases of epilepsy, verifying it as *epileptic* text. In doing so, Mahagin secures the poems' single, clinical reading. In his invocation of the clinical 'case,' a compilation of symptoms come to light. The intervals in which the definition appears, its chasms, signal the text's logic in terms of the cosine and the enjambment.

THE *EPILEPTIC* TEXT II

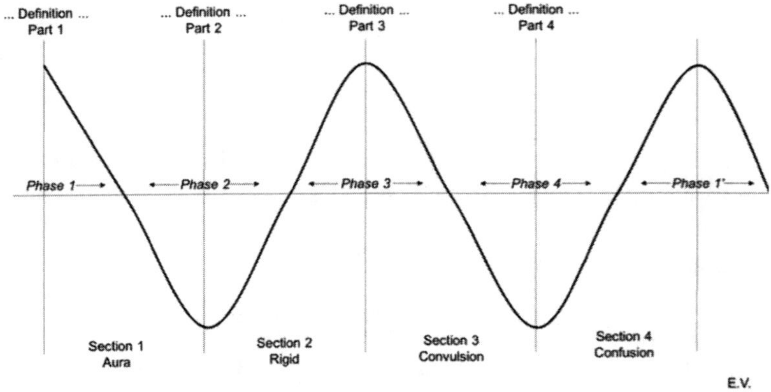

By exploring these positionings of the definition a bit further, as productive of a stabilizing and thus confining effect on the individual, it is worthwhile to reflect on the steady continuity with which these scissura materialize. It is a continuity that materializes in the number of poems and pages. To understand this, one needs to know that the collection is divided into four sections, each commenced by one part of the definition. In terms of the actual number of poems they encompass,[5] sections 1 and 2 contain thirteen poems, while sections 3 and 4 each consist of twelve poems. This slight difference in quantity might be due to the role of the page numbers, which stress a continuity of repetition. Between sections 1 and 2 there is a total of 30 pages, with 27 pages between sections 2 and 3, 29 pages between sections 3 and 4, and 31 pages between section 4 and the end—or as this analysis will argue, between sections 4 and 1'. Both the number of poems and the number of pages between sections evidence slight deviations in regularity,

5 For a better understanding of the terminology I am using:

phase 1 to phase 2	13 poems | 30 pages (section 1: aura)
phase 2 to phase 3	13 poems | 27 pages (section 2: rigid)
phase 3 to phase 4	12 poems | 29 pages (section 3: convulsion)
phase 4 to phase 1'	12 poems | 31 pages (section 4: confusion).

stressing the continuity, as intervals,[6] rather than counteracting it. Or put differently, 'the exeption proves the rule.' Taking the location of the definitions' parts into account, we see that they disclose the organizational logic of the poems, which obey a chronological order of continuity and repetition that resonates in the poems' topics as well as in their rhetoric, defining Mahagin's *dissecting poetics*.

This continuity and repetition that the readers—consciously or unconsciously—experience while working their way through the collection, underlines the chronological aspect of the *epileptic* text's logic. Instead of reducing epilepsy to the seizure, as *Lying* does, where the ellipse stresses the epileptic fit in one closed curve,[7] *Grand Mal*'s chronology attains a different, yet equally valid perspective on epilepsy. Its chronology mirrors the clinical classification of epilepsy, where singular fits denote exceptional seizures without the implication of an epileptic disorder.[8] Through the repetition of seizures, a continuity can be identified and diagnosed as epilepsy. This regularity—epilepsy being diagnosable through the probabilistic reoccurrence of seizures—can best be visually and mathematically described by way of the cosine function. The regularity in which the graph meets the x-axis as well as peaks and valleys at 1 at the y-axis portrays the clinical definition's chronology. It textually demarcates the definition as it repeats its overall generalization in the collection (*Grand Mal* 0, 31, 59, 89). The y-axis denotes the mountain and the valley of each section's epileptic phase, while the graph's rise and fall mark the duration of fading-out and fading-in of the neighboring epileptic phase. This means that no phase, although each is separate from the others, is experienced alone, but features the characteristics of both the preceding and the following phases. I argue, that this fading-in and fading-out of a phase is captured in the notion of the cosine—as the inserted graph shows. It thereby graphically stresses the 'run on' which in syntactical terms refers to the enjambment. This continuation then, allows us to think the repetition of epileptic seizures, since, in leaving phase 4, the fading-in to phase 1' begins.

---

6 The interval 12,5 poems | 29,25 pages allows to formulate the hypothetical case of: phase 1' to phase 2' 13 poems | 30 pages (section 1': aura').

7 See Chapter III.A.1 of this book.

8 See Chapter I.A as well as Chapter II.A of this book.

Its very momentum being a cosine instead of sine curve is bound to the syntax of the *epileptic* text as enjambment. This is due to the fact that each phase begins and ends with three dots—which are not, however, ellipsis or suspension marks in this text—relating to the preceding one as well as to the following. This does not appear striking, considering the fading from phase 1 to phase 2, 2 to 3, or 3 to 4, but the question thus arises as to why these three dots as a set of continuity, introduce phase 1 and conclude phase 4. It should be taken into account here that phase 1, due to the three dots, appears on page 0, and 'exchanges,' thereby, page 0 for 1. Phase 4 ends on page 120, erasing the slight deviations of page numbers between sections and underscoring the interval of each phase counting 30 pages. The eight "..." denote continuity within the text, marking its enjambment as subsuming poems into sections and thus into phases of epilepsy. Given the precision of *Grand Mal*'s positioning of the definition's parts, it emphasizes the continuity and thereby stability of the *epileptic* text. The three dots—in contrast to the suspense of the ellipsis—connect the parts of the definition and refers to additional text, namely to that of the poems. These poems are framed by the definition, stressing the *epileptic* text's chronology and syntax as underlining the a priori position of this pathological being that completely swallows the individual by turning his history, present and future into text.

In this sense, the mechanisms working on the individual, changing it into a *textualized* pathological being, generate the 'case' in the Foucauldian sense, where the meticulous recording of every sign yields a symptom that verifies the asserted disorder.[9] Each poem of each section can be seen as such a symptom, turning epilepsy into a linguistic sign that cannot denote anything other than itself and thereby generating the *textualized* pathological being. It does not require reference to its own history, as it does in *Lying*,[10] because the continuity of the repeating phases of the definition mani-

9 See Chapter II.A.1 of this book.

10 Although the poems work with epilepsy metaphors that, in many instances, capture their own history (e.g. *sleep*: "Puxatawnie In His Dun Period," "Stronger Than Dirt," e.g. *danger* (sex): "Banishing The Snakes," "Fare," "Gilded Cage Smacks Of Sanctuary," "Grand Mal W/Grown Up," "The Jefferson Theater," "Kindle Or Something Like It," "Porn Star's Sunday Song," "The Reins Supreme," "Spill," "This Poem Has Not Been Rated," "Trapper Don't Look

fests a structural objectification of the clinic and stabilizes the individual according to this *epileptic* text.

Looking at the sections' general topics, the single poems can be seen as representative of the respective symptoms of their respective phase. "section 1: aura" deals with various ways of addressing the aura: the wind—as in breathing or as nature's force—is the strongest metaphor in this section, emphasizing the etymological nomenclature of this term.[11] "section 2: rigid" addresses, almost exclusively, sex and pornography, objectifying the body in orgasm, while "section 3: convulsion" underscores the unconsciousness of this phase by switching from a predominantly lyrical-I in the previous two sections, to surrogate third-person speakers. The conscious experience in the first two sections is mainly captured in lyrical poems, while the unconscious state of the third section is rendered in narrative poems. Section 3 also deals with acting, staging and performance, imitating the spectacle of the convulsion for the audience. "section 4: confusion" consists of poems that primarily connote bewilderment and hospital experience, alluding to the upcoming auratic experience, stressing the continuity of the cosine and enjambment likewise. It is worthwhile noting that phase 4 underscores the chronological interval of roughly 30 pages as well as the syntactic enjambment between phase 4 and phase 1' because: "Flesh crawl like prelude / to epileptic aura, and it will be / all of 30 days before an

Back," e.g. *intelligence*: "Fence Fragment," "Green and Yellow Relocation Villanelle," "Hitchhickers Redux," "In A Green Dream Of Gregory Corse," "Jacks with Creeley," "Kreskin in Azure," "Layers & Layers of Meaning," "Mr. And Mrs Hughes Make Up And Wake the Dead"), they, nevertheless, push forward a fragmented interpretative approach which requires to skip extensively and exhaustingly between poems in order to affirm to the motifs' characters. The style in *Grand Mal*'s style as well as the referred to clinical experiences evolve and become clearer, however, through a reading of the text with the definition's a priori position. In sections 2 and 3 the historical motifs echo with the definition and can, therefore, be thought in accordance to it, but they are not explicitly analyzed in detail here. Furthermore, the general argument of this analysis shows that the individual can only experience its life as a patient through the clinical definition.

11 See Chapter I.A of this book.

Orkin Man" ("Grand Mal W/Landlord" 39-42), anticipating even on a content level the next phase: phase 1'.

In light of the *epileptic* text's logic, which manifests as enjambment and serves as the key rhetorical device of the poems, we will consider, more specifically, "Dr Dre In Passing Bedside Manor" in terms of Mahagin's *dissecting poetics* as well.

"Dr Dre In Passing Bedside Manor"
Dennis Mahagin

Forgive me, but an orderly
spaced out your chart. Luckily
we already know it by heart.
All these moments of flux,
be tough. I know because
like you, I was a mover
of furniture. Lasted 3 months
in the tail lights of my youth.
I needed bread. And the hours
worked for me. I pulled them
all, learned how loads
can shift, on the road
like the healthy

taking sick. Yet shakier still
were the customers who called
it down: smack in the middle
of their changes, to hear us
coming on, mornings, banging
open the quarter panel doors,
no banter amongst ourselves
per se (the public image of Dre)
but only softly spirit coughing,
all business, making ready
with the bungee straps, padded slip
covers, 2-wheeled dollies dumped
upon broadlawns. I was a musician
then, but still a long, long way

from doctor. Like you, I love
the people most, and was careful
with their stuff. Folks in deep flux,
their precious homes opened up
as rib spreader is to thorax
on a table. The moves I made
to get to MD, I cannot share.
Got to be that way. On account
of mortal moments shifting
away…unfair, I suppose
but back to

you: the chart, yes,
and results … but first, listen
to my freshest track to date
thanks to the polymorphic electric
bass harmonics carried along in 13 / 8
time by Echo Plex, the effects loop
with chorus: So much a series
of bone marrow aches
and pop, sounds a mind makes
for nausea solace watching raindrops
scoriate an oil slick, or sporadic
puddle. Like you, I only grew
into my skin comfortable when
I knew the pores to be slammed
open doors, transitory as our
music, and this
trouble. (Dennis Mahagin, "Dr Dre In Passing Bedside Manor" *Grand Mal* 10ff.)

The enjambment is, together with internal rhymes, a very prominent device in this poem because it aligns itself formally to a rap. The fast pace that rap embraces as one of its features, is met in the measured breathing and talking so that the continuity of enjambment is secured. This continuity of speaking is paralleled in this poem to the logic of the clinic. The uninterrupted word, the enjambment of the physician, the lyrical-I, objectifies the patient by emphasizing its own privilege through the monologue, namely in the systematic dissection of the patient.

"Dr Dre In Passing Bedside Manor" criticizes, ironically, the attitude physicians exhibit in the clinic while dealing with their patients. The fast pace with which physicians have to pass from bed to bed during their rounds finds its ironic counterpart in what appears to be a spontaneous (non-)diagnosis delivered to the patient in rap form, in four stanzas. In addition to the almost ridiculous image of a rapping physician, the irony lies in the doctor's lack of diagnosis. Being on rounds without the patient's chart–—"Forgive me, but an orderly / spaced out your chart. Luckily / we already know it by heart" (1-3)—the lyrical-I feels the urge to compensate for this mistake by providing the patient with supposedly soothing words. This compassion backfires, however, through the inappropriateness of the whole bizarre situation. The speaker/physician's spontaneous associations range from addressing his former job, hobbies and a line of inept parallelism between objects and people. What appears striking is that even the effort of trying to establish a bond of trust between doctor and patient becomes meaningless through the single word "trouble" (55). The lyrical-I ends the rap, and thus its round, leaving the patient not only as uninformed about the medical condition as before, but worse than that, with "trouble."

The success of the poem's critique lies in its enjambment, which adapts to the mechanisms of rap. The impact of the lines increase with the rapping skills of the lyrical-I to eloquently improvise and thus shatter the anticipated end of each line. Virtuously deploying its own point of view, moreover, the proficiency of a rapper goes hand-in-hand with the words that can be spoken in one run, breathing simultaneously without noticeable inhalation.

Like a good rap, the enjambments in this poem continuously disappoint, from the perspective of a patient, the hope for a longed-for revelation of his/her condition. The lyrical-I additionally deploys its own medical perspective on the patient reducing him/her to organs, rather than addressing him/her as an individual. Taking the first three lines as an example, where the lyrical-I plays with the hope of the patient by saying "Forgive me, but an orderly / spaced out your chart. *Luckily /*" (emphasis added, 1-2), due to the extra moment needed to move to the next line, the patient's hope can quickly manifest itself that s/he is lucky because s/he is healthy. Health is what annihilates the failure of a lost chart. However, the enjambment in this line only dashes the hopes of the patient more rigorously by revealing the exact opposite of health, that of chronic or lethal pathology which makes the loss of the chart as unimportant as health. The chart, the written down compilation of the symptomology, is already memorized by the physician, which might also stress the regularity with which the patient visits the clinic. So that the patient turns from a *textualized* pathological being into a mere *mnemonic* pathological being, thus becoming part of the physician and losing even this last form of individuality, as text, which separates patient from physician. The criticism delivered through this enjambment lies in the nonchalance with which the patient's needs for comfort and solace are met with the insensitivity of the physician.

The imprint of the lyrical-I's own ideology that reveals an objectification of the body follows a bonding moment between the lyrical-I and the patient. It establishes a connection through having shared the same profession, once (6-7), stressing however that this time is long ago for the lyrical-I (8-9), "Like you, I love / the people most, and was careful/ with their stuff" (28-30). After that, the own ideology of dissecting reveals itself, showing that the lyrical-I changed its way of thinking from moving objects from and into houses of moving itself into the body of patients, as the line continues "Folks in deep flux, / their precious homes opened up / as rib spreader is to thorax / on a table" (30-33). This simile of objects and organic material is repeated in the fourth stanza which refers to the first parallel between physician and patient before revealing the overall power that one has over another: ". . . . Like you, I only grew / into my skin comfortable when / I knew the pores to be slammed / opened doors, transitory as our" (50-53).

The lyrical-I views the body of the patient as an object that it can freely move in and out of, as something that can as easily be opened and closed as "homes" and "doors," forgetting that, to enter the body, implies a cut or at least penetration with the endoscope. Both will leave marks, possible even scars. A home is, in contrast to a body, built to be opened and closed. Of course intrusion will leave marks but the simile of the lyrical-I rests on the willingness of the home owner to open up their space. And the very difference between the home and the body arises within this willingness. An open door can be entered, the house explored without leaving a mark. The skin, the pores, will carry incisions and scars with them. The criticism in this passage lies in this exact enforcement of the lyrical-I projecting its language and profession onto the patient who thereby enters, imaginatively, its own death by following lyrical-I's steady movement into the body.

Staying with the body and combining the logic of the enjambment as it structures the whole collection and thus puts this poem in "section 1: aura," with its appearance as key device in the single poems, breathing becomes of central importance. If one takes the run-on lines as a rap technique of successfully breathing-in without stopping the flow of speech, one finds only two lines where the audible stop of the flow appears in all 55 lines (3, 8), not counting the final verse. Noticing that these lines appear close to the beginning of the poem, it seems as if the lyrical-I had to find its way into its own rhythm, to speak itself into the flow of the enjambment that even outpaces the demarcation or ignores the comfortable rest in-between stanzas. At this point it is worthwhile to look at the poem's title as well as the reference to Dr. Dre in line 21. With Dr. Dre, Mahagin chooses a rapper of international fame, someone who has perfected the rappers' ability to maintain the smoothness of the enjambement, by rapping and breathing almost simultaneously.

In the third and final step of this analysis of enjambment as the logical expression of this *epileptic* text, we will turn to the cover and the binding of *Grand Mal* which allude to the formulation of a *texture*alized pathological being. To establish this *texture*alized pathological being, the very surface of the book is scrutinized. Taking the color palate into account allows us to further underline the relation between clinic and society in protonormalistic terms—as they seem to have been experienced by Mahagin himself. The final step of my analysis addresses the central image on the book's cover that establishes the enjambment.

To see how this *epileptic* text can be articulated as a *texture*alized pathological being, the specific surface of the book's soft-cover is of importance, as it almost single-handedly internalizes the paradox of the clinic. Running one's fingers over the cover, they slightly stick to its surface, evoking childhood memories of playing with plasticine. At first stroke, the book feels as if it were malleable. Contrary to plasticine, though, which gives in to pressure because of its texture, the book only transmits a feeling, an illusion of malleability, without providing the materiality for something new to be created. To push this even further, the surface turns the touch from a gesture of motion into a steady grip. The coating enforces its own materiality onto the gesture. Instead of giving in to the influence, it influences the perceiver: one turns the touch into a grip, stopping the motion and resting the hand. The clinic, as experienced in this text, stresses this paradox of reversed influence. One could assume that the individual entering the clinic can participate in the formation of its treatment; the clinic, instead of adapting its definitions according to the patient, adapts the patient to the definition. In this sense the *texture*alized pathological being resonates with the *textualized* pathological being.

Grand Mal continues to push forward the notion of the clinic through its almost exclusively black and white finish. This black and white design of the cover is, nonetheless, interrupted twice by the signature trademark of the publishing house—the Rebel Satori Press' small, red rectangle that incorporates two white Japanese characters. The two tiny red rectangles, one of them placed on the bottom of the book's spine and the slightly bigger, second one on the back cover, at the left lower eighth of the book, resemble small incisions into the overall black and white cover, almost as if the book had been pierced—not severely pierced, however, but rather as if, for example, for measuring an epileptic patient's glucose level. Analogues to this *epileptic* text, these incisions measure its pathological state. Considering that the Rebel Satori Press views itself as "[p]ublishers on the frontiers of liminal space,"[12] providing a platform for upcoming author's from within the LGBT and disability movement as well as for artists that challenge the social status quo of normalcy, this trademark imprint can be seen as bringing to light what typically remains hidden in the clinic: the mechanisms of *protonormalism* that actively produce the pathological and excludes it. The experience of epilepsy as endured in the clinic that establishes this *epileptic* text becomes visible; in this *epileptic* text confidential information leaks out.

The enjambment of this *epileptic* text is mirrored in the image of a young woman's face that dominates both the front and the back of the book, making it impossible to hide from her gaze. The close-up picture of the young surgeon's or nurse's face is located at the right lower half of the white front-cover, while a zoomed-in augmentation of her gaze forms the entire backdrop of the back-cover. The book can, thus, only be put back into the shelf so that the spine is visible in order to protect oneself from her staring. Although it is a close up of her face, her eyes—her right eye in par-

12 <http://svendavisson.com/?page_id=287> consulted: 10/20/15, 11:06 p.m.

ticular—govern the picture. One cannot say if she is a surgeon or a nurse, but, due to her surgical mask and an operational cap, she certainly evokes the context of the clinic. The picture is reminiscent of the cinematic technique employed to represent the gaze of a newborn or a patient waking up from surgery, coma or just any other kind of unconsciousness, such as, for example, epilepsy. The latter reading parallels the theme of enjambment as continuity, since the picture continues on the back of the cover. Looking at the book, and adapting this logic, thus means that with each time the reader takes up the book s/he awakes out of a state of unconsciousness. The clinic, then, sets the overarching institutional parameters for what is conceived as normal. As an *epileptic* text, *Grand Mal* provides a look into the clinic and strengthens its a priori position through the enjambment of the staring woman on both sides of the book's cover.

In sum, through *Grand Mal* the reader experiences the effects of protonormalism on the individual who cannot but structure itself according to the logic of the *epileptic* text. Mahagin manages to formally endorse the clinical definition of epilepsy in such a manner that it marks his poetics as *dissecting*, incisive. In contrast to the first *protometaphor* that exhibited a chronology captured in the singular and uninterrupted clinical definition as mathematical ellipse, this text stresses the continuity of epileptic seizures and relies on the cosine function to capture this regularity. In terms of syntax this epileptic text relies on the enjambment, which enforces the chronology of the cosine in terms of its 'run on' line. In particular, *Grand Mal* stresses the *calculated individuation* of this *epileptic* text as displaying an interval of 13 poems | 30 pages. This *epileptic* text secures its ontological a priori even in the materiality of the book cover, equipping it with the feature of a *texture*alized pathological being that reiterates the power of the Foucauldian clinical gaze.

III.B Metaphor and Materiality: The Relational Body and Its Electric Individuation

III.B.1 Thom Jones' *The Pugilist at Rest*: Epilepsy as Compassion

"'—I saw the black lights'"
THOM JONES, "THE BLACK LIGHTS"

This chapter introduces epilepsy and boxing as a *relational metaphor* of compassion definitive of the short story collection *The Pugilist at Rest* by Thom Jones.[1] I will begin with a short overview of Thom Jones' literary oeuvre and critical reception, followed by a summary of the collection which highlights epilepsy and boxing as its central motifs. I will then turn to "The Pugilist at Rest," in particular, and offer a reading of the main character's individuation as marked by a metaphorization of epilepsy and box-

1 In a conversation with Bonny Lyons and Oliver Bill, Thom Jones addresses the connection between epilepsy, boxing, and compassion and thereby underscores this book' argument of a normative development from boxing to epilepsy that describes an individuation process: "I often wondered why I didn't go to Vietnam. I wanted to go, I was ready, but then I got injured in a boxing match, I developed epilepsy, which at the time seemed like a real bummer. As it turned out, though, everybody in my unit was killed, including my best friend, and presumably I would have been killed, too. The universe sends out a few prophets down to call it out, and Schopenhauer was one, and I am just mirroring it, channeling a lot of it" (120).

ing productive of an ethic of compassion. George Canguilhem's concepts of norm, normativity, and pain aid me in my unfolding of this first account of *electric individuation*.

Jones' oeuvre[2] encompasses three short story collections, *The Pugilist at Rest* (1993), shortly followed by *Cold Snap* (1995), and *Sonny Liston Was a Friend of Mine* (1999), which secured his presence as a newcomer on the literary plateau during the 1990s. Numerous stories from all three collections have been published in prestigious magazines and journals such as *The New Yorker*,[3] *Harper's*[4] and *The Mississippi Review*[5] as well as in magazines of a clearly masculine, mainstream orientation, promoting, if not favoring, the male gaze, such as *Esquire*, *GQ* and *Playboy*.[6] This fluctuation between high and popular culture might be one reason for the negligible academic reception of his oeuvre. Not knowing where to place his raw, out-dated 'machoism,' which oscillates between topics such as war veterans and boxing, scholars tend to compare him to writers of The Lost Generation. Jones' focus on boxing, in particular, leads one critic, for example, to compare his work "to the impact made by the young Hemingway, in the

---

2 His oeuvre has "[s]ince then . . . been anthologized frequently in The Best American Short Stories series and the O. Henry Awards collection" (Elieff and Jones 41).

3 *The New Yorker* published his first short story "The Pugilist at Rest" and continued to give Jones a literary platform and voice over the next decade.

4 *Harper's* published, similar to *The New Yorker*, one short story out of each collection, staying true to this author as well: "I Want to Live!" as well as "I Need a Man to Love Me"—published as "Nights in White Satin"—, and "Daddy's Girl." "I Want to Live!" also appeared in John Updike's and Katrina Kenison's collection *The Best American Short Stories of the Century* (2000), proving that with *The Pugilist at Rest*, Thom Jones made an impact on the 1990s literary scene, however short-lived his academic reception has been.

5 The *Mississippi Review* published "Rocket Man" as well as Jones' interview with Eden Elieff in 1998, which acknowledges his literary voice.

6 *Esquire* published "Wipeout" and "Ooh Baby Baby," covering Jones' first two collections, while *Playboy* included "Pickpocket," "Quicksand" and "Dynamite Hands," which were extracted from *Cold Snap* (1995), and "A Midnight Clear" found in *Sonny Liston Was a Friend of Mine* (1999).

early 1920s" (Lilly 123). But critical reception does not seem to go beyond this reading.

Jones' topics center on classically masculine issues such as war, friendship and bonding through fighting and an identification with boxing, and eventually, clash with the uprising gender discourses at the beginning of the 1990s (Lilly 129). Even Jones' other topics, such as medical drug abuse, urge critics to vehemently disparage his literary craftsmanship. But to read in boxing and addiction nothing more than the "boxer-warrior, macho maleness" (ibid.) is to miss out on what is actually a nuanced portrayal of the psychological intensity of the sport. In fact, the reduction of Jones' work to readings such as Lilly's and Bloom's does not give credit to the sensibility and honesty with which Jones approaches boxing as a philosophy of life. Additionally, what urges a more thoughtful consideration of his work, is his view on cancer (McCarron 59), his criticism on the state's health care system and the treatment of war veterans (Hennessy 204f.; Metzel 240), as well as the psychological and economical qualities of the American society on the threshold of institutionalized practices (Gerrig and Prentice 398). When Joyce Carol Oates writes in her *New York Times*' article that "[r]eading Thom Jones' fiction is like speeding in an open car: the landscape blurs, the momentum becomes intoxicating—and then the brakes are applied, with no warning" ("Their Bodies, Their Selves"), she highlights in his poetics, I argue, two leitmotifs—boxing and epilepsy—initiating a novel, more thoughtful approach to Jones' work.

The Pugilist at Rest divides into four parts, categorizing eleven short stories in sum. The three stories that define "Part I" center on an episode of epilepsy brought on in a momentous fight in the first-person narrator's life. "The Pugilist at Rest" focuses on this fight, while "Break on Through"[7] deals with the aftermath of the injury and "The Black Lights" portrays the hospitalization. "Part II" stresses the importance of incorporating a philosophy of boxing as fair fight into one's life. This can be seen in "Mosquitoes," where an ignorance of boxing parallels the negation of the charac-

7 With "Break on Through" by The Doors, "Wipeout," the song from the same-titled album by The Surfaris, "Unchain My Heart," by Ray Charles, and "Rocket Man," by Elton John, we can see Thom Jones' affiliation to poplar culture which is further explored in James D. Bloom's essay "Cultural Capital and Contrarian Investing: Roberts Stone, Thom Jones, and Others" (1995).

ter's vulnerability. This becomes even more obvious in "Wipeout," where the absence of epilepsy and boxing, and thus compassion, is mirrored in the first-person narrator who averts a 'fight' with his girlfriend, splits up with her and resumes his former gigolo persona, treating women as trophies. Meanwhile, in "Unchain My Heart" the protagonist fights for her first relationship until she is left heart-broken and pregnant, forced into an abortion where she has to "put [her] feet in the stainless-steel stirrups and the future heavyweight champion of the world is tossed into a plastic offal bag without throwing a punch" (127). In these short stories, the way in which the characters deal with their respective fights is linked to a philosophy of fair boxing.

"Part III" addresses the harsh inevitability and difficult acceptance of one's limitations in life and its social effect. While "As of July 6, I Am Responsible for No Debts Other Than My Own" connects not only thematically to "Part I," due to its first-person boxing narrator, it completes it on a structural level as well. The various narrators' experiences overlap with each other, suggesting these short stories are tied together through a diegetic connection. In "Silhouettes," the fear of dying from an epileptic seizure during sleep is embodied by the character Paul Palmer "who . . . had an epileptic seizure in his bed and suffocated facedown in his pillow" (148f.). This fear of death as the ultimate limitation to one's life becomes the leading topic of "I Want to Live!" where the main character, Mrs. Wilson, is dying of cancer. The reader enters into her experience of dying. The meticulous and nuanced descriptions of each step of the procedure demystify cancer and deprive character and reader alike of any guilt in observing it. Mrs. Wilson lives through fear and pain that can only be mitigated by her son-in-law, who seems to be the only one in the family capable of true compassion.

The last two short stories, "A White Horse" and "Rocket Man," define "Part IV" and serve to thematize the entire collection. While the first three parts focus either directly or indirectly on the experience of boxing, epilepsy or both, always from a first-person narrator perspective, "Part IV" changes the narrator's perspective. The compassionate view now comes from an omniscient narrator, allowing for the essence of boxing and epilepsy to transcend the terms of the 'fight' and manifest themselves as processes of individuation, establishing relations between individuals. In "A White Horse," the omniscient narrator takes on a merciful view of epilepsy allowing the epileptic protagonist, Ad Magic, to save a dying horse on the streets of India and then, for no other reason than compassion, pay for the tuition fees of an unknown child. "Rocket Man" addresses boxing and compassion again. Having won a fight, the young pugilist, Billy Preston, discusses his strategy for the upcoming fight with his trainer, W. L. Moore, who is in hospital. Finishing off the highly masculine-toned prep talk in an overflow of compassion for the old man,

> "Prestone squeezed Moore's shoulder and spoke, deliberately chopping off his words so his voice wouldn't break. 'I love you, champ. I love you more than anything. There's nothing in the world I wouldn't do for you. These are my true feelings. I love you. Don't fucking go south on me.'" (229)

As boxing and epilepsy permeate each story, then, capturing moments in the development of the first person narrator's life, one can connect the fighting scene from "The Pugilist at Rest," where the onset main character's epilepsy occurs, to the main character's psychiatric ward in "The Black Lights" and the humanitarian actions of Ad Magic from "A White Horse." To understand how boxing and epilepsy yield to compassion as a metaphor for this narrator's individuation, I will return to Canguilhem's concepts of norm, normativity, and pain. In viewing boxing and epilepsy as a *relational* account of the world which peaks in compassion, the history of epilepsy is demystified and boxing is portrayed as a metaphor for individual growth outside of the fight paradigm. Finally, epilepsy and boxing underscore the etymological heritage of "compassion"—suffering together—and, thus, the inherent connection between individuals.

"The Pugilist at Rest" deals with the first person narrator's memory of his time as a Marine, before, in and after the Vietnam War. The story evolves around him and two other Marines: his friend Jorgeson, who got killed on the war field while saving the narrator's life and Hey Baby, who used to bully Jorgeson for being sensitive. Beginning chronologically, with the obligatory training camp, the narrator gets back at Hey Baby for mistreating his friend Jorgeson, beating Hey Baby mercilessly until he is in need of neurosurgery, diagnosed with a fractured skull. It is the first mentioning of the narrator being a "skilled boxer" ("The Pugilist at Rest" 8). Being then in Vietnam, Jorgeson dies in the heroic act of saving his friend's life on the battlefield while the narrator "cut and ran from that field in

Southeast Asia" (19). After Jorgeson's death an interlude follows, wherein the narrator relays the story of the ancient Greek boxer, Theogenes, whose statue 'The Pugilist at Rest' lends the story its title. The narrator delves into the innumerable brave fights Theogenes won during his lifetime, painting the picture of an iconic boxer. After this interlude the story's setting shifts to the U.S., leaving Jorgeson and Theogenes as these two fighters. Back home, the narrator is caught up in a boxing fight against a superior opponent who hits him so hard that he develops epilepsy a year later. At the end of the story the narrator compares his friend Jorgeson with Theogenes, despising himself for being alive while his friend is dead. Similar to the Theogenes interlude, the narrator relays an account of Dostoyevsky and his epilepsy, thereby covering the two subjects that he identifies with: boxing and epilepsy. The story, told in hindsight, closes with the first person narrator thinking back to Hey Baby and what he had done to him along with the prospect of a surgery for controlling his seizures.

"The Pugilist at Rest" effectively portrays how the first person narrator's life develops from one norm into another, changing in *relation* to his respective milieu and stressing thereby the underlying principle of normativity. These two norms describe him before and after war, while his war experience echoes the normativity as in-between these two norms. War itself comes to serve a drastic if not traumatic event in his life. This does not, however, oppose Canguilhem's concepts of norm or normativity, as it applies to the individual and how it relates in a situation regardless of this situation's intensity. Posttraumatic Stress Disorder describes as much a norm as does epilepsy or any other physical or mental condition, and although one could easily focus on PTSD in this short story, the leitmotif of "The Pugilist at Rest" requires an analysis of the relation between boxing and epilepsy. Understanding thus that these norms describe how the individual participates in and is influenced by its milieu, these norms do not display separate, singular moments of the individuation process. And this process is furthermore defined as the normativity that actually positions the individual as in relation to "dynamic polarities."[8]

The narrator's individuation process leads to the compassion that comes from the experience of pain. He starts off, however, as a hard-boiled, almost naïve young man striving for heroism, yet eventually disillusioned by

8 See Chapter II.B of this book.

the trauma of war. His tale ends with mercy toward himself and to those he has inflicted pain on, feeling with them, without a sentimental wish for forgiveness: he becomes compassionate. Hence, as he enters the Marine Corps as a young man, he shows a strong identification with the drilling of the training conditions, viewing physical and psychical stability and fitness as the only means for achieving integrity. He does not accept any similarities between himself and his other recruits who cannot keep up with the required toughness:

> "In the course of training, lots of the recruits dropped out of the original platoon. Some couldn't pass the physical-fitness tests and had to go to a special camp for pussies. This was a particularly shameful shortcoming, the most humiliating apart from bed-wetting. Other recruits would get pneumonia, strep throat, infected foot blisters, or whatever, and lose time that way. Some didn't qualify at the rifle range. One would break a leg. Another would have a nervous breakdown (and this was also deplorable). People dropped out right and left." (5f.)

Although this description invites us to view the military as a microcosm of society in its normalization practices, where drop-outs range from gender, sex, ethnicity, age or ability, what is striking is that the narrator feels immune from these limitations; he distances himself from the idea of being vulnerable. There is no hint of empathy or understanding. He identifies himself through this distance between himself and the weak others. With the decrease of recruits the increase of his strong, fit, masculinity stabilizes and, moreover, stresses his singularity as privilege. And this view, strengthened by his respective military milieu, mirrors his understanding of boxing at that time.

His norm of war echoes in his understanding of boxing until it loses its sportive character and turns into war itself. He comes to see boxing as less a contest of physical and psychological finesse and more as a means of destruction. Being the "skilled boxer" (8) that he was, when he hits his fellow recruit Hey Baby, pursuing his weakest spot, he severely injures him:

> "There was blood from the scalp wound as well as froth of blood emitting from his nostrils and his mouth. Blood was leaking from his right ear. Did I see skull fragments and brain tissue? It seemed that I did. To tell you the truth, I wouldn't have cared in the least if I had killed him, but like most criminals I was very much afraid of getting caught." (9)

Even the fact that the person opposite from him turns into a spectacle of pain and death, turning his inner organs out, does not trigger any form of compassion but only strengthens his norm as the milieu to which he has adapted and on which he himself is exercising. There is nothing of boxing left, as there is nothing of his own vulnerability or compassion left. This passage shows clearly that the physical and mental norm that he displays at that incisive time before war echoes in his understanding of boxing.

From the training field to the battlefield, the narrator demystifies the heroism of war and pushes forward normativity as a principle of life. Being trapped by the NVA, losing his best friend Jorgeson, together with almost all of his platoon, while he can return without "a scratch [from] Vietnam" (20), his former norm is decisively tackled. Having deprived himself of heroism because he "cut and ran" (19), he resigns and falls into a rage against himself and others where he "grieved for [him]self and what [he] has lost" (20). Disconnecting himself from this distorted glorification of war, he is lost and in need of refiguring himself and his life. It is at this point, that his normativity as a life principle works upon figuring a new way for proceeding through and sustaining life. As war has broken away as a means for structuring his life, his boxing style has had to readjust accordingly. This search is the "apparently stable" moment that marks normativity. It is apparently stable in this case because he knows that his main tool for approaching the world is boxing, though in need of redefinition beyond a means for destruction.

This new orientation enters the text in the form of the interlude on Theogenes. Counting on this ancient figure's successes, where out of "[f]ourteen hundred and twenty-five times Theogenes was strapped to the stone and fourteen hundred and twenty-five times he emerged a victor" (18), Theogenes is the example *par excellence* of his former norm. Theogenes, however, whom the narrator views in the statue of 'The Pugilist at Rest,' does not embody glory and heroism but

". . . is sitting on a rock with his forearms balanced on his thighs . . . . There is a slight look of befuddlement on his face, but there is no trace of fear. There is an air about him that suggests that he is eager to proceed and does not wish to cause anyone any trouble or to create a delay, even though his life will soon be on the line. Besides the deformities of his noble face, there is also the suggestion of weariness and philosophical resignation. *All the world's a stage, and all the men and women merely players.*" (original emphasis 19)

The pugilist's posture and his concentrated, humble yet exhausted expression, stand in contrast to the image the narrator had of the perfect fighter. The narrator has to bring these nuances of Theogenes together, as they are carved into the statue. They provide a novel means for stabilizing his life according to boxing. Or, put differently, he can, through the statue as medium of self-reflection, allow for the unfolding of a life through boxing disconnected from the chimera of glorious fights.

He thus dives into a world of boxing that marks, through epilepsy and, hence, through pain, his individuation as in *relation* to others. In this manner Canguilhem's notion of pain and disease as "new ways of life" enter the narrator's normativity and manifest, at least for this narrator, as compassion. This decisive step in the narrator's individuation requires a short detour in order to understand the impact of this fighting scene. Throughout the whole short story collection the fight is repeatedly referred to, especially in the first part, where the argument that sustains the fight, reveals itself as the impetus for the narrator to relate to others. The titles "The Pugilist at Rest" and "The Black Lights" contribute to this correlation of boxing and epilepsy. The first title clearly issues from the fatigue that results from a life in continuity of fighting, stressing, thereby, the moment of pause that demarcates Theogenes. While the first story builds up and finds its climax in the fight, the latter deals with the aftermath of having seen "the black lights" (66) in the clinic.

Taking a look at this specific fighting scene in both stories, the semantic field elicits attention on light as electricity, on this singular electric event, and, thereby, signals its reception as the moment the narrator relates newly to his milieu: "He put me down almost immediately, and when I got up I was terribly afraid. I was tight and could not breathe. It felt like he was hitting me in the face with a ball-peen hammer. *It felt like he was busting light bulbs in my face*" (emphasis added, "The Pugilist at Rest" 20). The experience of this great force which is first compared to a hammer and then to bursting light bulbs is worth attention. While a ball-peen hammer is an object capable of great force through the extension of one's own bodily movement, imitating an arm and a fist, light bulbs appear as more complex, delicate objects, their force coming from their ability to generate electric light. Furthermore, while a hammer appears from a technological standpoint to be an object that has reached the apex of its developmental refinement, the light bulb, as an invention and product of the nineteenth century, transmits, on a material level, *enlightenment* and continues to be technologically refined. And it is in line with this simplicity and complexity that the hammer and the light bulb appear in this hierarchical order of endured pain for the individual.

This stress on light and electricity as the incisive measure for inflicting *pain* resonates with two passages in "The Black Lights," emphasizing the succession once more but also the entrance into "new ways of life":

> "I was a boxer with over a hundred and fifty fights, and I had taken a lot of shots, but this last punch was the hardest I had ever received and the first punch ever to put me down. I had seen stars before from big punches; I had seen pinwheels; but after that shot to the temple I saw the worst thing you ever see in boxing—I saw the black lights." (66)

This metaphor of the black lights, of being switched off, finds its mirror image in epilepsy when, in the same story, the narrator takes this metaphor and notes that "[j]ust before the fits, instead of having otherworldly spells, I felt only fear and would see the black lights of boxing. I was having very violent fits" (79). Hence, both boxing and epilepsy overlap and begin to establish a new norm for the individual almost immediately after this experience when the narrator states that "[s]uddenly I began to feel sympathetic to the cares and sufferings of all living creatures. You lose your health and you start thinking this way" ("The Pugilist at Rest" 22). This overflow of compassion regulates itself in the narrator and becomes a part of his life because he now relates himself to others, seeing himself not, as in the beginning of the story, in what distinguishes but, rather, what connects him with everyone else. It is not so much that this experience is bound to epilepsy as such, as it is that epilepsy stands metaphorically for any experience of vulnerability.

The former expression of war turns out to be a means of relationality. This becomes clear when the narrator ends the story remembering his former norm, thinking of Hey Baby, and wondering how he is feeling. The very person he had almost killed becomes a companion in suffering, through the relatability of being vulnerable. This form of compassion manifests throughout the entire story collection, never leaving boxing or epilepsy, until in the last part where the narrator affirms to his new compassionate stance toward the world. This is achieved formally through the switch to an omniscient perspective in "A White Horse," where the main character, who cannot tolerate the suffering of an animal, adopts a horse (199, 208).

In sum, *The Pugilist at Rest* is more than a display of machoism (Lilly 129) or failure of American pop cultural capital (Bloom 490f.). Attention to the ways in which boxing and epilepsy lead the narrator to compassion, requires a refusal of categorizing the text along such obvious readings that view boxing as an expression of masculinity or epilepsy as the violation of a person's consciousness. Furthermore, it displays the individuation process of the narrator that clearly outreaches any reduction to these two obvious first readings. In his refusal to aestheticize or diminish the pain of boxing or epilepsy, the first person narrator finds a means to connect to those others from which he initially alienated himself. In that sense Jones' works deprive epilepsy of its stigma and establish a new reading that stresses the fragility of health leading to compassion.

III.B Metaphor and Materiality: The Relational Body and Its Electric Individuation

III.B.2 Rodman Philbrick's *The Last Book in the Universe*: Epilepsy as Archive

> "First the smell of lightning fills my nose, the clean electric smell of the air after a thunderstorm, and then the blackness rises up and takes me down."
> RODMAN PHILBRICK, *THE LAST BOOK IN THE UNIVERSE*

With Rodman Philbrick's teenage cyberpunk novel *The Last Book in the Universe* (2000), this chapter provides a second account of how epilepsy as a *relational metaphor* gives rise to motifs outside of the historical. In this particular novel, the main character's epileptic brain serves as an archive for storing memories. When we apply the concepts of norm,[1] normativity,[2] pain[3] and patient[4] as introduced by George Canguilhem, we can retrace how the main character, Spaz, individuates according to epilepsy and, hence, gains this archiving quality. My analysis begins with a short summary of the novel's plot and an introduction of its characters. This is fol-

1 See Chapter II.B of this book.

2 See Chapter II.B of this book.

3 See Chapter II.B of this book.

4 See Chapter II.B of this book.

lowed by a reading of the history of epilepsy as presented in this novel in accordance to Canguilhem's concepts of social norms.[5] After providing a distinction between social and vital norms, the analysis shifts toward an understanding of the main character's individuation through epilepsy. Both parts of the analysis unfold alongside the plot due to the novel's epic diegesis, resonating with Canguilhem's understanding of normativity as it unfolds successively throughout one's life. A focal point for the second part of the analysis will be the *organ in sound*,[6] describing the main character's seizures. This chapter concludes with a discussion of the newly acquired norm of the protagonist as 'vital archive,' who furthermore learns to own his normativity and thereby matures as an individual.

The Last Book in the Universe is set in a not too distant future evolving along Spaz' journey to find a cure for his sick little sister, Bean, who is dying of leukemia. In this dystopia, Spaz must navigate between two complementary social models, Eden and Urb, which are acting out an imbalance in power distribution; the first secures its power by reigning over the second. Epilepsy comes to play a decisive role in this relationship between Eden and Urb preventing Spaz from participating in the poisonous antagonism between those two through an immunity to "mindprobe" addiction. Mindprobes function through electrode needles, which stimulate an individual's brain according to its favored bodily experiences, inducing corporeal hallucinations. Spaz' brain reacts with a seizure to this intervention, which means that his condition turns his epileptic brain into a shield (Philbrick 39). These mindprobes are futuristic drugs used by genetically engineered humans, so-called "proovs," who live in a secured district, "Eden," to control the "normals" living in "the Urb." The Urb encompasses a huge territory surrounding Eden which splits up into three districts referred to as "latches." The plot develops alongside Spaz' journey through these latches as he looks to find a medication for his sister Bean. In order to save his little sister's life, Spaz and his acquaintances, Ryter, Little Face and the "proov" of the group, Layana, enter Eden. The novel ends with Bean being 'cured' of her leukemia, Little Face staying in Eden, Ryter being massacred, and Spaz being the only one of this group outside of Eden able to tell their story. He becomes a 'vital archive' of his own experience

5 See Chapter II.B of this book.

6 See Chapter II.B of this book.

as well as that of the others. Spaz' individuation is inextricably bound to his epilepsy and describes, respectively, how he relates to the world.

Spaz' social norms begin with his early encounters with what it means to be different because of his epilepsy, experiencing normalization practices of exclusion. He grew up in a foster family living in a latch that was located close to Eden and free of mindprobes. The novel begins with Spaz' in his teenage years. He lives in the latch flooded with mindprobes and devastation, ruled by a latch boss named Billy Bizmo, who we learn, at the end of the novel, is his biological father. Spaz is Billy's henchman, stealing for him. Expelled from the home of his foster father, because "[n]obody wants to claim a spaz boy, that's for sure," his stepfather "got it fixed in his head that [Spaz] was growing up dangerous and that somehow Bean might get infected with whatever it was that made [him] a spaz" (37). At the beginning of the novel Spaz shows that he has internalized what people with epilepsy have suffered from throughout history—that is, those features categorized in this thesis under the motif of *danger*:[7] contagiousness, abandonment and exclusion. He himself adapts to these discrimination practices and leans in to his future as a person of lower value who earns his living by stealing.

While his foster parents and his direct milieu treat him as a "spaz boy," he encounters a completely different treatment from a character named Ryter, who introduces Spaz to famous epileptics. Here, Philbrick covers the historical motif of *intelligence*.[8] Ryter, is an old guy, a "gummie," awaiting Spaz to rob him. He willingly hands him out everything that he owns, except for his most valuable treasure: a book, a historical cultural artifact. Spaz cannot see the reason for protecting something as impracticable as a story—"What's the point if you can't touch it or steal it or shoot it into your brain?" (19)—not knowing, however, that he himself will become a story, or, rather, that his brain will form a book to archive memories. Intrigued by Spaz' epilepsy, Ryter begins to liken Spaz to all the famous epileptics that he has read about (38). This shakes Spaz' worldview tremendously, having endured only stigmatization and discrimination.[9] After the robbery, when Spaz has taken all of Ryter's belongings, except for the book, he runs into a

---

7 See Chapter I.A of this book.

8 See Chapter I.A of this book.

9 See Chapter I.A of this book.

"proov" called Layana, a girl about his age, who sneaks out into the Urb to provide the starving people with food. Disturbed by this surreal image of the perfect human among the normals, he heads back home where he receives a message from a "runner." Runners are people that move in-between the latches, a highly risky task since every latch forms a dictatorship of its own, punishing them, if caught, with death. The runner tells him that his little sister Bean's sickness has become worse and that she might be dying.

This message leads Spaz to embark on a dangerous journey to visit his sister one last time; it requires moving between latches and initiates his individuation. Refused of a safe passage by Billy Bizmo, Spaz plans to leave the Urb "out along the Edge" (51), stressing the transitional space he is actually and metaphorically moving in—that is, actually and metaphorically in terms of his individuation through epilepsy. Accordingly, seizures take up a decisive role in this chapter, as Spaz thinks back to his first epileptic attack which led to his abandonment: a seizure triggered by his excitement over his little sister's alleged recovery. His vital norm at that time exposed an overwhelming joy while, in contrast, the social norm labeled him deviant and dangerous. Thinking back to this first seizure, then, Spaz collapses in front of a wild mob that wants to "cut his red" (54) because they recognize him as one of Billy Bizmo's henchmen. This time the seizure is the result of tremendous fear. Ryter, who has observed the seizure, decides to accompany Spaz on his adventure through the latches and begins to familiarize Spaz with the history of his condition. Ryter again focuses on the motif of *intelligence*, enlisting famous epileptics.

"'Shut up about the spaz, okay? I don't want to hear about it. I don't want to talk about it.' 'And you don't want to think about it,' Ryter adds. 'Fine. Agreed. I shall not speak of the innumerable famous and successful human beings who shared your condition. I shall not speak of Julius Caesar, Napoleon Bonaparte, Leonardo da Vinci, Agatha Christie, Lewis Carrol, or Harriet Tubman. I will never again mention Joan of Arc, Vincent van Gogh, Sir Isaac Newton, Alfred Lord Tennyson, Edgar Allan Poe, or the great Paganini. Done. Finished. My lips are zipped.'" (60)

Spaz' reaction to this extreme juxtaposition between his memory of abandonment and degradation, on the one hand, and Ryter's praising, on the other hand, stresses clearly that both sides do not capture the actual experience of having epilepsy, which means that the actual experience of epilepsy cannot be grasped by its socio-historic motifs.

Moving through old water pipes into the first latch, Spaz and Ryter meet Little Face who is incapable of verbal communication and joins their group, which by now includes a person with epilepsy, an old man, and this mute child. They are a group of outsiders in a time of hunger, depression and devastation. To get to Bean's latch, which is ruled by a boss called Lotti Getts, marking the only mindprobe-forbidden-zone outside of Eden, they first have to pass Mongo's district. As it turns out, this boss is addicted to mindprobes and lives in a decaying body while his mind is peacefully plugged into a constant "loop" (84) in Eden. Little Face, Ryter and Spaz pass through this latch as they assist a new latch boss in gaining power. In return, he ensures a free escort through the next latch, where they go on to rescue the proov Lanaya from a mob of starving people. Lanaya becomes the fourth member of this group, arriving safely in Lotti Getts' latch where Bean lives and mindprobes are forbidden. In this particular community epilepsy again reiterates the history of its disorder when Spaz is accused of having "bad blood" (112) and is referred to as "deef" (149), which designates the epileptics motif of *danger*, as it serves as shorthand for genetic defects. Bean's condition is comatose so the group of four take her to Eden to find a cure.

As it turns out, the main purpose of the people of Eden is to form a new, better species of humans, which can easily be read as resembling an eugenicist's[10] ideal (180f.). This is further stressed due to the geographically-secluded area that is, as the name alludes to, a paradise in a beautiful natural landscape equipped, however, with advanced technology. To coin it "Eden" evokes a creationist's and eugenicist's reading, where humans, through genetic engineering, take in a position of godlike superiority. Layana views the hierarchical position of her people over "the normal" critically, culminating in her statement: "'[w]e despise the very idea of being 'normal,' and yet those who are normal do not despise us for our apparent 'perfection'" (207). The group has to leave Eden after a cure for Bean is genetically engineered. The alteration of Bean's DNA was necessary for that matter since medical knowledge is obsolete in Eden because no one ever gets sick. This invention evokes Canguilhem's view on cure as chime-

10 See Chapter I.A of this book.

ra, since a body never gets back to his former norm but establishes a new one. Here the new norm marks not the restoring of biological innocence but its enhancement, altering the body's own normativity.

Leaving Eden, it becomes obvious that both of the two extremes that structure the cosmos of *The Last Book of the Universe*, the Urb and Eden, are not fitting for Spaz, who is the only one who does not belong to either world's schema. His epilepsy makes him an outsider. In some latches of the Urb his epilepsy hinders him from experiencing mindprobes while in mindprobe-free districts his epilepsy is viewed as a degeneration; in Eden he does not fit in because he is considered genetically imperfect. This position in-between extremes defines him, nevertheless, as the only possible safe archive for storing humanity's knowledge. The people of Eden control and manipulate all surrounding districts, keeping knowledge to themselves with the greater aim of allowing the normals to die in their addiction to mindprobes, being captured in decaying bodies with a supposedly free mind. In fact, the only free mind left is Spaz'. Back in the Urb, the importance of Spaz' brain becomes apparent when Ryter is massacred in front of Spaz' eyes. Before Spaz can be traumatized by the volatile spectacle of his friend's gory death scene, his brain's protective function snaps in and pushes him out of consciousness. The last words that he hears his friend say, "save my pages" (221), assign Spaz with the task of securing his witnessing of their era. Spaz takes on the task to write down his own story in an archive for future generations. As the task of writing down one's history has gained importance for Spaz during their adventure so has his own biography and life.

In Canguilhem terms, Spaz' brain clearly displays the epistemological distinction between social and vital norms. Looking at the universe of *The Last Book in the Universe*, we see that social norms can work as a means for securing a position of power for an elite minority—the people of Eden—which stigmatizes and controls the vital norms of a majority, the normals. The fact that the people of the Urb are called normals underscores the differentiation Canguilhem opens up when he states that social norms secure normalization while vital norms display normativity. Spaz' epileptic brain is vital and detached from normalization practices since its very nature marks a clear distinction between him and the people of Eden but, moreover, due to his vital norm, he is protected against their normalization practices: the mindprobes. His brain thus preserves what is considered almost given nowadays—that is, being the owner of one's consciousness—and thereby reverses what has always been the most fearful aspect of epilepsy: the loss of control. Here, losing consciousness describes a vital norm of the mind and body to strongly fight for ownership of the self. It is not as much a reinterpretation of the history of epilepsy—as Spaz experiences the social exclusion—but an invitation from the author to sensitize the audience for the differentiation between social practices and bodily alteration. The socio-cultural sphere is experienced as oppressing by the individual, yet, it is the individual's normativity that upholds its uniqueness. A momentary blackout, such as in Spaz' epileptic attacks, is more desirable than the complete loss of one's identity. It thereby marks the individual's norm as one outside of the statistical differentiation between pathology and health, displaying "life as dynamic polarity."

In line with Canguilhem's thought, I argue that the main character's vital norm needs to be separated from the social norms that mirror the history that discriminates against him. From the first chapter on, where Spaz is discriminated against, the reader can detect the novel meaning given to epilepsy. In order to understand how Spaz' epilepsy marks an 'original account of the world'[11] and establishes a destigmatizing *relational metaphor*, a closer look at the mindprobes is necessary. Spaz is one of the few characters capable of long-term memory and thus the of preserving his own identity. In a world where minds are manipulated and controlled and other people's brains have been "softened by needle probes . . . . [l]ong-term memory is a thing of the past, no pun intended" (18). Spaz' originality is secured by being aware of who he is. Among people decaying in their own bodies, having been "normalized" into a homogenized controllable group, Spaz remains resistant to normalization, upholding his own original account of the world. His relation to the world is implied in his epilepsy as counteracting comparability and upholding individuality. Epilepsy secures his identity, which means that he can distinguish himself from others; his body and mind are literally convulsing against intervention. In that sense, the shivering, shaking and convulsing, the former loss of control and momentary loss of identity, uphold the overall stability of the individual as individual.

11 See Chapter II.B of this book.

In this relation of epilepsy and milieu, epilepsy also serves as a metaphor for the rebellion against and liberation of an oppressive regime. While the majority accepts willingly and unquestionably self-destructing norms—one can say that they factually incorporate them—the ruling minority elite can reign unimpeded. Spaz' vital norm, his originality, is to define the moment of chance without, however, drifting into heroism. He cannot, however, appreciate the liberty that comes with his vital norm at the beginning of the novel, as he experienced too much discrimination because of his epilepsy. This is important to mention because the novel does not aestheticize epilepsy or diminishes the pain or the experience of being discriminated. It does however introduce different, new relations between bodies and society, enabling the necessary nuance that lies in the alterity of the first. To take up the energetic power of the expression 'to spark,' Spaz' brain can be seen, due to its epilepsy, to provide the needed stability for archiving memories and thus sparking a revolution for future societies to embrace individuality. This is Spaz' way of finding orientation in the world that is *epilepsy,*[12] because it is individual. An individuality that, for him, is undesirable at the beginning of the novel, as his 'spark' results in an outburst leading to his deportation.

This outburst describes, on two levels, his epilepsy as *electric way of life*: ". . . I've got this serious medical condition that means I'm allergic to electrode needles" (1). Electrode needles are typically used to measure the electrical activity of muscles or nerves. Allowing for the mindprobes to be seen as infusing experience into the receiver, these experiences work on the body's own electrical charge and regulation, stimulating the brain in such a way that it is deprived of its own neuronal function. In this sense the social means to control the people is electrically infused into their biology, altering it. Spaz' brain can, in contrast to others, communicate directly, on the same level of materiality. Furthermore, electricity as the communication device of the social and vital within the individual is artificially linked to the social while remaining naturally part of the vital. This allergic reaction thereby highlights the brain's answer to the manipulation: it repels vigorously. This strategy is employed again when the society, as a phenomenon, clashes against the vital, because it tries to use one of its own phenomena

12 See Chapter II.B of this book.

against it; here, the clash stresses the principle of the living in its vital materiality.

An additional reading of the outburst as *electric way of life* can be located in what Canguilhem linked to the notion of pain: "[d]iseases are new ways of life." Considering pain as a parameter for displaying the body's normativity, we can read pain as that which converts into electricity, beginning in the body and becoming visible to the outside world. Concerning the individual, pain and electricity describe the two ends of this *electric way of life*. The pain itself is not experienced in the actual outburst but in the aftermath whereas electricity describes the other end of the spectrum as it comes to light only in the preliminary stages. The individual, Spaz, is thus aware of being in an apparently stable equilibrium of life. It is the electrical charge of his neurons that echoes the equilibrium's sensitivity. Electricity and pain thus form a bond with each other that encompasses the actual outburst. In as much as electricity is the inner body's communication, pain defines the aftermath of this communication that turned from within the individual body toward its milieu and back to the individual. In this sense, it can be seen as a communication of the body, where the individual's corporeal disposition negotiates between the dynamic polarities of life: the individual normativity voice's itself.

With Spaz, this normativity becomes clear when situations overwhelm him, as in joy or in fear. Therefore, the term of *organ in sound* refers to his body which speaks to him in an electric way, defining the first seizure in the novel when Spaz claims that "I can't keep it from happening, no matter how hard I try. It always begins this way. First the smell of lightning fills my nose, the clean electric smell of the air after a thunderstorm, and the blackness rises up and takes me down" (55). Keeping in mind that it is the *organ in sound*, Spaz has no direct way of stopping this sound from voicing itself because it is his normativity navigating through life, measuring itself in-between extreme influences. This particular seizure overcomes him at the beginning of his journey, marking the first visible step, for the reader, of Spaz' individuation.

Since epilepsy defines the framework through which Spaz experiences his journey as a process of individuation, the metaphor of electricity in "my blood still feels electrified" has to be read in this particular way. This electrified feeling spreads through him shortly before he and his friends arrive at his sister's place. It marks, thereby, epilepsy as his normativity, as the apparently stable equilibrium which resides in him constantly and not only in the moments of its outburst. A final outburst of his normativity as *electric way of life* appears at the end of the novel, thus bringing his journey to a close and, as far as the reader can participate in it, his individuation. In an almost identical formulation to the beginning of his journey he describes the onset of his seizure, "... then the smell of lightning fills my nose, the clean electric smell that comes after a thunderstorm, and the blackness rises up and takes me down" (226). In this instant, his brain kicks in his protective ability and shuts him out of consciousness since what he would have been watching in a conscious state of mind would be the massacre of his friend. Not being traumatized, however, he can fulfill his friend's last wish, stating that Spaz is "the last book in the universe" (225).

With this statement, Spaz has moved, not changed, into his next norm, which describes his individuation through epilepsy. And thus echoes Canguilhem's thought, in as much as the cure is not the answer of the individual in its relation to the world, but a movement from one homeostasis to another. Spaz still has his epilepsy, but his relation to his epilepsy has changed significantly: "[t]hey call me Spaz, which is kind of a mope name, but I don't mind, *not any more*" (emphasis added, 8). Spaz tells his story in hindsight, beginning at a time when he did not like his name—the one which, at the end of the novel, changes. Spaz' story corresponds to Canguilhem's view on the *patient* arguing that it is the patient who has the power to decide whether or not to seek and accept medical advice. While, at the beginning of the novel, Spaz can only focus on the socially enforced norms that discriminated against him, he can, at the end of the novel, appreciate his brain's ability to protect himself from forgetting his identity and his beloved ones. Now, he is aware of his epilepsy as an orientation toward the world as well as a means of securing his individuality and the history of his time, urging him to write down his story.

In this novel of epilepsy as *relational metaphor* that works, I argue, through Canguilhem's notion of norms, normativity, pain, and patient, epilepsy acquires the metaphor of an archive. This metaphor can stabilize itself through the notion of epilepsy as an orientation of the individual toward the world. Considering the distinction between social and vital norms, this book shows quite vividly how historical ascriptions to epilepsy continue to serve as a strong force in social discrimination. The main character Spaz endures stereotypical stigmatization, be it exclusion or praise, hindering him from including epilepsy into his perception of the world and from ascribing an individual meaning to it. His social status at the beginning of the novel oscillates between the motifs of *danger* and *intelligence*, describing however a completely unrelated, separated understanding of his epilepsy for himself. Looking at epilepsy as part of his vital norm, however, the character individuates according to himself until he turns into a vital archive. This distinction in ascription between social and vital norm has a liberating meaning for the notion of epilepsy as well as for the individual. Over the centuries, epilepsy has been feared because it ostensibly deprives the individual of itself through the uncontrollable loss of consciousness. In this novel, however, the opposite occurs: the seizure secures the individual in remaining and, moreover, becoming itself. It is in this second instance of *relational metaphors* of epilepsy that the multiplicity of new epilepsy metaphors can, together with the multiplicity of main characters displaying and experiencing epilepsy, liberate epilepsy from a normalizing and stigmatizing perspective.

III.B Metaphor and Materiality: The Relational Body and Its Electric Individuation

III.B.3 Reif Larsen's *I Am Radar*: Epilepsy as Communication

> "This is the lesson: find your own frequency."
>
> REIF LARSEN, *I AM RADAR*

With Reif Larsen's *I Am Radar* (2015)[1] epilepsy as a *relational metaphor* finds its most potent expression of the individual becoming an *organ in sound*,[2] allowing the body's vital materiality to communicate effectively with the world via electricity. The emphasis here lies on the effective communication, since the *organ in sound* defines a language from within the individual that turns itself toward the world, though is not understood by it. It thus distinguishes sharply between the vital and the social.[3] This novel, thereby, envisions how the vital becomes relatable to the social without being normalized. Canguilhem's concepts of vital and social norm help us to

1 *I Am Radar* is the second novel by Reif Larsen published six years after the great success of *The Selected Works by T.S. Pivet* (2009) which became a motion picture in 2013, entitled *The Young & Prodigious Spivet*, directed by Jean-Pierre Jeunet starring, among others, Helena Bonham Carter.

2 See Chapter II.B of this book.

3 See Chapter II.B of this book.

further grasp how the main character's epilepsy defines his normativity,[4] stressing that no "biological innocence" can be achieved. *I Am Radar* articulates, in particular, through the unique materiality of the main character, an *electric way of life*.[5] Although Canguilhem's notion of normativity as well as the interplay of vital and social norms apply to many characters in this novel, highlighting, with each of them, how the respective individual copes with changes by establishing a new relation to its milieu, the focus of this analysis lies on the main character's, Radar's, individuation process. It is preceded with a short outline of the novel's central themes.

With over 650 pages *I Am Radar* stretches over four continents, incorporates wars and scientific breakthroughs of the twentieth century and unfolds, meticulously, the biography of minor characters, linking all these events to a secretive group of performance artists that goes by the name of "the Kirkensferda performance group." Although the first formation of artists to found this group met during World War II in Kirkenes, Norway, *I Am Radar* begins in New Jersey, 1975, with the birth of the main character Radar, and ends with the beginning of a spectacular performance staged in The Democratic Republic of the Congo in 2012. Over the course of roughly 70 years, the novel addresses the lives of the performance artists and their histories. Addressing the Khmer Rouge in Cambodia, from the end of the 1960s to 1975, and travels through former Yugoslavia, from 1975 to the beginning of the Croatian War of Independence in 1991. All characters experience war and refugee crises. They also develop each their own ability to grapple with the radical scientific breakthroughs of their respective times. Among the manifold physical topics that this novel thus addresses, it refers especially to Nicola Tesla's idea of a worldwide communication system—which was almost realized in the Wardenclyff Tower in 1901—and discusses Werner Heisenberg's uncertainty principle as well as Erwin Schrödinger's superposition of eigenstates.[6] This group of performance artists

4 See Chapter II.B of this book.

5 See Chapter II.B of this book.

6 The superposition of eigenstates permeates the whole novel and could be treated as a motif of its own. Beginning with Radar, who is black and white, this juxtaposition continues in the supposed death of three characters whose death is never witnessed or affirmed. They merely vanish, leaving their beloved ones completely clueless; they are, thus, simultaneously dead and alive. One of these

specializes in puppeteering and quantum physics, archiving their performances in a book called "Spesielle Particles." At the intersection of science, political revolution and performance, this novel delineates the similarities between these three areas, treating them as one epistemological category that yields an understanding of the present as it takes place:

> "The staging itself is the art form. They aren't meant to be seen—they're meant to happen . . . . I think for us, the notion of audience is not limited to a group of people sitting in chairs, watching the stage. The universe can also be an observer. The atoms, the quarks, the elemental bonds—all of these can pay witness to the show. There are many ways to alter the course of time." (Larsen 572)

The main character Radar Radmanovic joins this group at the end of the novel, and participates in one of their performances. It is through his own normativity, that the core of the group's ideology is exposed.

What will be of interest in the following analysis is, thus, how epilepsy exhibits Radar's own original being.[7] The main story evolves around Radar, a radio conductor from New Jersey, who has epilepsy and joins the Kirkensferda performance group on their way to their next great act which is to take place in The Democratic Republic of the Congo. Radar's life develops almost analogously to that of a superhero. With a technological expertise beyond imagination, Radar experiences social exclusion as a child and lives a rather isolated life as an adult. To continue the superhero theme, he is a shy, humble, and responsible person who falls deeply in love with the 'girl next door,' Ana Cristina, who loves him in return. This mutual love must be put on hold, however, as Radar's journey across the Atlantic begins immediately after he and Ana confessed their affection for each other. The immediacy of the journey is due to a blackout caused by his father, Kermin Radmanovic—a radio conductor as well who built a so-called vircator to reverse the effects of epilepsy in Radar brought on by his exposure to an experiment on electromagnetic waves when he was a child. Since Radar's father, Kermin, a member of the Kirkensferda performance group, vanishes as a result of the blackout, Radar must take his place in the group.

---

characters is Kermin Radmanovic, Radar's father, who vanishes after causing a total blackout in the entire state of New Jersey.

7 See Chapter II.B of this book.

What makes Radar worthy of participation in this group is his own specific organic materiality: he can communicate with technical objects as well as with nature through his own electrical waves, feeling their electrical charge and being in resonance with them.

Verging on scientific possibility and magic, Radar Radmanovic's birth already poses a conundrum to parents, doctors and society alike, who push forward normalization practices in order to understand this child's organic materiality. It is not clear if either his body's frequency initiated the total blackout during his birth or if the total collapse of electricity was a mere coincidence; either way, Radar comes into life during "a new kind of darkness" (4). The exceptionality of his being continues: although both parents are white, Radar is born black, "a negative image of "[him]self" (8). Any speculations of adultery are immediately taken off the board since Radar exhibits the exact same facial features as his father Kermin Radmanovic, merely in black. Without any possible explanation for his vital norm Radar is, at the same time, "the whitest of whites," and "the blackest of black," (14). In that respect, his originality strikes against too many social norms to be accepted as he is. Driven by curiosity, guilt, stigmatization and discrimination, his mother drags the child through an infinitesimal amount of doctors, until a group of Norwegian researchers promises to change the child's skin color by exposing it to electromagnetic waves that will "manipulate the physical composition of these melanosome radios to our [scientists'] liking. We can change their structure. And thus their appearance" (95).

Such drastic measures—where one's child is willingly exposed to a room full of electromagnetic waves that penetrate its skin in order to reconfigure its biological texture—show how strongly social norms enforce themselves on the conduct of people. Radar's mother Charlene, however, who is caught in this vicious circle of normalization, regrets her decision once Radar's vital norm becomes threatened. His skin begins to "peel" off (126), making him vulnerable to light, temperature and texture; his hair falls out and he seems to have developed epilepsy, turning him, again into an object of discrimination, and thus highlighting that the adjustment to a norm set outside of the individual not only counteracts the individuation process as it dictates the parameters, but also emphasizes that discrimination cannot be avoided through adaptation. Furthermore, it stresses the ontological difference between social and vital norms. While social norms require the establishment of increasingly more organization/organs in order to sustain normalization, vital norms reside in the organism where they establish its normativity.

Taking a closer look at Radar's vital normativity, then, one can already read an *electric way of life* in his name "'Radar,' [Kermin] confirmed, bouncing and recalling his fingers from an invisible barrier. 'Like this: Signal. Echo. Return'" (11). This bouncing and recalling of fingers visualizes how Radar will relate to the world, his own vital materiality pointing to waves radiating into the world and back to their receiver. His normativity is his constant electrical pulse, which is sent out by his body trying to configure his position in the world and to the world always anew. This means he is embodied in the world as perceiving the waves of each object surrounding him while sending out his own frequency, being in a constant exchange with the world without always being consciously aware of it. There is no decoding necessary, because the communication is transmitted through the wave lengths that, in contrast to electromagnetic light,[8] can move through objects, allowing this communication to take on an almost omniscient power, reminiscent of an eighteenth century notion of ether. In fact, in naming his son Radar, Kermin gives him the name of what he himself considers a medium for communicating with God (29). Radar's normativity, although apparently always part of his life, displays itself differently in his childhood years than as an adult, showing that it maintains as a principle but refines together with the individual's conscious and elaborate way of relating to his surroundings.

As a child Radar's electricity displays itself in two rather extremely opposed ways, echoing the manipulation of his vital norm but also visualizing his body's normativity. Radar exhibits an understanding of technical objects that transcends any knowledge of schoolmates or teachers alike (289). He builds, connects, reconnects and establishes new communication networks via telephone boxes throughout the whole city, making the boxes ring to his command. This love of technical objects could, however, merely be the product of observing his father's dedication to them. Through his epilepsy, Radar's own vital materiality, his normativity comes to light as a novel form of relating to the world:

---

8 One character is named Raksmey which means "Ray of Light" (436) in Cambodian. His account of the world is given as a 'visible' display of knowledge, being enlightened, while Radar's is 'invisible' in the form of electricity.

"From the kitchen, Charlene sensed a misplaced stillness in the air. She came into the room and found her son sitting like a statue, his torso rigid and strangely arched backwards, a motherboard lying in the palm of one hand. And then a wave passed through him, and his entire frame began to shiver and shake uncontrollably, sending him tumbling into the pile of radio parts splayed out before him. At first she thought he might have electrocuted himself accidentally, but when he continued to shake, she ran over and held him as his eyes rolled backwards and his arms popped and trembled in their sockets. A wilted smell of urine filled the air. She put her hand on his face and felt his jaw balling and grinding into itself with an uncanny mechanical persistence. His hat fell to the ground, revealing the lonely lateral tuft. On the television, the picture of Godzilla went soft and then split into a static that pulsed and thrummed with each of Radar's convulsion. A stench of burnt wires wafted through the room" (128f.).

Radar's first epileptic attack reveals a connection between his electrical current and that of the technical objects surrounding him. The television's frozen image can be seen as a metonym for Radar's seizure which is a "disruption of the electrical communication between neurons."[9] Similar to the television's disturbance of transmitting a moving image and being on hold and bound to this one image, Radar's motions are interrupted and display a single movement. Already, in this first seizure, one can see that Radar's relation to the world is an *electric way of life* which is trying to find a way to effectively communicate with the world. His materiality makes itself seen, heard, and smelled, thus serving as an *organ in sound* where the vital is effectively mediated to its social surrounding via technology. While Radar's body is on high voltage anticipating his succeeding pain in the cramping organs, joints, and bones, his pain as internal language[10] has left his body and speaks to the world via the humming picture. The smell of "burnt wires" is especially fitting for the *organ in sound*, as the *organ in sound* does not allude to the mere perception of sound but describes the experience of pain.

---

9 <http://www.epilepsy.com/learn/about-epilepsy-basics> consulted: 08/06/15, 1:35 p.m.

10 See Chapter II.B of this book.

Along with the novel's leap into Radar's adult years, his normativity as electricity becomes a means for him to relate to the world—not only through the *organ in sound*, not only through his pain, but on a daily basis that underlines his own notion of normal. This becomes clear in those moments when Radar describes his experience of automatic doors as in relation to a "[r]adio signal [which] felt much more organic—like swimming in the ocean versus swimming laps in a tiny pool, though he didn't know how to swim, so he couldn't be sure if such an analogy was entirely accurate" (270). The term organic, highlights Radar's vital materiality in resonance with electromagnetic waves, incorporating electricity as physical phenomenon into the biological and thus bridging the gap of what in the vitalist tradition is treated as two separate spheres: the physico-chemical and the biological describe two forms in which living can take place. Radar's normativity, however, combines both, envisioning thereby the same principle. This does not mean, however, that Radar's unique connection to machines annihilates the distinction between technical objects and humans. Radar communicates on a different level with machines than with humans. When he has a seizure the machines take care of themselves, feeling his electrical discharge and reacting accordingly: "they had looked after themselves while he had shifted into another plane [seizure]. They had felt his contractions, felt the throbbing agony of his synapses, but they had not faltered in his absence" (294). It rather broadens the notion of actively-participating entities in the world, or "actors" in a Latourian sense, in order to re-invent the notion of both of these concepts as well as their relation toward one another.

Following Radar's normativity as communicating his electrical current with that of his milieu, he resonates with technical objects as well as with nature, connecting with each entity's own vital norm, being on the search to "find [his] own frequency" (317). After the big blackout that his father caused in order to reverse the "reversed electrocution" of Radar's childhood years that triggered his seizures, Radar meets "[a] wary duck [...] eyeing him from a little spit of marsh water just beyond. He nodded to the bird, conspiratorially, as if what had just transpired had all been on purpose. The duck had nodded back" (299). This mutual understanding becomes even stronger on his way to The Democratic Republic of the Congo, where shipping across The Atlantic Ocean "[t]he salt water had an electromagnetic frequency all its own, but it was a frequency with which he [Radar] was not familiar. Its note was singular, ancient, without end. He had come from a symphony [the city], and now he was listening to an old man singing in the dark" (528).

This ensemble of three entities, each of which is in communication with Radar in its own "frequency"—the duck, the city, and the ocean—is further enriched by the ship. Radar senses the ship's pain as it roars under the upcoming storm:

> "It was one of the more horrible sounds he had ever heard—a groan sustained and amplified into a curdling wail that came and went, came and went. Like the wail of a mother who has just lost her son. Except that this wail came not from any living creature but from the ship itself. The bones of the ship were crying" (548).

While the duck nods, the city and the ocean sing, and the ship cries. None of these entities are, however, humanized in this novel, so that a reading of these verbs as a personification would not give the book its due credit. In line with the tenor of this novel, Radar searches for a way to explain the interconnectedness, the entanglement of particles. With Radar and his relation to the world, Larsen establishes a means for visualizing this (quantum) entanglement.

When Radar and the duck nod, it is not at all a mirroring but the superposition of all the several implications that can be made with a nod. Both Radar and the duck seem to know about the blackout, but the reader never gets to know how deep this knowledge on both sides is, knowing only that the duck and Radar registered this mysterious event. Similarly, the city's and the sea's individual music as well as the ship's cry are considered in a similar fashion. Both the electrical current of the city and of the sea echo within Radar, entangling with his own frequency, thereby creating this particular music, or cry. Everything in Radar gets entangled with everything of the duck, the city, the sea and the ship; electricity serves as the means for translating this entanglement of Radar's normativity in communicative gestures and sounds such as nodding, singing and crying. Larsen thereby finds a way to avoid the immediacy of verbs that would denote a "touch," because they would immediately demarcate where one particle ends and the other begins. Gestures and sounds show that the entanglement of particles needs to be understood as being held together by "invisible strings," as the elemental bonds between them.

In seeing Radar's normativity as an *electric way of life* that stands metaphorically for the communication between different particles/entities, it is worth remembering that epilepsy serves as the catalyst for his *electric way of life*. In the first sequence, where the *electric way of life* appears as the language of pain to Radar's mother via the flickering television screen, the father, driven by the love for his son, tries to build a machine that reverses his son's epilepsy: a machine that reverses the "reverse[d] electrocution" (96). This "vircator" causes a blackout of almost nuclear impact, shutting down electricity for all of New Jersey. The force with which this reversal, this cure, explodes, emphasizes, on the one hand, the parental desire to free the child from pain; on the other hand, it radically addresses the impossibility of returning to a former state of vital norm, of establishing "biological innocence." Although Radar does not have any seizures after the blackout, he still is not cured. His body continues to anticipate the electrical current surrounding him, always reminding him of a past experience that would have resulted in a seizure but now causes déjà-vu (520, 602f.).

Radar is thus completely aware of his normativity; he can actively feel the dynamic "polarity of life," since he can feel his electrical current as it unfolds as his own life principle. Therefore, we can say that Radar turns into a new *organ in sound*. The *organ in sound* relies on pain, because in good health it does not communicate this sustainability to the individual. It is for this reason that pain is prerequisite for an *organ in sound* to be in the first place. With Radar, however, the situation is different. His underlying epilepsy which, on the one hand, causes electricity to become his normativity, allows him, on the other hand, to actually feel his organs in health. His body turns into a vital materiality that finds a means to unfold as such in a principle beyond the bio-physical boundaries of the individual. It connects to the normativity/frequency of other entities, speaking its own language which can be understood by its milieu because it permeates all the living:

"On the third evening, [Radar] figured out how to wire the radios to himself. Using very sensitive electrical nodes adapted from a heart rate monitor he had found in a forgotten drawer inside *Moby-Dikt* [the ship], he connected the radios to several contact points on his temples, wrist, and chest. It took him a while to adjust the sensitivity of the connection and to figure out exactly how he could control the dials without touching them, but once he had determined the correct voltage and resistance, the rest came fairly easily. It was as if the radios had become a natural extension of him. All he had to do was simply envision the radio switching channels and it would change, just like that. When he came upon something in the spectrum that felt right, the radio would hold, as if it too knew what was needed for the performance." (628f.)

In sum, this final novel was deliberately chosen to close this Chapter III.B, as it establishes, with Radar, another character whose epilepsy, on the one hand, describes his coming into being as his own form of normal which works to counteract the hegemony of the historical motifs. Canguilhem's notion of vital and social norm enabled us to see how the social permeates and enforces itself on the vital differentiating between the originality of the first and the homogenization of the second. On the other hand, Radar's epilepsy determines his individuation in so far as it establishes his own normativity as a way to connect, to entangle with the world, and to communicate on a new level with humans and technical objects alike using radar, the language of electricity. Radar's normativity needs to be understood similarly to the adjustment of a radio channel. A radio channel's reception is not only bound to its own frequency but also depends on the position of the surrounding objects in order to receive a clear signal. In this sense, Radar is the only character to turn into an *organ of sound* that does not rely on pain; his constant repositioning in the world stresses his relation to it and adjusts him to the appropriate frequency for an effective communication via his body's vital materiality.

III.C Metaphor and Idioms: Siri Hustvedt's Metastable Rhetoric as Transindividuation

III.C.1 *The Blindfold*: Falling as Fragility

> "I fell into a world of only liminal consciousness."
>
> SIRI HUSTVEDT, *THE BLINDFOLD*

Siri Hustvedt's literary debut *The Blindfold* (1992) exhibits, besides a captivating story about Iris Vegan's years as a graduate student at Columbia University, an innovative rhetorical style which echoes in her chosen topics through her intelligent and subtle usage of idiomatic language. She challenges, ever so slightly yet very effectively, the stability of concepts such as gender, health, desire, and identity, eventually arriving at an understanding of metastability that defines her poetics.[1] Hustvedt manages, thereby, to think movement together with stability. The conceptual metaphor of EPILEPSY IS METASTABILITY[2] helps to capture Hustvedt's rhetorical finesse, which lies in her use of the idiomatic expression 'to fall,'—its placement in the text, its references, as well as the continuity in which it appears. From this perspective, I will derive *falling* as *fragility* which marks a first means to dive into Hustvedt's unique rhetoric that designates her poetics.

1 See Chapter II.C of this book.

2 See Chapter II.C of this book.

To develop an understanding of her rhetoric in terms of this conceptual metaphor, this chapter will begin by looking at the tenor of her work's reception. I will then show that EPILEPSY IS METASTABILITY by analyzing the idioms of falling in her text. In order to fully grasp this, we need to first look closely at Simondon's expression of the individual as "falling out of step with itself." It is this particular aspect of metastability—dephasing––that highlights Hustvedt's rhetoric and alludes to what can be read as a poetics of individuation. I will also read *The Blindfold* chapter by chapter, first by way of a short summary and then through Simondon's theory, in order to show their resonance with each other. Since *The Blindfold*'s four chapters address different layers of individuations, they concentrate on single phases of Iris' life.[3] Although told in hindsight, the four chapters do not infer a linearity of chronological accuracy, but rather an intensity of individuation. Showing, thus, that individuation describes a discontinuous continuity of phases that, in spite of their distinguished spatiotemporal impact, need to be seen as part of one process. This implies that while some phases can define daily episodes of Iris' biography, others evolve over a longer period of time and in a greater number of places. With respect to this intensification of falling, the rhetoric of *falling* as *fragility* increases respectively.

Within the scant reception of Hustvedt's literary debut, three topics stand out: chronology, genre, and gendered power relations. The unique chronology of *The Blindfold* presents Iris Vegan's life in four short stories, rather than in four integrated episodes characterizes Hustvedt's narratologically-novel style (Knirsch n. pag.). However insightful, this reading stands rather secluded from the general tenor of researchers that emphasizes her genre categorization. Researchers tend to feature Hustvedt as a writer of modern Gothic fiction who explores the abject (T. Johnson 48f.) and the paranoid (Dallmann 68; Flieger 90f.). In line with this affiliation of a clearly psychological agenda stands Alison Jameson's reading of Hustvedt, in which she sees, in the display of the female-male power relations, an endangerment of the protagonist's identity. Her exact words are of importance as she "argue[s] that the multifaceted nature of power causes the protagonist to experience nothing less than a self-shattering, a dangerous destabilization of any sense of personal identity" (422). Contrary to this common

3 The timeline is not explicitly referred to as such but several clues allow for this timespan.

understanding of Hustvedt's *The Blindfold* as putting forward a notion of self-shattering and destabilization,[4] I believe that Hustvedt's oeuvre requires a new, different reading. Hustvedt, as this chapter shows, does not shatter and thereby destroy the identity of her characters but, rather, develops a new mode of process that is applicable to objects and individuals alike, stressing their inherent "event structure" that incorporates moments of incision contributing to their individuation instead of their destruction.

To see this, we must turn precisely to what critics have labeled as fractured, paranoid or destroyed. Hustvedt's exploration of all moments and notions of falling, lead to such readings because, from a cognitivist point of view, falling demarcates a downward movement that goes hand in hand with a notion of loss. This reading is as well mirrored in the history of epilepsy which shows the devaluation and stigmatization of the individual. Such a reading of her work is further accentuated, as it connects the motif of *falling* with epilepsy,[5] characterizing the fallen or possessed, who are 'struck down' from above, or who have lost consciousness—and are thus fractured, destroyed or perceived as paranoid. In allowing everything and everyone to constantly 'fall, drop, collapse, and sink' without, however, denoting a loss, but merely movement, Hustvedt subtly emphasizes the process of individuation, stressing the significance of the act of *falling* for individuation rather than for evaluating a direction. In order to understand this movement, Hustvedt explores the individual in confrontation with itself and others,[6] characterizing this mediation as *fragile*, but not as "self-shattering," as Jameson argues. It is the acceptance of one's own and other's *fragility* that allows for relationships to either emerge, be restored or be abandoned through the ability to successfully *fall*. This new perspective on *falling* as *fragility*, describes how the individual reacts in psychic tension and how this leads toward its becoming. *Falling* as *fragility* marks the new ontological correspondence[7] that is pointed to in the conceptual metaphor EPILEPSY IS METASTABILITY. The epistemological impact of conceptual metaphors manifest throughout *The Blindfold*, residing in the idioms

4 See Mats Bjerke's "Siri Hustvedt's *The Blindfold* and *What I Loved.* A Study of Destructiveness in Art and Human Psyche" (2014).

5 See Chapter I.A of this book.

6 See Chapter II.C of this book.

7 See Chapter II.C of this book.

and the plot alike, since it is daily language that describes, holds true to, or initiates a shift in belief systems.[8]

Let us return to Simondon's call for the individual to "fall out of step with itself," "*se déphaser*," and the three characteristics which define it: the haecceity of the individual, being as "more-than-identity" and the discontinuity of the process.[9] Haecceity stresses the present state of the individual as displaying its own being as simultaneously stable-in-itself and in-process. This is important, since it stresses the identity of the individual with itself at each moment of its individuation process, which should not be mistaken for identification as a doubling. This is possible since the individual moves into a new phase of its being, which defines the idea of 'being-more-than-identity' because it marks, simultaneously, an identity and a non-identity. The fact that these shifts are considered to be discontinuous lies in the mediation of the individual and its "psychic tension." Each posed problem, so to speak, has a different impact on the individual, given its experiences in the past as well as its experience of the present moment. To "fall out of step with itself" thus demarcates the individual's shift during its individuation process, allowing for *falling*, and although it characterizes a sudden movement, denoting the *fragility*, it by no means implies its loss.

The first chapter of *The Blindfold* deals with Iris Vegan's part-time job, while a student living in New York, constantly broke. A writer named Herbert B. Morning hires her to describe, as precisely as possible, the objects that belonged to a young woman, Sherri Zalewski, who was murdered in his building three years ago. Morning keeps Zalewski's belongings, counting trash among them, in separate boxes, and asks Iris to not only describe these objects but to whisper her descriptions into a tape recorder. For him, the whispering is crucial as it prevents the speaker's voice from distorting and thus influencing the description. Having described the objects first by himself, Morning later on realized that his knowledge of Zalewski tainted his longed-for objectivity in capturing this woman's identity. The whispering marks thus another step, after handing the task of describing to someone else, in his quest to possess a post mortem knowledge of Zalewski. The eeriness of this task lies in as much in the impossibility of Iris achieving an exact verbal representation of the objects in front of her, as it does in Morn-

8 See Chapter II.C of this book.

9 See Chapter II.C of this book.

ing's obsession with these whispered descriptions. The act of describing is a task that is bound to fail from the onset. As the objects tend to lose their vividness the harder Iris tries to capture them, Zalewski becomes more difficult for Morning to grasp, the more he tries to reach her through objectivity. The job comes to an end when Iris demands an explanation for her task, afraid that Morning might have murdered Zalewski himself three years ago. She walks out of the apartment and leaves behind her, as Morning asks her to, an object of herself: a green eraser.

Leaping a couple of months back in time, the second chapter deals with the circulation of a disturbing picture showing Iris in spasms of ecstacy. Involved in what seems like an obscure love triangle between Iris, her short time boyfriend Stephen, and his friend George, this picture emanates a fascination for any beholder other than Iris, who is confronted with the distortion of herself. This powerful picture is taken after all three are enjoying the day on the roof of a building. On the roof top, George, the "artist who took photographs" (42), Stephen and Iris' attention is suddenly caught by "a loud bestial whine that went through [Iris] like electricity" (47).[10] This whine is the echo of a young woman suffering a "grand mal" (49) attack down on the streets. While George captures this moment with his camera, Stephen observes it eagerly as an entertaining spectacle.[11] Only Iris' gaze is defined by compassion and fear. Inspired by this scene, George wants to take a picture of Iris. The upcoming photography session oscillates between euphoria, eroticism and voyeurism, ending with an imbalance of a satisfied George and an ashamed Iris who feels that she has given her innermost away. This feeling affirms itself when she sees the picture, while her relationship with Stephen ends anti-climatically, after he obsesses about the picture. The rumors of her picture rule the New York art and academic scene and are highly anticipated by everyone at George's forthcoming exhibition. George plans to pair Iris' portrait with the grand mal photograph; however, Iris' portrait gets stolen and leaves a symbolic blank space in the art gallery next to the grand mal display.

10 See Chapter III.B of this book for the relation between electricity and epilepsy.

11 See Chapter I.A of this book.

Eight months after these incidents, right before her oral exams, Iris experiences excruciating migraines that put her in a female psychiatric ward[12] for ten days. Two closely connected aspects are of importance in this chapter, her pain as well as the focus on women. Focusing on the first parameter, this chapter deals with Iris being in-and-out of constant pain and sleep. When Iris notes that "[she] fell into a world of only liminal consciousness" (107), she refers to this oscillation between being intensified through pain and the loss of it in unconscious sleep. This in-between state poses a problem to her therapist, Dr. Fisher, who cannot seem to control her migraines and thus puts her on drugs, an act that Iris is generally afraid of, because drugs, therapeutic or not, counteract "[her] interest [which] has always been in maintaining balance, not tipping it" (160). Another important aspect of this chapter is the absence of men. Iris shares her room with two older women. The relationship between these women is stressed spatially and pathologically. First, it appears in the positioning of beds. Iris occupies bed number two, bed one remains empty, Mrs. O. and Mrs. M., beds three and four. In terms of pathological hierarchy, Iris, the "migraineur" (91), is at the bottom, followed by Mrs. M.'s nervous disorder having "her 'mind' . . . unaffected" (96) and Mrs. O., whose condition causes her to stumble over the question of her own name. Mrs. O. whose, mental instability poses "a conundrum to everyone" (98), is drawn to Iris.

Chapter four, the final and longest chapter, overarches all three preceding episodes of Iris' life in New York. This chapter contains the master narrative of Iris' individuation process, with the three former incidents defining her daily struggles, each one with its own significance: finding a job (chapter one), love life (chapter two), hospitalization (chapter three). In this chapter Iris wanders through the city at night with a new short haircut and in a man's suit, trying to experience gender liminality. Two other characters play a part in this chapter that are of significance in Iris' "dephasing": Pro-

12 Consider Chapter III.A.3 and Chapter III.B.1 of this book, to see that the experience of being analyzed overpowers the individual in the clinic. Contrary to Dennis Mahagin who refers to Thom Jones' short story "A White Horse," and Jones' indirect reference to Ken Kesey's *One Flew Over the Cuckoo's Nest* by adapting the Salem clinic as institution in "The Black Lights," Siri Hustvedt avoids this direct link between psychiatric ward and the loss of the individual in it by placing her protagonist at the Mount Olympus Hospital.

fessor Michael Rose, her lecturer, and Paris, an art critic. With the former she begins a love affair defined by admiration, intellectual stimulation and great physical attraction, while her relationship with the latter turns out to be an abusive friendship. These two men form separate plotlines in her life and while Professor Rose initiates and terminates Iris' gender exploration, Paris is amused by it. Iris' relationship with each of these men is marked by an imbalanced distribution of power, which she at first gives in to, from which, however, she liberates herself by asserting her independence and thus tipping the imbalance of power in her favor. Both relationships end with sexual abuse that Iris is able to free herself from. To capture these decisive three years in Iris' life, they begin with her arrival in New York for her studies and end with her job as a lecturer, after she has passed her final exams. As a young student, she becomes Professor Rose's research assistant where one of her tasks includes the translation into English of the German novella "Der Brutale Junge, [The Brutal Boy]" by the (fictitious) author Krüger. It deals with the sadistic imagination of a young boy named Klaus, the name Iris adopts and adapts—as Klaus(ina) Krüger—during her nights wandering the streets and bars of New York as a man, exploring the malleability of gender identity.

As stated earlier, we will now focus on EPILEPSY IS METASTABILITY, to derive Hustvedt's poetics from her rhetoric of *falling* as *fragility*. I will do so by subsequently analyzing the chapters to show how Hustvedt applies the idioms of falling in them. While the first chapter deals with falling objects, the second concentrates on the protagonist's falling photograph, the third chapter portrays falling as an organic reaction, while the fourth chapter provides on overall notion of falling as part of Iris' individuation process. In addition to objects, images, organs and the individual, this analysis of EPILEPSY IS METASTABILITY stresses this conceptual metaphor's "event structure"[13] because of its encompassing notion of the individuation process per se. Hustvedt manages to transmit a movement that she observes in her milieu and characterizes it as *fragile*, evidencing a poetics that emphasizes disturbance as essential for individuation.

Looking back to chapter one and the boxes, the intimacy that ostensibly ordinary objects, such as bed sheets or mirrors, radiate, is tightly linked to the value ascribed to them, raising their status to that of individuals—in a

13 See Chapter II.C of this book.

Simondonian sense—rather than being perceived as *mere* objects.[14] We see this, first of all, in Morning's effort to assemble all of the deceased's belongings before finding boxes of every shape to match and store them. This 'customized fitting' of boxes to objects, works to efficiently shield them from exposure. Furthermore, since Morning is neither a relative nor a friend of the deceased, a certain mystery builds up regarding the means by which he acquired the objects; he must have gone through some kind of trouble to attain them. In addition to that, contrary to a person close to the victim, Morning is not interested in preserving the picture of the deceased by leaving all of her objects untouched and in place, but, rather, to disclose from each de-contextualized thing, a meaning of its own that is representative of Zalewski's being. This value is further underscored by Iris' tasks to describe them in whispers and Morning's expectations of her results. She strives for accuracy in these "painstaking descriptions" (14), such as in her approach to the first object given to her—a single glove. She forgets, however, to include the glove's smell into her description. Morning points out to Iris, that by forgetting to describe the glove's smell, she has missed out to capture its unique note. I argue that by doing so, he treats these objects as individuals. When, hence, Iris accidentally pushes one of Morning's boxes to the floor, it is a movement that dominates and echoes throughout the whole chapter because its *falling* is the *falling* of an individual, stressing its *fragility*:

> "My head was bent over the box when I heard him coming toward the door, and I leapt backward, accidentally pushing the box off the counter. It fell to the floor but didn't open. I was able to return it to its place before Mr. Morning appeared in the doorway. Whether or not he saw my hands dart away from the box, I still don't know, but when the box fell, whatever was inside it made a loud, hollow, rattling noise, and he must have heard that." (20)

In this *falling* of the box, with respect to *falling* as *fragility*, we see metastability unfold itself. Like an individual that is hiding something, the box attracts Iris to open and look into it, characterizing this scene in terms of a relationship between an alluring object and an interested woman. Although it then falls, emphasizing its fragility in terms of its position and weight, it

14 See Chapter II.C of this book.

does not tear open or give any other hint as to its interior other than the noise it makes. Through this fragility, it protects itself from the planned intrusion by the protagonist and reassures itself in its being because it persists as an individual protecting its interior from the outside. A steady, stable box would not have fallen to the ground, not made a noise and could have easily been opened by the protagonist since the latches are not difficult to open. This one, however, is able to fall, to exercise its fragility by reacting to the clumsy reaction. The noise is therefore a mediation between the exercised force that is implied in Iris' interest in it and its owner's wish to hide it, providing no clue to Iris but rather informing Morning.

The mediation resonates in this fall for the next five pages as "I[ris] remember[s] his [Morning's] trouble breathing as he spoke, the letters on the page, the white box falling, his hand on [her] arm" (25). Looking at this created imagery, the letters are fixed on the page, and Morning's hand is fixed on Iris' arm. Only the acts of the troublesome breathing and of the falling box mark a dynamic: both verbs appear in the present progressive, stressing continuation. This is interesting because breathing implies a continuation per se, even if not in the present progressive. 'To breathe' is different in meaning from a single act of inhalation and exhalation. To breathe is a necessity for living and one cannot escape its inevitability. 'To fall' however is a concept that is normally conceived of in terms of a downward movement: height and ground. To fall denotes, usually, a single movement. Here, however, falling and the fall participate in the "event structure" that denotes a movement due to the two aspects of the fallen box so far. On the one hand, it defines the reference to the box as individual, implying life. On the other hand, the present progressive suggests its parallel with breathing. Falling, thus, does not appear as a movement that is reduced to a single downward direction.

This notion of falling which stresses the "event structure" is not reduced to the box alone, but reiterates its conceptual outline with the final box that Iris receives from Morning:

> "I opened my bag, took out the check, ripped it to pieces and threw it into a large trash. Then I threw away the tape recorder and the unopened box. I can still see the small black machine lying askew on the garbage heap and the smaller box as it tumbled farther into the bin. It upset a Styrofoam cup as it fell, and I turned away just as a stream of pale brown coffee dregs ran over its lid." (38)

Taking the personification of the unopened box as another means for underlining the status of these objects as individuals that is expressed in the box' "tumbl[ing]" as well as in its ability to "upset" other objects, the relationship between the tape recorder and the unopened box takes on significance. As the machine finds a position of metastability due to its being "askew," the "unopened box" mirrors how the metastability breaks and thus the individual's need to "fall out of step with itself." Both objects display, together, how the metastability as "event structure" emerges: as the oscillation between the states of being askew and of falling out of it. Iris' turning away leaves these two states as they are because she does not stay to witness the trashed tape recorder or box reach the bottom of the bin. Although, for her, the relation to the box has ceased—mirroring the end of her work for Morning—the box and the tape recorder continue to individuate. Following the lines of the "coffee dregs," the box continues to exercise a novel mediation in accordance to its new milieu outside of the protagonist's storyline.

As the second chapter revolves around the witnessing of an epileptic fit, let us now address the way in which epilepsy positions itself in the general argumentative outline of this chapter. At the center of this phase in Iris' life is a picture of her in what appear to be spasms of ecstasy. This picture is juxtaposed with the observed epileptic fit of this chapter. The "grand mal," whose violent cramps and convulsions, which are described in elaborate detail over two pages (47ff.), scares the heroine and fascinates the two minor characters, displays the historical motif of *danger.*[15] Fear and fascination are both restaged later on when Iris, Stephen and George behold Iris' picture. This overlap of epilepsy with *danger* manifests the stereotype of its history only on the level of figurative language, while the general renegotiation of *falling* articulates a new concept in the sphere of idiomatic language. Put differently, while the motif of *danger* rests on the level of poetic metaphors, the renegotiation of *falling* describes conceptual metaphors, describing how thought upholds structures according to embodiment. This distinction juxtaposes the figurative with the epistemological. The renegotiation of *falling*, then, offers an understanding of processes of individuation.

Considering the epileptic fit and the photograph, the second chapter allows us to consider how the conceptual metaphor of EPILEPSY IS METASTABILITY requires the distinction between *falling* as *fragility* and *falling*

15 See Chapter I.A of this book.

or *fragility*, the latter denoting destruction or fragmentation. As destruction or fragmentation, they affirm Jameson's reading of a shattered individual. *Falling* as *fragility* preserves the individuation process, while *falling* or *fragility*, as destruction or fragmentation, ends it. The first pushes forward the idea of metastability, while the second defines, as Jameson, herself, states, destabilization. To convey this delicate but decisive distinction, Iris' picture and Iris need to be seen as two completely separate individuals, not only in terms of different modes of existence, but in terms of signifier and signified. The following passage highlights Iris' perception of the picture for the first time. Looking at the picture, she cannot recognize herself at all, before she then tries to understand how this lack of identification with herself is explainable:

> "It wasn't a full-body shot. I was cut off below my breasts, and my extended arms were severed at the elbows. Photographs are cropped in all sorts of ways, and the results are seldom disturbing. The viewer fills in the missing pieces, but this picture was different. The convention didn't seem to work, and I had the awful impression that the parts of me that weren't in the photo were really absent . . . . A long piece of hair was swept across my right cheek and part of my mouth, slicing my face in two. A dark shadow beneath my uplifted chin made my head appear to float away from my body. My whole face lacked clarity, in part because the light was obscure, but also because the expression I had was nonsensical, an inward leer or grimace that signified no definite emotion or even sensation. It was a face without reason, and I hated it." (62f.)

This picture, the frozen fragmentation of a person, being cut and "sliced," triggers in Iris the immediate desire to annihilate an identification with it: "I am not that, I thought, and let the photograph fall from my hands to the table" (63).

The fact that Iris does not violently throw it away, but simply lets go of it, underscores this separation of signifier and signified. After her hateful reaction, she parts from the image, realizing that holding on to an identification would require a destruction of herself, since the picture shows the falling apart of a woman. The *falling* of this picture from her hands is thus an act of accepting her *fragility* in order to preserve herself. An act that will later on, while searching for the picture and forcing herself to look at it—holding it instead of letting go—initiate a dissolution of herself: "There was no sound in me, and I watched as the hole began to swallow the picture's frame. I feared for my fingers but didn't think to drop the photograph. It was bonded to my hands, a part of my limbs, and I was blind. I don't know when my vision returned" (67). This feeling of being tied to the picture represents the urge to be stronger than her own metastability and stresses the importance of the individual to be able to "fall out of step with itself" and not remain in a situation of unbearable "psychic tension." Her near dissolution into the picture, adapting to the fragmentation and destruction, gives insight into how instability effects the individual in contrast to metastability.

Another factor that needs to be taken into account, is the destructive nature of Iris' and Stephen's relationship which materializes in their individual approaches to the picture. In contrast to Iris' needs to let go of it in order to protect herself and her identity, "Stephen picked it up immediately and held it out in front of him. He made a sound between his teeth, a long breathy whistle I[ris] had never heard from him before and his face, which I[ris] saw in profile, had *collapsed* into an unfamiliar softness" (emphasis added, 63). Here, Stephen falls in love with the woman in the picture (69), marking the end of his relationship with Iris. This ending is implied in the way Iris perceives his softness. It is not only the unfamiliarity of the softness, which she witnesses for the first time on his face, it is also the way in which his face adapts to this tender feeling. For Iris his face "collapses into an unfamiliar softness" because he directs his love toward another woman. She witnesses her betrayal in this softness, marking it, thus, as unfamiliar and his whole mimicry thereby as collapsing. Her boyfriend is gone the moment he gazes at the picture. The realization of this collapsing face concurs with her letting go of the picture. Both acts of *falling* preserve her individuation process as they secure her shift into her next metastable state, preventing her from remaining in an unbearable situation. The first protects her from identifying with a fragmented I, while the second protects her from staying in a relationship with an unfaithful partner.

We find evidence linking Iris' "falling out of step with [her]self" to her break-up with Stephen in two other locations. In the first chapter, Iris thinks back to Stephen, remembering when his body was "still enchanted; it had a power that I battled against for months. Later that enchantment fell away, and he passed into a banality I never would have thought possible" (18). The leap from enchantment to banality defines the emotional rigor with which the shift actually takes place. It visualizes how the "falling out of step with [her]self" does not mean a "doubling," but how the being, Iris, still remains herself while becoming. Iris is herself during and after the relationship; nevertheless, she has moved on. While she had been jealous, insecure and left longing in her relationship, she actually pursues her life afterwards. Stephen's enchanted body, on the one hand, and his banality on the other hand, mark the respective states of Iris at that time, shifting from the one to the other through the simple gesture of letting the picture fall to the table. The second reference to Stephen linked to the notion of *falling* appears in chapter three.

The third chapter deals with the act of vomiting as preserving metastability, drastically marking the shift of the individual from one phase to another. Two situations lead to Iris' throwing up. Iris is, on the one hand, alarmingly allured by the mentally instable Mrs. O.—she identifies with her—while, on the other hand, she is caught in the unbearable oscillation between pain and sleep. In both situations, the dangerous identification with instability as well as the alternation between unbearable being and unconsciousness, resolve themselves through *falling* as *fragility*. The instability of Mrs. O.'s mental condition is decisive here, because it visualizes drastically its difference to the notion of metastability. In the same manner the push to mediate herself between the two extremes of pain and unconsciousness emphasizes the need for a metastable individuation mediating between two intensified forces instead of being caught in either one. *Falling* as *fragility* appears here not in a voluntary motion of letting go, as in chapter two, but in the violent bodily reaction of throwing up. This act closes the chapter which allows Iris to maintain her metastability and not give in to instability, securing herself, once again, from fragmentation or destruction.

In the first of these two situations, after pinching Iris lightly one night, Mrs. O. kisses her passionately while she is asleep (105). Their connection, which begins, for Iris, with abjection, turns into what Julia Kristeva calls a "hysteric conversion" (45) that finds its peak when Iris catches Mrs. O.'s searching gaze. While Mrs. O. cries out her own name, for the first time, she is staring at Iris as if she is recognizing herself in the young woman opposing her. The latter instinctively responds to the old lady by reassuringly screaming "'I am here!'" (112), blurring her identity with Mrs. O.'s. This raw scene triggers the notion of a mirror reflecting either the beholder's lost youth or her approaching future, depending on which of the two characters functions as the other's image: Iris, as the young version of Mrs. O. or Mrs. O. as an old Iris, both dressed in the clinical wardrobe, looking at each other while lying opposite of one another, agree on sharing an identity, depriving both of any individuation while being caught up in the other. After this scene, Mrs. O. is mysteriously taken away overnight, and Iris falls into a comatose sleep, her immediate reaction to this withdrawal is the body's struggle for metastability:

> "I vomited. My intestines cramped horribly, and my bowels fell out of me. The paroxysms seemed to send all my internal organs into the toilet. I steadied myself on the sink and looked at my hideous face in the mirror . . . . It was dark outside, and large snowflakes were falling steadily." (115)

This passage also applies to the second of these two situations in which Iris finally regains her ability to mediate herself between pain and dreamless sleeps (114). While the entire chapter revolves around these two states, they reinforce each other until they blur the demarcation between imagination and reality for Iris. This blurring ends through her vomiting and positions her finally in relation to these extremes instead of living in them. The end of the chapter, which concludes with her vomiting and the end of her institutionalization, portrays Iris observing the snowflakes. And this second notion of *falling*, captured in falling snowflakes, shows *falling* as *fragility* describing the leading "event structure." Although delicate, the snowflakes distinguish themselves sharply against the backdrop of the dark sky. It is through their continuous *falling* that they achieve their status as the event of 'snowing.'

These two moments of falling, her "bowels" and the "snowflakes," display metastability as well as Iris' individuation and the metastability of physical processes. Iris can thereby finally distinguish and relate herself according to binaries such as day and night, outside and inside, mirror image and self, without losing herself in either position. The difficulty for Iris to maintain her metastability between pain and unconsciousness, echoing nature's dynamics, comes up again in chapter four, when Iris "walked home through the park in the *snow*. As soon as I was inside my apartment, I *fell* into bed . . . . I slept for two days, waking *intermittently to the pain* and then *falling again into unconsciousness*" (emphasis added, 180), and then again when "[w]e went on *into the spring*, and I was well. From time to time, I would *fall* into bed and chant when my head *fogged with an oncoming migraine*, but the pain was negligible" (188).

Still in light of this chapter's main topic, Iris' vomiting is decisive in preserving Iris' metastability. A minor detour into one of Hustvedt's rhetoric innuendos in this novel might be worth of consideration here. Looking at the names in this chapter together with the lineup of beds in the patients' room, Iris Vegan would be called Mrs. V., 'V' indexing her last name. Based on the fact that the initial 'O' in Mrs. O.'s. name does not refer to her first name, which is Eleanor, we can deduce that Iris Vegan's corresponding abbreviated name would be Mrs. V. Considering Hustvedt's constant play with the ambiguity of names as identity markers, we are invited to read into the term formed when combining the patients' initials—V, O and M (M, for Mrs. M., the third patient in the room)—the acronym 'VOM,' hinting toward the word/notion of 'vomit.' The lineup of beds is described in the chapter's opening lines and as the chapter ends in the vomiting and snow scene, *falling* as *fragility* is the framing and dominant metaphor of the whole chapter.

The last and longest of the chapters provides a framework for chronologically organizing these three episodes of Iris' life, highlighting each episode as a moment in Iris' individuation process. Since the focus in this novel is on the shift, the "stepping out of [her]self," it is in this last chapter that *falling* as *fragility* fortifies in the rhetoric finesse and subtly manifests the conceptual metaphor. Hustvedt has, at this point, familiarized the reader with the notion of *falling*, allowing her heroine to constantly relate to *falling* while continuing to love, live, think and individuate. In addition to that, Hustvedt builds through her rhetoric the willingness to accept *falling* as a necessity for maintaining balance; this is what defines Iris' life as metastable. This metastability is best captured in her blindfolded walk close to the end of the novel.

Each chapter of the novel stresses the individual's need "to fall step out of itself." While the first chapter envisions how this can be thought with respect to objects, the second and third chapter display the protagonist's attempt to shift into her new phases without losing herself. To be more precise, while in chapter two Iris' individuation was initiated by her act of letting the picture drop to the table, it increases in the painful vomiting scene in chapter three. In both of these episodes, Iris is at the verge of fragmentation, of losing her identity, and both times *falling* as *fragility* prevents her from following this destructive path. In chapter four, Iris continues to initiate and endure dramatic shifts which almost always lead to her annihilation only to secure and strengthen her in the end.

In this fourth chapter Iris undergoes her first decisive shift in her individuation as she switches genders at night. She dresses like a man and adapts the name of the fictional sadistic boy, Klaus(ina), of the novella she had translated as a research assistant for Prof. Michael Rose. As Klaus, she strolls through the streets of New York at night and hangs out in bars. Completely broke, hungry and in need of financial and emotional support, Prof. Rose saves her by becoming her lover. Their relationship ends when he hits her and forces her into obedience during sex. Her next shift is triggered after his physical abuse which repeats itself in the person of her cynical friend Paris, who also tries to overstep her physical boundaries. Both times Iris stands up for herself and ends the relationship. This is a continuation of her strength and integrity.

In this last chapter, the many instances of falling, of shifting, which are echoed in the rhetoric of *falling* in *fragility* can be parallelized to Iris' shifts in herself. From confined hair that frees itself while falling down (129), to hands (132, 193), mouths (139), knees (139), arms (185, 220), coverings (206), heads (209), blankets (210), tears (210), and faces (212), Hustvedt lets everything fall, defining the inner metastable balance of these individuals anew. In the frequency and nonchalance of her use of *falling*, she introduces the conceptual metaphor, shaping idiomatic language. Her rhetoric becomes the key device for understanding Iris' approach to her milieu, transporting with it a poetics of life that follows the laws of metastability. The manifold ways in which these *fallings* appear stress even more so that this is a principle defining the acting out of individuation: everything becomes as it falls. One example that visualizes how *falling* as *fragility* establishes itself as new conceptual metaphor of individual life, experienced in its metastability, is Iris' friend Rebecca.

Rebecca expects Iris to show a certain reaction when she tells Iris about her engagement. As Iris' reaction does not seem to fit her expectations "[h]er face fell" (212). The manner in which this *falling* appears gives no reason to interpret anything other than Rebecca being disappointed in her friend's ostensible disapproval of her marriage. The reader can immediately read disappointment, even though their friendship marks only a short passage in the book so that an elaborate account of this character's traits is not obvious. The easiness with which this new understanding of falling is accepted is because we already have a conceptual metaphor for grasping expectations. Expectations follow a conceptual metaphor that delineate a movement from high to low, up to down; expectations can thus rise/grow or fall. Hustvedt uses this existing metaphor and resettles the focus of attention. The fact that the face "falls" displays not a downward movement but rather an emotion; something that is of passing nature. Through the steadiness of the face, since it cannot literally fall, as in losing itself, or being destroyed, Hustvedt shows how metastability, the momentary stepping out of itself, enlarges the existing notions of "event structures."

The final scene that fortifies this novel's poetics as metastability that echoes through the rhetoric of *falling* as *fragility* is the blindfolded walk that the heroine successfully masters at the end of the novel. It stands metaphorically for her general determination to always reestablish balance while living a life that repeatedly throws her out of it. Initiated by a bet with Prof. Rose, Iris allows him to blindfold her for the last blocks on her walk to her home. Putting herself in this position of walking without sight she "walked slowly forward, feeling for the curb with every step, determined not to fall" (202). Taking into account that the possibility of *falling* is inherent with each step that she takes, she nevertheless makes the walk. It is difficult because it articulates the sensibility of the equilibrium: "Those six blocks were an odyssey. My equilibrium was gone with my sight, and I lurched and tottered forward, marking each block in my head" (ibid.). It is not so much gone as it is constantly at stake. This blindfolded walk is the shift into her new phase, where she embraces her *fragility*. Throughout the novel Iris confronts possibilities of destroying herself, however, she always decides to turn away from them. She accepts this side of hers and incorporates it as a means to individuate.

In sum, this first analysis of Hustvedt's rhetoric focuses on the conceptual metaphor of EPILEPSY IS METASTABILITY which finds its way into the text through new modes for thinking *falling*—epilepsy—and modifying it as *fragility*. Throughout the novel, Hustvedt marks the coming into being of her protagonist through the moments where her meditative ability to deal with "psychic tensions" is put under scrutiny. With her rhetoric she manages, to envision a poetics that allows individuals to accept moment of crisis, even dive into them, and thereby mirror what surrounds us in daily life. The fact that her debut is read as a novel promoting self-destruction only confirms how strongly the ideal of a stable self is rooted in society, labeling every form of fragility as a "dangerous destabilization" (Jameson 422) or analyzing it under the heading of "destruction" (Bjerke). With *The Blindfold*, the focus of metastability is clearly on the shifting of phases, allowing the reader to participate in Iris' exhausting, fearful and also optimistic journey. Iris' need to "fall out of step with [her]self" stresses Hustvedt's ability to indulge in the notion of *falling* while drawing a sharp demarcation between *falling* as *fragility* and *falling* as the destruction of identity. It defines her poetics at the nexus of psychology, gender and disability studies. As she manages to transmit this through her conceptual metaphors, one can say that her rhetoric becomes a transindividual of its own, providing a means for her audience to participate in a shared experienced through the emergence of a new idiomatic and, thus, relatable language.

III.C Metaphor and Idioms: Siri Hustvedt's Metastable Rhetoric as Transindividuation

III.C.2 *The Enchantment of Lily Dahl*: Shaking as Vulnerability

> "The stillness of that body was absolute, and Lily screamed."
> SIRI HUSTVEDT, *THE ENCHANTMENT OF LILY DAHL*

In Hustvedt's second novel *The Enchantment of Lily Dahl* (1996), her poetics manifest in the characters' willingness to relate to others, and forwards a reading of their respective shaking, trembling and quivering as a means of visualizing this disposition. While *The Blindfold* stressed the actual shift individuals[1] undergo in their processes of individuation, *The Enchantment of Lily Dahl* focuses on the states of characters on the brink of these shifts. Both novels participate, however, in the respective rhetoric of the other, allowing individuals to *fall* (*Blindfold*) and *shake* (*Enchantment*), respectively. Hustvedt's exploration of shaking, enables her to introduce the *vulnerable* as a refined notion of the metastable as "sensitive equilibrium." This means that her poetics in both *The Blindfold* and *The Enchantment of Lily Dahl* revolve around the same conceptual metaphor of EPILEPSY IS METASTABILITY. While the first novel works to denaturalize epilepsy's central motif of *falling*, the latter dedicates itself to the reintroduction of a

1 See Chapter II.C as well as Chapter III.C.1 of this book.

novel approach to *shaking* as a means for connecting individuals. The conceptual metaphor adds to *falling* as *fragility*, *shaking* as *vulnerability*. It thereby elevates the vulnerable for any individuation process which arises through a relational approach of an individual to its milieu. That means, participating in the social and emotional life of others, influences and shapes one's surrounding through an openness to actively receive information.

Hustvedt's poetics persist in challenging the superiority of the strong, young, healthy and abled over the weak, old, sick and disabled, in order to establish a general mode of living freed from these categories and urging, instead, the notion of life as individuals in relation to other individuals. To develop this idea, I will first offer a short overview of metastability as "sensitive equilibrium"[2] wherein the notion of *a praesenti* (original emphasis "Ontogenesis" Footnote 18)[3] will work to provide the theoretical background of Hustvedt's relational poetics. I will then draw the connection between metastability and Hustvedt's notion of *vulnerability* which will be followed by a short summary of the novel. This summary will serve as the toolbox for analyzing the characters' individuation as emerging in relation to one another. In *The Enchantment of Lily Dahl*, this individuation through relationality is mediated for the reader through the variety and degrees of the characters' *shaking*, arguing for a rhetoric of vulnerability based on the plurality of being in a sensitive balance, paradigmatic for Hustvedt's poetics. I argue that the characters in *The Enchantment of Lily Dahl* participate in life as active and resonant beings with their environment because they are vulnerable.

In order to understand metastability as "sensitive equilibrium," we must first consider what Simondon calls the "*a praesenti.*" But as a short recapitulation of the mestabable equilibrium, a system is "in metastable equilibrium (or false equilibrium) when the least modification to the parameters of the system (pressure, temperature, etc.) is sufficient for breaking the equilibrium of the system" (Combes 3). What is important here is that the energy in the metastable system is not actualized but potential, residing within the system, ready to be released. Metastability is, thus, a sensitive equilibrium, an equilibrium nevertheless, with the decisive feature of being able to

2 See Chapter II.C of this book.

3 See Chapter II.C of this book.

be thrown off its own balance, so to speak, out of itself,[4] keeping its state at the highest possible energy. Simondon sees in this inherent potentiality within a system a principle that he transfers to individuals. That is, Simondon thinks the individual and its individuation as it lives in the moment, *a praesenti*. The individual is a distinct unit in resonance with itself, and, in that manner, stable and with an identity, while simultaneously allowing its actualized past, its experience, as well as its potential future to reside in the present moment, being, thereby, always liminal in the sense of a possible release of energy.

It is difficult for a literary studies' project to capture the 'potential' energy of a text, since this feature of metastability, is invisible, contrary to the 'actual' shift, which was the center of attention in the previous chapter.[5] The sensitivity of the metastable system forms a paradigm of Simondon's philosophical thought. It requires careful consideration as, in contrast to stability and instability, it denotes the relational moment as liminal—i.e. that which can account for identity and change, for continuity and discontinuity. It is in this liminality that the notion of vulnerability is best explicated. But how does this moment and therefore, the *vulnerable* become visible? Furthermore, as the very foundation of individuation, how can this feature of metastability be detected within a text? By presenting the variety of involuntary bodily motions this liminality becomes visible to the reader in the materialization of quivers; not yet a smooth motion but also not static and therefore neither instable nor stable. It is this corporeal mediation that is essential for fathoming the characters' interactions with each other and for piecing together the elements contributing to their individuation.

Before diving into Hustvedt's rhetoric of *shaking* as *vulnerability*, a short summary will serve to introduce the main characters. It should be mentioned at this point that this summary does not require an elaborate unfolding of the plot as did *The Blindfold.* My reading of *The Blindfold* examined the various shifts in individuation that Iris Vegan goes through, while *The Enchantment of Lily Dahl* explores the momentary interaction between characters. Nineteen-year-old Lily Dahl is the heroine of this gothic tale, set in Webster, Minnesota at the end of the twentieth century. Lily is an aspiring actress, working part-time as a waitress in the local Ideal Café, who

4 See Chapter II.C as well as Chapter III.C.1 of this book.

5 See Chapter III.C.1 of this book.

falls obsessively in love with middle-aged artist Edward Shapiro from New York. The plot revolves around the mysterious, premature burial of a former citizen of Webster, Helen Bodler, whose murder seems to have cast an eerie spell on the inhabitants that outreaches her descendants and turns every character in the novel into a suspect of murderous intentions. The novel contains, at first glance, central aspects of gothic fiction, from the haunted mind of the heroine to the premature burial, to violence and murder, to the atmosphere of utmost anxiety, oscillating between imagination and reality in a nightmarish setting which, on top of all these strikingly gothic features, calls for psychoanalytic exploration.

Each of the characters in this novel are, in their own particular way, flawed and could be regarded as misfits. Although young Lily Dahl appears to be beautiful and smart she could also be considered naïve, pursuing a career in acting despite her mediocre acting skills. Her close friend and neighbor Mabel is an old, quirky woman who lives alone and is trying to finish her autobiography, a task that will end, given the fact of her constant writing, with her death. Martin is a stutterer; he is Lily's childhood friend, with whom she shares a friendly if not unique bond. Being bullied by the other teenagers in town, Martin can only speak smoothly while performing on stage. In contrast to Lily, he is considered to have great acting talent. His obsession with Lily, epitomized in a puppet he builds resembling her, ends in a dramatic showdown at the end of the novel, when he shoots himself in front of Lily's eyes. Dolores, the local prostitute, along with the Bodler brothers—two middle-aged single men who live in a messy, secluded house—do their share in completing the ensemble's weirdness. Edward Shapiro, Lily's lover, appears to be the only well-situated, educated and stable character. However, even his composure is severely threatened by his stay in Webster, Minnesota. By painting portraits of Mabel, Dolores, and the Bodlers, Edward dives into their world. These characters' individuality, together with the mysterious and gloomy atmosphere that Hustvedt creates through her eerie tone, beg for a consideration of the gothic influence on modern notions of 'the weird.'

Resisting the temptation of this obvious reading and thereby reducing Hustvedt's novel to the plot and to a genre without considering her poetics, I argue, instead, that her work mediates between the scientific, the neurological, the aesthetic and the psychological, culminating in a notion of the vulnerable articulated in an exploration of the liminal space in-between forces. She zooms in on the relational that exists between extremes—in the act of falling asleep, for example, or in the encounter of the male in the female and vice versa, tackling those concepts of identity that rely on a strict demarcation. Moreover, in this novel, characters relate to one another through their reciprocal dependency, the liminal becomes relational. It is thereby the connecting moment between individuals necessary for interaction and individual development. It encompasses the old and the young, the healthy and the sick, and puts them all under the category of vulnerability, making any of the former classifications of 'abled' and 'disabled' obsolete.

The first character to expose Hustvedt's rhetoric of *shaking* as *vulnerability* is Mabel Wasley.

> "Mabel poured Lily a cup of tea, her hands trembling as she held the pot in the air. The woman always looked cold. But the room was warm, and Lily had gotten used to Mabel's tremors and quakes and her constantly moving hands. She wasn't sick. She was nervous, so tightly strung that Lily half expected to hear the woman's body hum from the strain." (34)

Here, the plurality of synonyms with which Mabel's *shaking* is described in this rather short passage, allows to argue for a poetics within the rhetoric. Mabel's "trembling . . . tremors and quakes" and her being "nervous, so tightly strung" characterize her as a constantly "shaking woman"[6] and thereby emphasize her individuality. Shaking is her mode of existence, counteracting any form of weakness or exposition that is usually accompanied by the observation of someone trembling. The fact that Lily only knows her friend as a shaking woman, not being at least irritated or worried that this old woman might not be strong enough, shows the novelty with which Hustvedt defamiliarizes a familiar concept. Mabel's *shaking*, her *vulnerability*, is a testament of her age, so to speak, an earned *shaking* and, thus, a moment which highlights her strength. The synonyms for *shaking* also characterize the closeness between these two women. Similar to nick-

6 This expression of the "shaking woman" is found in Hustvedt's "The Shaking Woman: Or a History of My Nerves" (2010), an essay where the author presents her scientific investigations on the notion of embodiment and consciousness throughout varies disciplines, focusing on the impact of epilepsy and hysteria thereby.

names, which express intimacy within a relationship as well as the individuality of each member, Mabel's unique feature is her *vulnerability*.

Secondly, what becomes important here, the constantly trembling Mabel, whose voice becomes hysterically high-pitched every time she is agitated (4f.), is Lily's focalization. The nonchalant observation of Mabel's body makes the metastability visible to the reader without creating the expectation of breaking it. Quite the contrary: the calmness reinforces the sensitivity, its delicate state. In addition to this, Lily perceives the potential energy as an upcoming sound that resides in Mabel as a "sensitive equilibrium," implying that Mabel's energy is at such a peak that it almost becomes hearable. Mabel remains in this sphere between silence and sound, echoed in her *shaking* that is neither clear movement nor rigidity. In the light of *vulnerability* as a life force that urges one to connect with others, it is safe to say that her acquired metastability, her "body's hum from strain," is her individuated being expressed in this moment of "almost" humming, being hence: *a praesenti*.

This characterization of *shaking* Mabel, embracing her *vulnerability* as a testament to her life and as impetus to continue it, defines such a strong feature of her being that it proliferates even in Ed Shapiro's portrait of her:

> "Then she [Iris] moved her hand out of Ed's grip and looked down at the drawings. In all of them, Mabel was sitting in the canvas chair, her position only slightly different in each one. Her expression, however, was never the same. One fiercely animated face after another looked up at Lily from the floor. Mabel glared in one, squinted and frowned in another, her lips were parted, her lips were closed, her hands were raised from her elbows or splayed at either side of her face. These were images of the intense, shivering Mabel she knew, and despite the fact that they were still, Lily could almost feel them move." (150f.)

At this point, one has to consider that Mabel gave her child away when she was too young to take care of it. She watched her husband die and witnesses her own mortality in the loss of the smoothness of her fingers which hurt in their deterioration from writing. Considering that each drawing is only "slightly different" and yet clearly distinguishable from the others, these nuances follow the stream of thought with respect to *shaking* as they carefully allude to the difference residing in similarity. The drawings all show the same person, similar in that sense, different however in expression and, again, similar in capturing the individual's being as *shaking*. And this acquisition of *shaking* marks Mabel's character whose force strikes Lily even through the stillness of the portraits. Mabel's individuation challenges the portrait's raison d'être of stability, because Mabel *is* her very own *shaking*. In accordance with this painted *shaking*, the previous passage envisions resemblance to it through the anticipation of sound, both evoking the feeling of movement.

It is here, in the fulfillment of an expectation for sound and movement to work in harmony, as they appear to do on a daily basis in the utterance of words, that Hustvedt deploys her rhetoric of *shaking* as *vulnerability* in the character of Martin. Being a stutterer, Martin's vulnerability is the *shaking* word. At the beginning of the novel, this form of *shaking* defines a special bond that he and Lily share, a communication of their own, which, similar to the various synonyms for Mabel's *shaking,* displays an intimacy. When Martin orders his daily breakfast at the Ideal Café where Lily works, she can tell that

> "[h]e wanted an exchange, so instead of Martin stammering out an order and getting flustered, he tapped out a little rhythm on the tabletop with his fingers, rat-tat-a-tat-tat, and Lily answered him with two raps of her own, tat-tat . . . . No one else was in on it. Those beats were a little language all their own, and Martin seemed so happy to order his breakfast in code, it made Lily happy, too." (10)

This private exchange transforms the spoken word into a sound and a gesture, as already the attempt at speaking would break Martin's metastability. His tapping shows how novel ways of interaction can be established. These new interactions only function if both parties, as in the case of Lily and Martin, meet half-way, and fill the zone between speech and silence with their own form of communication. Looking more closely at this new communication, the *shaking* word merely requires a different medium in order to be understood. Translated from a "stammering out" to a "tapped out," the latter, due to the new medium, becomes a relatable sound—that is, a rhythm that can be adapted by both parties. It is, thus, not that the *shaking* as *vulnerability* is overcome, but on the contrary: Martin and Lily articulate through it a new plateau, which for Martin is a means for initiating their friendship. The importance of sustaining this relationship on this plateau becomes clear when Martin actually speaks to Lily. She interrupts him viciously; an act that she does subconsciously, because Martin's obsession annoys and scares her (158).

Although Martin's stutter narrows down the group of people with whom he can relate to—a small circle—it is, nevertheless, his own metastability, his ability to connect with others, that, once lost, ends in his death. To see this, one has to also realize that, for the people in Webster, the fascination with Martin lies in his transformation from a stutterer into an actor. On stage he loses his stuttering and everything else that discloses his vulnerability. This alleged perfection that he obtains, amazes the other actors and leads everyone, including Lily, to be in awe of his great talent. However, this perfection comes at a price. Being deprived of all flaws, he is deprived of himself, becoming for the others "like somebody, no, Lily thought, something else" (61). With the loss of his *shaking*, since "—he didn't stutter" (ibid.), he lives a different mode of existence. That is, he no longer lives as a social being that stands in relation to others, but, most prominently, he is elevated to an object—on stage—and admired. Actors on stage are precisely not themselves, but perform different personas, trying to hide as much of themselves as possible. It is not a position of balanced social interaction but one of entertainment. So when Martin puts on his stage make-up and walks into the Ideal Café pointing a gun at Lily "[h]e blinked, and she saw his head wobble for an instant. I am going to die right now, she thought. He's going to kill me in the Ideal Café. Right now, these are my last seconds. Lily felt her face convulse" (248). It is important to note that Lily realizes the impossibility of establishing a connection to Martin in the moment she sees his *vulnerability* fading away. The juxtaposition of Martin's last short "wobble" and Lily's face "convuls[ing]," which will lead to her losing control over her bladder as well, shows clearly that metastability has been lost for both of them. While Martin has lost it completely, shooting himself in the head in a steady motion, Lily convulses and shifts into a new phase of herself.

Focusing on Lily Dahl, the heroine of this novel, we see that the sensitive equilibrium points to, not only the means of her own individuation, but also to her way of perceiving the world. Contrary to Mabel and Martin who are both constantly *shaking*, the first one through her age and the second one through his stutter, Lily's metastability is set in what, from a general point of view, is a healthy, young woman. Despite this classification, Hustvedt allows her to shake as well and in such a continuous manner that she awakens *vulnerability* in the obviously flawed to a moment of shared individual experience. For Lily, everyone and everything individuates through the intensity of its *shaking*. The abundance of this *shaking* resembles the frequent instances of *falling* in the previous chapter. Here is a small selection of examples of how Lily's character and her perception of the world is relayed through her *shaking*: the "vague spasm of her abdomen" (13), "the shiver of excitement" (31), "her lip as it quivered" (74), "the faint tremor of his [Edward's] orgasm" (79), "her legs trembl[ing] with exhaustion" (81), her "vibrating [nerves] just beneath her skin" (165), her "jaw [shaking]" from release (172), her "voice [as it] shook" (202) and her actual "shaking" (226).

Lily expresses this relatable vulnerability when she thinks about her direct milieu: "[Lily] remembered Dolores's ankle buckling in Ed's room, and it made her think of Mabel's shaking hands and of Martin's stutter, that word he had started but never finished outside the Arts Guild. She felt unsteady herself. Everybody's quivering, she thought. Everybody except Ed" (163). She understands others because of the liminality they are in. For her, everyone is liminal, yet, expresses this liminality in their own individual way. Because others display *vulnerability*, as in "buckling," "shaking," "stutter," she can meet them there, in this liminal space, being "unsteady" herself. *Shaking* and, thus, the *vulnerability* of others is the relatable moment, which becomes even clearer in Edward's loss of it.

Pivotal for their relationship is the fact that Lily does not contact her lover, strong and steady Edward Shapiro, after the traumatic experience of witnessing Martin's suicide. Instead, she seeks shelter and help with Mabel. Keeping in mind that the latter is in constant tremor, an embodied *vulnerability* so to say, and Edward does not even shiver once, up until this point in the novel, it is paradoxical that Lily contacts the *vulnerable* over the steady. It is, nevertheless, Mabel's *vulnerability*, especially its constant exposition, which shows that her sensitive equilibrium has so many times reestablished itself that the continuity of its resetting, is proof of her life so far. Her *shaking* reassures Lily. Edward, however, lacks what is crucial for social life in this Simondonian sense. Moreover, never having observed him display his *vulnerability*, evokes the question of his ability to deal with crises for Lily. The shivers are the body's essential motion for social interaction, connecting characters as disparate as Dolores, the alcoholic prostitute; Mabel, the constantly nervous, almost 'hysterically intense' old woman; Martin, the small town's stutterer; and Lily, whose adoration for Marilyn Monroe takes on childish projections of identification.

Outside of this group of easily labeled and classified deviants, Edward Shapiro's comparative motionlessness begs for attention. He presents strength, control and independence, a middle-aged, beautiful man whose creative skill turns canvases into art (1), and whose outmost expressions of indecision are mere wrinkles of concern (172). Therefore, up until the very end, Edward will remain a mystery to the reader, a character full of ostensibly desirable attributes, however, not individuating. Despite of his affair with Lily, and despite his supposed friendships with Mabel and Dolores, he lacks individuation because he holds back *vulnerability*. His lack of importance for the plot, given his diegetic involvement as the heroine's lover, can only be understood in Hustvedt's deliberate exclusion of him from the rhetorics of the novel. At the end of the novel, nevertheless, Edward shivers and his metastability comes to light. His vulnerability begins to take over, beginning in the face and flowing through his body until his knees start "jiggling" (265) and he finally gives in. This moment resonates with Lily in as much as she "felt her chin begin to shake, then her neck and shoulders. She didn't try to stop the shuddering. It seemed alright now, like a seizure that had been a long time in coming" (226). Lily continues until the very end to relate to others on this level of her metastability.

With Lily Dahl, however, this metastable means of perceiving the world takes two other experimental forms worth considering. Two instances show Lily being shaken as well as shaking another person, each intensifying as well as inducing life. In the first scene, Lily is shaken by her former boyfriend Hank, while in the second scene, she shakes an unconscious woman.

"Her head bobbed forward and her spine collapsed . . . . He [Hank] clutched her upper arms harder to hold her up. If he let go, she knew she would fall . . . . Before she knew what she was doing, she was smiling like an idiot into Hank's outraged face. He started to shake her. Lily's head flew backward, then whipped forward again. She lost her footing and stumbled forward into Hank who continued to shake her. His fury amazed Lily, and she heard herself cry out in surprise." (44)

"Taking the woman by the shoulders, Lily started to shake her. She shook her gently at first, waiting for a response, but the woman's head seemed as heavy as a bowling ball. Lily shook harder . . . and that was when she realized she was enjoying it, that this shaking had an energy, a life all of its own, and that it felt so good she didn't want to stop, and shook more." (176)

In both passages the *shaking* does not come from within the respective person but is forcefully, in a manner of agitation—anger and ecstasy—inflicted on the other person, making this not a movement of relational interaction but, rather, a demonstration of power. Lily gets to experience both sides. Considering that she relates to the world through *shaking*, understanding others and experiencing herself in that manner, always, however, in respect for the sensitivity of the respective person's state of mind and body, it is the strength of Hank's *shaking* that not only deprives it of its sensitivity but also withdraws her ability to connect with him. In the second scene, nevertheless, she abuses the vulnerability of another person, which is followed by a feeling of shame later on. What begins as the helpful intention to bring someone back to consciousness, turns into an act of omnipotence. Lily finds herself not in a position where she reads the metastability of another person and can thus meet her or him that way, but turns into a life force herself, indulging in ecstasy over it. These two scenes, however, form an exception to Lily's approach to her milieu.

In sum, only a solipsistic individual, in search for total control over itself, can immunize itself from the unexpected, the loss of control. On the grounds of this vulnerability the development of the individual characters is manifested through their own intensity and way of *shaking* residing in their metastable equilibrium, highlighting the sensitivity of this state. Hustvedt thus ascertains a concept of social bodily motion that is present in the characters' relation to each other and unfolds itself to the readers through the rhetoric of jiggling, stuttering, stammering, trembling, buckling, quivering, shaking, shivers, spasms and convulsions. Through Mabel's constant tremors, Hustvedt defines metastability as a testament of life, implying that it has been gained through a successive dephasing, where the individual has fallen so many times out of step with itself that this denotes the ability to constantly reassure metastability. With Martin, one can see that the burden of living a metastable existence in a society where the vulnerable are excluded, can lead to the individual's denying of itself, resulting in a worst case scenario of death. The character of Lily Dahl stresses that metastability and, thus, vulnerability is not a state for an excluded group easily defined as 'different,' but a means for approaching the world. Finally, with Edward Shapiro's character the last pillar of normal classification is torn down as he joins his girlfriend in *shaking*. EPILEPSY IS METASTABILITY thus manifests the liminal as the central component of individuation.

III.C Metaphor and Idioms: Siri Hustvedt's Metastable Rhetoric as Transindividuation

III.C.3 *The Summer Without Men*: Em Dash as Endurance

> "Can we change and stay the same?
> I remember. I repeat."
> SIRI HUSTVEDT, *THE SUMMER WITHOUT MEN*

Siri Hustvedt's fifth novel, *The Summer Without Men* (2011), which deals with a married couple pausing their relationship for a summer, occupies the final position in this investigation of her rhetoric, as it plays a pivotal role in her oeuvre, establishing next to, *fragility* (*Blindfold*) and *vulnerability* (*Enchantment*), *endurance* (*Summer*) as part of her poetics. In addition to marking a sharp intensification of her rhetoric, *The Summer Without Men* prepares the form for Hustvedt's sixth novel *The Blazing World*, published in 2014. By continuing the conceptual metaphor of EPILEPSY IS META-STABILITY in *falling* as *fragility*[1] and *shaking* as *vulnerability*,[2] Hustvedt stays true to her rhetoric. *The Summer Without Men* stands out in its very syntax, calling for an analysis of her punctuation. In her previous novels, the *em dash* came to take on an increasingly stronger significance, becoming an indispensable means for fathoming her rhetoric as poetics. Thus, *The*

1 See Chapter III.C.1 of this book.

2 See Chapter III.C.2 of this book.

Summer Without Men can be seen to form the nexus between Hustvedt's beginnings and her most recent work.

In order to contextualize the argument, this chapter will begin with a short outline of the reception of Hustvedt's fifth novel. After that, the argument for reading this chapter's epilepsy metaphor will be accompanied by a short overview of what Gilbert Simondon means in the statement, "[t]he living [is] both agent and theater of individuation."[3] A first concise overview of the plot is followed by an analysis of Hustvedt's versatile usages of the *em dash*. Reading it in its larger context of colons, commas, semi colons, periods and parentheses, the *em dash*, first of all, stresses their common feature of pausing the reading, be it a pause within single or between multiple sentences. Due to this common feature, the surplus of *em dashes* stresses the *em dash* as a connector that works along the different degrees of implied pauses. Securing the preservation of these degrees through the syntax, the *em dash* is not a tool for erasing the differences between these various punctuation marks, but hints at an overall poetics of pause.

Before focusing on Hustvedt's usage of the *em dash*, though, it is important to note, that although critical reception of her work is scant, critics tend to focus on the idiosyncratic form that unfolds in a remarkably eloquent manner in this fifth novel. *The Summer Without Men* consists of a pastiche of various texts and images, including "#Entries," drawings, poems, songs, messages, semantic innuendos, cross-references to Hustvedt's entire oeuvre, puns, as well as capitalizations and italics. Her critics' view of her as a postmodern author finds therefore a solid ground. Furthermore, her relentless exploration of the thresholds between neuroscience and psychoanalysis and body and mind make her prone to being read in this tradition (Hartmann, Marks and Zapf 130). This thesis, however, proposes a different view on Hustvedt—one that fosters an appreciation of her unique style of approaching the liminal through the conceptual metaphor of EPILEPSY IS METASTABILITY as it emerges in her work on the notion of the pause.

To derive Hustvedt's poetics from her rhetoric of the conceptual metaphor of EPILEPSY IS METASTABILITY, the utilization of the *em dash* appears to be of exceptional significance as it stresses, on a formal ground,

3 See Chapter II.C of this book.

the importance of *endurance* for individuation. This means actively living through the moment of felt stagnation. Considering for a moment the leading topic of this novel, the cliché "*pause*" (original emphasis 1) between long-married couples—due to an affair—finds itself reiterated and formally enforced in the manifold appearances of the *em dashes* that populate the text. Hustvedt's precise grammatical knowledge of this punctuation device echoes the various meanings of pauses, stressing its characteristic feature as being a momentum that, although still, favors continuation: pause over stagnation. Ranging from the signification of colons, commas, semi colons, periods and parentheses, the *em dash*'s versatility plays out its full being in this novel. It is here, that epilepsy is destigmatized on formal grounds, just as the aftermath after a seizure marks a pause for the individual who experienced it. Pauses as moments of felt stagnation stand, hence, for the loss and regeneration of consciousness, which, despite their ostensible absolute character, mark individuation as process and not as the accumulation of fragments of experiences. Similar to the previous two chapters, where the range and abundance of *falling* and *shaking* introduced novel meanings of these idiomatic terms for the individual, the *em dash* redefines the meaning of the pause for the individual. Moreover, by exploring, the whole range of the *em dash* and leaving the reader in a conundrum about the couple's reunification, Hustvedt stresses the importance of *endurance* for individuation.[4]

Hence, the *em dash* as pause takes on a double meaning, configuring the metastable rhetoric and introducing *endurance* as part of individuation. Starting with this double meaning, the *em dash* is, on the one hand, a grammatical device, while, on the other hand, it carries with it the novel's central topic. It is simultaneously form and content and can, thereby, illuminate how metastability means for "[t]he living [to be] both agent and theater of individuation[.]"[5] Considering for a moment then that the *em dash* denotes in this reading the living, it helps to understand the significance behind the roles of "the agent" and "the theater of individuation." In the role of "agent," the *em dash* exercises its syntactic function by organizing and structuring the text. Yet, here it also goes beyond this function: in the role of "theater," it transports the overall leitmotif of the text—the pause. Each

4 See Chapter II.C of this book.

5 See Chapter II.C of this book.

time, the *em dash* appears, the pause manifests itself. Thinking this reinforcement of form and content both ways, the content's focus allows for the scrutiny of the form for possible markers that underline its leitmotif. Thinking Simondon's notion of metastability alongside the *em dashes* in this text, then, illuminates Hustvedt's ability to explore the richness of experience for the individual living through a pause. This requires thinking in line with the other two aspects of metastability: "falling out of step with itself"[6] and the "sensitive equilibrium,"[7] both of which emphasize "psychic tension"[8] necessary for individuation.

The importance of the pause in the novel is evident from the beginning until the end. The main character Mia Fredricksen, a fifty-five year old writer and lecturer, is left by her husband for a younger woman referred to as "[t]he Pause" (2), with a capital P. This euphemistic nickname hovers over Mia's thoughts throughout the novel. Her husband, Boris Izcovich, coins the name during his confession of the affair and asked for a "*pause*, not [a] *stop* to keep the narrative open, in case he changed his mind" (original emphasis 3). The novel begins, similar to the aftermath of an epileptic attack, after Mia's psychological breakdown, and denotes her mediation of herself in this new phase of her life, wherein she has to reestablish herself, or in the terminology of this thesis, familiarize herself with her new metastability. This new form of metastability, defines *endurance* as the main theme. Mia must endure the betrayal. In order to do that, the protagonist moves from her flat in Brooklyn to her hometown in Minnesota where she stays until the novel ends, with Boris regretting the "Pause" and returning to his wife. The reconciliation is palpable but not explicit as Mia does not answer him right away, when he rings the door bell, but instead says: "Let him come to me" (182). This last utterance precedes the cinematic direction "FADE TO BLACK" (ibid.) which closes the novel, stressing the plot's theatrical framework introduced in the prologue by way of an excerpt from the comedy *The Awful Truth* (1937). In contrast to the comedy, starring Cary Grant and Irene Dunne, Mia Fredricksen and Boris Izcovich neither slide accidently into their near-divorce, nor do they reaffirm their marriage. The pause was one-sided and deliberately chosen by Boris, and Mia

6 See Chapter II.C as well as Chapter III.C.1 of this book.

7 See Chapter II.C as well as Chapter III.C.2 of this book.

8 See Chapter II.C of this book.

endured it, experiencing a summer that, in hindsight, helped her to individuate.

Mia's summer without men, then, which begins after her psychological breakdown and ends with gaining reassurance in herself, is characterized by her different relationships to the women in her milieu, the first of which form a group named the "Five Swans" (8) which includes Mia's mother, George (Georgiana), Peg, Abigail, and Regina. During the course of the summer, the 'pause,' Regina loses her memory and Abigail dies from a stroke, reducing the group to four. With Abigail in particular, Mia develops a bond of trust where the former shows Mia her artwork of "the masturbators" (67) and shares her memories with her. The second group of women are seven teenage girls that enrolled in Mia's summer poetry writing class: Peyton Berg, Jessica Lorquat, Ashley Larsen, Emma Hartley, Nikki Borned, Joan Kavacek, Alice Wright. Four of these girls will form for Mia the "Gang of Four" (19). In both groups Mia will function as a mediator at the end. While she directs a group discussion on Jane Austen with the "Five Swans," she intervenes in the bullying Ashley is facing by calling each of the girls and their mothers together for a talk. In addition to these nine women, each with her own story to tell and problem to face, Mia befriends her neighbor Lola, who finds herself in an abusive relationship with her husband Pete. Again, Mia will serve as a center of solace and trust for this woman. Finally, Mia maintains her good relationship with her daughter Daisy and her sister Beatrice, called Bea. All of these women are connected to Mia and, with their stories and lives, they enrich Mia's seeming stagnation, bring movement into it, and thereby define the pause. The gathering of and focus on female characters in this novel thus leads one to rethink the title *The Summer Without Men* as *The Summer of Women.*

The many women defining Mia's summer and, hence, her metastability as pause, are the only clue for deciphering why the title refers to men and not to a 'man.' Only two other men besides Boris play a role in Mia's summer, both of which relate to Boris and their relationship. She sometimes thinks back to Stefan, Boris' brother who kissed Mia and confessed his love for her, before he committed suicide. She also receives mysterious, destructive notes from a "Mr. Nobody" who could, however, be a phantasm of hers, given that she is diagnosed with a psychosis close to the end of the novel. Either way, these two men, or the ideas and memories of these men, serve as rather small detours her mind takes while thinking about Boris and their paused relationship. They therefore do not give a satisfying explanation as to why the title refers to several men. Given that the novel focuses on portraying women in their various stages in life—as teenagers (her poetry class), young adults (her daughter), young parents (her neighbor), in midlife (Mia and her sister Bea), and as old women of almost 102 (George)—Mia's pause allows her to enter the lives of each of these women, undefined by partners or lovers, experiencing *The Summer Without Men*. Diving into these two titles, then, they specify why the pause as *endurance* is necessary for Mia's individuation. She reflects in this pause on the past, present and future of her as being a woman; it becomes the agent and theater of her individuation. Similar to Mia's pause, which orchestrates the various lives of the characters in the novel, bringing them together, and thereby defining her individuation, the pause of the *em dash* needs to be read, that is, as defining the metastability of the text in its transindividuality.

The first *em dash*, located in the position of colons stresses a rather informal than formal usage.[9] The *em dash* in this position adapts the colon's usage in concluding or summing up a thought, while simultaneously lending it an insistent, personal tone. It indicates a pause, insinuating, however, the urgency of a conclusion. One can already see that these two features of the *em dash* alone change the immediacy of the text and plot. The two examples we will consider in depth in the next paragraphs, are exemplary for how Hustvedt prefers the *em dash* over the colon: she deliberately upholds grammatical function while utilizing its expressiveness of the pause. The pause in the form of the colon is exchanged for the *em dash* in order to stress the text's general leitmotif. By mediating to the reader that the pause is decisive, it cannot simply be scanned but requires attention to be recognized in its very being. Besides this attention to the pause, which defines it as *endurance*, the *em dash* carries the significance of the pause on the content level for Mia's individuation. The *em dash*'s first means for establishing metastability works through its exchange for the colon.

9 For the syntactic positionings of the em dashes used in this chapter, see <http://www.thepunctuationguide.com/em-dash.html> consulted: 10/05/16, 7:54 a.m.

From the start of the novel, Mia's metastability mediating space and time, is pushed forward by the *em dash.* When Mia is still adjusting to her new situation she states that "there is no living without a ground, without a sense of space that is not only external but internal—mental loci . . . . A man tells his wife he is taking a stroll and doesn't come home for dinner—ever again" (11). These two *em dashes* appear in close proximity to one another, transporting Mia's general state of mind onto the *em dash.* They characterize how she endures her state, while they respectively enforce her *endurance*. The first *em dash* sums up the preceding part of the sentence as "mental loci," while the second stresses the length of the current state she feels herself exposed to: "ever again." The absoluteness of both of these states, mind and time, define the two focal points, or forces between which Mia feels herself trapped. What she defines as the necessary ground for any living, is the stability of the mind from which she, nevertheless, was momentarily deprived of. Knowing about the fragility of this living ground, then, she also experiences it as an opportunity to restructure herself. Although anything but solid or stable, she puts the mind into the position of a life force that defines her inner space, her being. Taking this space as the first pole, she opposes it with the loss of repetition or, contrarily, with the infinity of loneliness, making time an inevitable counterpoint.

Between these two forces highlighted by the mere visual significance of the *em dashes* over colons, Mia *endures*. She feels herself trapped between the instability of the mind and the deprivation of love. She regards both of these states as necessary for her life because she has experienced how they withdraw themselves from her total control. Hustvedt continues to use the *em dash* instead of the colon to mark metastability as that which mediates between two forces: inside and outside, emptiness and abundance, light and shape, men and women (63,72,101,104). The reader participates in Mia's *endurance* through the empathic and informal quality in which the *em dash* inheres and thereby transports. It is almost as if she has to refigure her metastability anew against all classic binaries, learning what it means to be inside a house without losing the connection to the outside. Learning anew how not to be scared off by the emptiness of a vast open field but to see it as a composition of "—corn and sky" (72). She also learns her eroticism anew "that erotic explosion . . . —any or all may have done it" (101). When she finally directs her attention to the exchange of men and women, the *em dash* takes on a comical value. It becomes the pause necessary for marking the punch line. She thinks of a biblical story which moralizes that in masturbation "wasted" semen, which spilled on the ground does not fulfill its purpose of landing "—inside of a woman" (104), showing that the *endurance*, although still balancing between poles, has lost its painfulness and has subsided into relief.

Taking this value of *endurance* as relief, we can now consider the *em dash* in the position of the comma. The comma stands in close relation to the semicolons and periods with regard to its grammatical alliance with the *em dash*. Grammatically, the *em dash* is said to be a stronger pause than the comma and weaker than a period. It is perhaps, then, closest to the semicolon. Its informality, however, sets it apart from the others, lending, as it does, a personal tone to the text. Three examples allow insights into the three relationships that define Mia's summer of pause and display the metastability in terms of *endurance*. In the first example Mia describes Abigail's table runner of "the rendered female onanist" (66), tainting the notion of *endurance* with the agony of anticipated relief and tension. In the second example, in which the *em dash* is preferred over the semicolon, Mia finds herself in a situation where she has to listen, involuntarily, to her friend Lola fighting with her husband. The *em dash* connects both women in their *endurance* through the cracks in their respective relationships. The last example in this section refers to the *em dash* functioning in the position of the period and relates to Mia's relationship to her young students.

Especially with respect to the comma and the *em dash*, the following passage shows how subtly and deliberately Hustvedt chooses punctuation and how it denotes the metastability of the text as sexual *endurance*:

> "Slender sylph reclines in easy chair, strategically dandling a feather between her open legs. Dark lady lies at edge of bed, legs in the air, two hands hidden beneath disordered petticoats. Chunky redhead straddles the bar of a trapeze, head thrown back, mouth open in orgasmic extremity. Grinning blonde with shower nozzle—spray stitched in neat fanning lines of blue thread. And, finally, a white-haired woman lying in bed clad in a long nightgown, her hands pressed over the cloth against her genitals." (66f.)

This passage shows five women in ecstasy. There is a certain balance in the description of these five sentences with the *em dash* exposing, however, the possibility of a disturbance in the fourth sentence. The onset of each masturbation scene is identical in its composition, beginning with the distinctive feature of each woman: "[s]lender sylph," "[d]ark lady," "[c]hunky redhead," "[g]rinning blonde," "[a]nd, finally a white-haired woman." After that, the symmetry continues for the first three and the final sentence in the grammatical structure of "subject verb object": the nymph "reclines in easy chair," the lady "lies at edge of bed," the redhead "straddles the bar of a trapeze," and the woman "l[ies] in bed clad in a long nightgown." With the first three women the beholder knows their location and can anticipate their pose. The same is true for the last one. Growing continually more familiar with this descriptive mode and pace, the fourth scenery allures the naratee to visualize the blonde woman in the same manner before being deprived of the grammatical balance. It is one sentence that shows how the grammatical structure and devices can shift emphasis and expose the metastability of the text.

The blonde stands out, she grins, her pose, location, clothes or motions are not described, nor is her masturbation explicated in any way that facilitates the imagination. The sexual action is rather implied through the three women before and the one following her, and looking at their grammatical resemblance, it is precisely the comma—in contrast to the *em dash*—that produces this disruption. With the other women, the commas thread the single elements of the masturbation together, giving just about enough detail for the reader to visualize them. The *em dash*, however, works quite differently, by shifting the entire focus from the portrayal of the women's sexual endurances onto the materiality of the artwork itself. These five women in ecstacy are stitched pictures on a table runner, it is, however, only with the picture of the blonde woman that this materiality is mentioned at all. Thereby, and only here, the reader is reminded of the actual materiality of the cloth. On the one hand, there is the abundance of material, tactile information, while on the other hand, the description lacks information of sexual details. It is the metastability of this simultaneous lack of, as well as abundance of information that define it as sexual *endurance*. By means of the *em dash* and the fixation on materiality Hustvedt sustains the tension of the passage, not giving in to relief, maintaining metastability.

A different form that brings the tension of *endurance* to light derives from the *em dash* in place of semicolons. In the following passage, Mia does not yet know her neighbor Lola whom she will become close friends with. When she thus finds herself involuntarily exposed to one of the frequent fights of the couple living next to her, she describes it in the following manner: "What carried into my domain was anger: the screech of her voice that changed register when it cracked into sobs, and his booming tenor—both of which were occasionally punctuated by a crash" (45). The tension between this couple becomes palpable to Mia and scares her. This passage relies on the emphatic power of the *em dash* as its function as marked pause distinguishes it from the semicolon. Both the sobs and the tenor are "punctuated by a crash" defining a rhythm of fight that is orchestrated and intensified by the *em dash*. Forced to listen to them, Mia thereby endures this scenario of marital screaming. Mia, as she is still recovering from the sudden pause of her own marriage that was, at no stage, marked by these loud rhythms, is suddenly confronted with the sufferings of the unknown couple.

Another scene wherein Mia enriches her summer of pause, is with her students. Here, Hustvedt, uses the *em dash* instead of a period. Reducing the intensity of the pause between two sentences that are otherwise clearly distinguishable from each other, they are now brought together. When Mia is talking to Dr. S. about her students, the latter notes that "'You [Mia] seem to have struck a chord with your young poets.' (I heard a chord on a guitar—metaphors often do this to me, even the deadest of the dead)" (50f.). The fact that Mia is hearing the chord, although she does not want to, indicates the *em dash*'s forceful power which could signify the inner sound that is building up inside of her. A period would have required a longer pause—for hearing the sound of the chord without any judgment about the echo. The *em dash* however initiates a continuation of this perceived metaphor of sound and categorizes it among the "deadest of the dead." This value judgement ascribed to the vivid, embodied reaction of Mia, infuses the conceptual metaphor of "striking a chord" with death. The *em dash* counterbalances, once again, a classic binary and denotes the metastability's position in between two forces.

Finally, the metastability in which the *em dash* inheres, achieves its fullest force in superseding parentheses. The *em dash* highlights, besides providing a grammatical informal outline, the parenthetical content. Furthermore, it is intrusive and can thus indicate a sudden change in thought. Given these features, three groups of two examples mirror how the *em dash* as metastability defines *endurance*. In these three groups, the *em dashes*' metastability marks *endurance* because it plays with the hierarchical order of the content, sometimes even to the point of reversing it. The reader has to mediate between the different information, rereading and re-structuring it. The first pair is a contrasting juxtaposition that mirrors and thereby reverses the two female characters, while the second group rearranges the order of important information, before the last pair plays with the order of attention and provides jokes as comic relief to *endurance*.

The first pair, then, juxtaposes Mia and Lola who are both distraught by their love life. In the first example, Mia has just been "sobbing" when her neighbor's daughter, Flora, approaches her. Accompanying Flora back to her mother Lola, "I [Mia] saw Lola register my face, what it looked like I have no idea—a red-gray mash of tears and mascara, probably—but her brow furrowed for a fraction of a second in sympathy" (57). So far, the *em dashes* do not disclose any other function than drawing attention to Mia's emotional state. As Mia's and Lola's friendship grows deeper after this incident, given that one has exposed her fragility[10] to the other and both share the experiences of motherhood and difficult marriages, a second sequence emerges that manifests the *em dashes*' metastability. Again, the initiator of the gathering will be Flora, underscoring a possible comparison of the two scenes. This time, however, Mia observes Lola: "She [Lola] did not appear to have shed any tears—her cheeks were dry and the whites of her eyes were untouched by redness—but her chest rose and fell as she breathed deeply, like a person who had been running" (133). After Lola and her husband Pete fight intensively, surpassing even their fighting standards, Mia sees her friend in agony. Both sequences begin in the same way and center on the same topic. The metastability occurs due to the exchangeability and yet difference between these two women dealing with their situations. The *em dash*'s content displays, first, a woman's face as missing any contour due to smudged mascara and puffy eyes, before it then sets apart a woman in complete composure, despite a previous dispute. Through the reverse perspective it becomes clear that the *em dash* points toward the *endurance* of the situation, for each of these women is in psychic tension.

Looking at the second pair, metastability is established through the additional information that nevertheless takes up the importance of the main clause. While Mia is curiously "spy[ing]" (64) on her students as they leave her poetry class, she observes a group of teenage boys: "With a single ex-

10 See Chapter III.C.1 of this book.

ception—a tall boy in wide shorts and a baseball cap turned backward on his head—they were runty amours, much shorter than most of the girls, but all five—towering boy included—were engaged in what appeared to be a clumsy, testosterone-infused form of group gymnastics" (65). Before looking into this quote, it shall be stated that pages 64 and 65 display a frequency of eight *em dashes*, none of which is used in direct speech as interruption, but all of which fulfill one of the thus far explicated grammatical punctuation devices. Returning to this scene, the four *em dashes* zoom into the group of boys, marking one of them as standing out from the others, due to his height, his being a "towering boy." Given that four *em dashes* alone accompany the towering boy throughout this observation, he can easily be seen to be the center of attraction for the girls as well as for the reader.

A similar topic centers on sexuality and reverses the importance of the *em dash* by challenging the main clause again. Mia thinks back to "a couple of years ago at a discussion group on sex and the brain, I was SHOCKED when a colleague of Boris's assured me that in the animal kingdom—or, rather, in the female side of the animal kingdom, in other words, in the whole animal queendom—only human women experience orgasm" (original emphasis 103). With the neologism in the *em dash*'s content, "queendom," the attention is drawn to all female living beings, a mass of incredible magnitude that stands in direct analogy to human women as well as to the main characters in this novel. This is further elevated as the capitalized "SHOCKED" serves as the direct link to this magnitude and reserves the experience of orgasmic pleasure solitarily to human women. It is also the moment to settle in *endurance*; for Mia this information challenges her scientific belief as well as triggers her empathy for all female living beings experiencing sex for procreational purposes alone: enduring the act.

With this procreational perspective on sex, the last section of this chapter, reflects on the *em dashes*' serving to reverse the order of truth and lie/exaggeration, pursuing the funny side of *endurance*. Teaching her students D.H. Lawrence, Mia is confronted with a highly conservative mother, Mrs. Lorquat, who sees in the poem "Snake" a threat to her daughter's innocence (78). Mia's reaction: for she measures the woman opposing her:

> "The woman did to not look stupid. She looked dangerous. In Bonden, a rumor, a bit of gossip, even outright slander could spread with preternatural speed. I mollified her, asserting my great respect for beliefs of all kinds—an outright lie—and by the end of our conversation, I felt I had assuaged her worries" (78).

Mia has to *endure* the narrow-mindedness and tackle it, at least for herself, for the integrity of her belief system, by lying.

In line with this, the final passage relays a funny daydream of Mia's, where she imagines one of her talks filmed and directed. It is a scene wherein she shares an experience of her own teenage years with her students. While telling this story Mia imagines herself in a

> ". . . most all-knowing, authoritative, good-teacher-beloved-by-the-students expression, a cross between Mr. Chops and Miss Jean Brodie and then I slapped Theodore Roethke shut, stood up, and made my exit. In the film, the camera would follow my back to the door, my high heels—sandals in reality–clipping smartly on the floorboards, and then I pause, just for a moment, and turn to look over my shoulder." (91)

With this whole scene she manages to *endure* the disarming deprivation that can accompany the youthful glance upon older people while sharing a moment of her own life. The loss in height and style likewise, from high heels to sandals, strengthens how decisively an image can shift into another phase of itself by changing parameters as ostensibly insignificant as shoes.

In conclusion, the *em dash* denotes the moment necessary for individuation as it provides the means for the individual to build its strength to endure difficult and psychologically challenging situations. The experience of a pause might evoke the notion of stagnation in life but, quite contrary to that, it also opens up the possibility to shift and resettle focus. It removes the pace and forces the individual to stay present in a situation, mirroring, thus, the haecceity[11] that served as the past in *The Blindfold* and the *a praesenti*[12] in *The Enchantment of Lily Dahl.* This part of the conceptual metaphor of EPILEPSY IS METASTABILITY refers to the very aspect of the epileptic attack that for the individual marks the aftermath, the regathering of strength and reorientation. Exemplified alongside epilepsy, *endurance*

11 See Chapter III.C.1 of this book.

12 See Chapter III.C.2 of this book.

becomes visible in the same manner as the *em dash* connotes a visible pause in the text, emphasizing, in its syntactical form both the emphatic and the incisive. Through the *em dash* as *endurance* Hustvedt introduces a variety of experiences that rest in this state, be it sexual endurance, the reorganization of hierarchical positions, or comic relief. To encompass such a variety of experiences with this grammatical device, Hustvedt underlines her rhetoric as a metastable transindividual.

Conclusion

This book shows that in American literature, between 1990 and 2015, a profound corpus of epilepsy metaphors emerges and both reasserts the discriminating image of epilepsy as well as tackles it decisively. In order to approach these metaphors and their engagement in the perpetuation of or breaking with the stigmata attached to epilepsy, a first step required to look at the history of epilepsy. I compiled and categorized the stigmata with which people with epilepsy were approached and discriminated over the centuries, such as prophetic, devout, possessed, imbecile/genius and spiritual, according to the motifs of *sleep, falling, danger, intelligence* and *religiousness*, in order to account for the different nuances with which these attributions reappeared and before the appearance of what came to be known the "epileptic" in the twentieth century. These motifs endure over such a long period of time because they cover up the five levels of stigma persistence, on the "affective," "emotional" and "linguistic level," followed by the "level of conduct" and the "cognitive level," which were identified by Lerita M. Coleman Brown. However, given the time that is of interest for this thesis, another level emerges that mirrors the epistemological outlines epilepsy has been prone to over the centuries. As stated in the introduction, the two explanatory models of epilepsy which have persisted through the centuries are medicine and religion; together they have played crucial roles in the formation of stigma persistence and form what I came to call the *ratio-spiritual* level.

This history of stigma and discrimination provoked, on the one hand, the scrutiny of the scarce critical attention to epilepsy in American literature and, on the other hand, the exploration of the academic field of cultural disability studies, in order to derive a fresh means for dealing with this topic. With these motifs in mind, I needed to see whether or not they gave rise to certain interpretative approaches of famous authors such as Edgar Allan Poe, Emily Dickinson, Walker Percy and Thomas Pynchon. The reception showed a clear alignment between these motifs and the dominant readings of these authors, reducing their work to the medical accuracy of or insights they might offer on epilepsy. Given the persistence of the history of epilepsy, I demonstrated that the dominant perception of epilepsy is, indeed, that of a disability. What came, then, to be the most debatable topic at hand was the use of metaphors in relation to disabilities in general. Be it that they flagrantly strengthen rigid belief systems circulating in a society or subtly permeate daily language, their discriminating power was attested to. It was here, that the given literary corpus of epilepsy metaphors in the time from 1990-2015 called for a new theorization as they tackled these rigid belief systems and provided a new perspective on idiomatic expressions. When Amy Vidali, thus, called for metaphors to capture "the full range of disability," I argued that the novels at hand provided new metaphors, using epilepsy, which not only tackled the notion of the normal on three levels—the society, the body and language—but highlighted the individual in it.

Being aware that these three fields at hand, and their relation to the concept of normal, not only provide, each, a book of its own, but also acknowledge their reinforcement of each other, I argued that the distinction is, of course, not absolute, but merely helpful in accounting for the different emphases of the respective metaphors. The first theorization thus focused on metaphors that, at their core, tackled or reinforced the perceived 'everydayness' of a society, which, in Jürgen Link's research, can be said to ask the question of 'who is normal?'. This attempt was further refined given Michel Foucault's elaborations on the clinic, since one means for labeling epilepsy as 'deviant,' besides its history, stems from a medical framework and thereby enters society. In line with these two theories, I coined the two terms of *protometaphors* and *flexmetaphors*. Since *protometaphors* split up into two sections, as some metaphors reinforce the stigma of epilepsy by conflating it with its history, while others strengthen the clinical outline of epilepsy, I attributed to the second metaphor the power to transform a text into an *epileptic* text, as it is the medical and clinical notion of epilepsy that define the authorities in our society for dealing with this disorder. A liminal space that allows for the individual to come to light was said to be part of *flexmetaphors*, as these metaphors point toward epilepsy and a moment of shared experience.

With a focus on the 'normal' body, the second theorization took George Canguilhem's work into account. Given his own background as a physician and philosopher, it was especially helpful to consider that his understanding of the normal body stresses the individuality of each body. Instead of comparing the body to a normal ideal, measuring how far it deviates from it, Canguilhem postulates that each body bears its own normativity and norm, that is, its own means of relating to its milieu. This stress on the individual body let me to coin the notion of *relational metaphors*. It is with Canguilhem that the notion of liminal space comes vividly into focus since these *relational*, single bodies require an understanding of them as in constant process of sufficiently stabilizing themselves. As these metaphors rely on the materiality of the body and the bodies in question deal with epilepsy, I derived the notion of an *electric way of life* as well as the *organ in sound.* Although both of these terms emphasize a common moment in the materiality of epilepsy, the metaphors take on different interpration, stressing the individual experience.

Taking the last level of metaphors into account—idiomatic and, thereby, perceived 'normal' language—I started off with the central criticism at hand which stated, from a disability studies perspective, that "conceptual metaphors" as introduced by George Lakoff and Mark Johnson, mirror a society's ideal of an able and healthy body. Without counteracting either this statement nor the theory of conceptual metaphors, I looked into Siri Hustvedt's rhetoric and saw in her work a new mode for perceiving the world which called for a new conceptual metaphor. Taking Gilbert Simondon's notion of metastability into account I coined the conceptual metaphor of EPILEPSY IS METASTABILITY, as both of these concepts overlap in their "event structure" because they display the idea of a simultaneity of movement and rest. I argued that, similar to other conceptual metaphors, both epilepsy and metastability become more relatable if put in relation to one another. The very fact that this conceptual metaphor accounts, on an ontological level, for daily language, enables it to encompass words that are used to describe epilepsy, such as shiver, spasms, falling, into metaphors. This means that both the historical and the clinical are left aside to function as explanatory models. The term transindividual was supposed to stress that through language as a means of social interaction and exchange, this new understanding of epilepsy is introduced.

Moving over to the novels which inspired this dissertation, I ordered them according to the different foci of their respective epilepsy metaphor. The first group, which includes Lauren Slater, Audrey Niffenegger, and Dennis Mahagin, displayed what I coined *calculated individuation*, and showed that texts focusing on the notion of a social 'normal' are prone to the mechanisms of *protometaphors* and, even more so, to the formation of an *epileptic* text emphasizing thereby the clinical impact on our society. With respect to the second group and the emphasis on the body, electricity indeed verified itself as a common denominator of all three *relational metaphors* that were detected in the works of Thom Jones, Rodman Philbrick and Reif Larsen. Staying true, however, to Canguilhem's idea, they each push forward a completely distinct metaphor, strenghening its individuality. I thereby argued that, with epilepsy, the *organ in sound* as well as the *electric way of life* describe how the body's materiality can take on its own meaning if it is deprived from social stigmatization or normalization practice. I coined this emphasis on the individual: *electric individuation*. It is also interesting to see, that especially these *relational metaphors* and the works analyzed in this section, overarch the whole timeframe (1990-2015), highlighting even more so that with electricity one can account for a stable moment to relate to epilepsy, providing a liminal space to secure individualization. It is here, with Canguilhem, that the neurological affiliation of the 1990s, together with the disability studies' movement, finds its literary and philosophical counterpart. Finally, looking into a selection of Siri Hustvedt's work, and focusing on the idioms therein, epilepsy not only verified itself in the text as a conceptual metaphor but helped to distinguish Hustvedt's particular poetics as displaying metastability: EPILEPSY IS METASTABILITY. By finding a way to connect epilepsy, on an ontological level, with movement and rest, partaking thereby in the concept of a transindividual, Hustvedt introduces epilepsy as a means for understanding life through a shared experience of *fragility*, *vulnerability* and *endurance*: life is metastable.

Bibliography

The New Oxford Annotated Bible with Apocrypha. Ed. Michael D. Coogan. 4th ed. Oxford: Oxford University Press, 2010. Print.

Andermatt, Michael. "Epilepsie als Metapher. Zum Bild der Epilepsie in der Literatur." *Epileptologie* 24 (2007): 106-112. Print.

Boever, Arne, et al., eds. *Gilbert Simondon. Being and Technology*. Edinburgh: Edinburgh University Press, 2012. Print.

Baker, Brian. "The Pathologies of Mobility: Time Travel as Syndrome in *The Time Traveler's Wife*, *La Jetée*, and *Twelve Monkeys*." Diseases and Disorders in Contemporary Fiction. *The Syndrome Syndrome*. Ed. Tim J. Lustig and James Peacock. New York: Routledge, 2013. 83-97. Print.

Bardin, Andrea. *Epistemology and Political Philosophy in Gilbert Simondon. Individuation, Technics, and Social Systems*. Heidelberg: Springer 2015. Print. Philosophy of Engineering and Technology 19.

Bazil, Carl W. "Seizures in the Life and Works of Edgar Allan Poe." *Arch Neurol*. 56 (1999): 740-743. Print.

Beard, David, and Kate Vo Thi-Beard. "Rethinking the Book: New Theories for Reader's Advisory." *Reference & User Services Quarterly* 47.4 (2008): 331-335. Print.

Becker, Howard S. *Outsiders. Studies in the Sociology of Deviance*. New York: Simon & Schuster Inc., 1963. Print.

Berg, Anne T., and Ingrid E. Scheffer. "New Concepts in Classification of the Epilepsies: Entering the 21st Century." *Epilepsia* 52.6 (2011): 1058-1062. Print.

Bjerke, Mats. "Siri Hustvedt's *The Blindfold* and *What I Loved*. A Study of Destructiveness in Art and Human Psyche" *MA thesis*. University of Oslo, 2014. Print.

Bladin, Peter F. "Historical Note: 'The Epileptic Constitution': The Psychoanalytic Concept of Epilepsy." *Journal of the History of Neuroscience* 9.1 (2000): 95-100. Print.

---. "Historical Note: History of 'Epileptic Vertigo': Its Medical, Social, and Forensic Problems." *Epilepsia* 99.4 (1998): 442-447. Print.

Blistein, Burton. *The Design of 'The Waste Land.'* Lanham: University Press of America, 2008. Print.

Bloom, James D. "Cultural Capital and Contrarian Investing: Roberts Stone, Thom Jones, and Others" *Contemporary Literature* 36.3 (Autumn 1995): 490-507. Print.

Caeners, Stefanie. "The Locus Amoenus in Audrey Niffenegger's *The Time Traveler's Wife*." *Literatur in Wissenschaft und Unterricht* 44.4 (2011): 265-275. Print.

Caeton, D. A. "'Veux-Tu Regarder, Bourreau!': The Somanormative Dimensions of the Diderotian Citoyen." *Journal of Literary & Cultural Disability Studies* 4.1 (2010): 73-88. Print.

Canguilhem, George. *Knowledge of Life*. 1965. Trans. Stefanos Geroulanos and Daniela Ginsburg. New York: Fordham University of Press, 2008. Print.

---. *New Reflections on the Normal and the Pathological (1963-1966)*. Trans. Carolyn R. Fawcett and Robert S. Cohen. 2nd ed. New York: Zone Books, 1991. Print.

---. *The Normal and the Pathological*. 1943. Trans. Carolyn R. Fawcett and Robert S. Cohen. 2nd ed. New York: Zone Books, 1991. Print.

Cavanna, Andrea E. "Epilepsy as a Pathology of Consciousness." *Epilepsy & Behavior* 30:1 (January 2014). Print.

Cazeaux, Clive. *Metaphor and Continental Philosophy. From Kant to Derrida*. London: Routledge, 2007. Print.

Chaudhary, Umair J., John S. Duncan, and Louis Lemieux. "A Dialogue with Historical Concepts of Epilepsy from the Babylonians to Hughlings Jackson: Persistent Beliefs." *Epilepsy & Behavior* 21 (2011): 109-114.

Coleman Brown, Lerita M. "Stigma: An Enigma Demistified." *The Disability Studies Reader*. Ed. Lennard J. Davis. 3rd ed. New York: Routledge, 2013. 179-192. Print.

Combes, Murial. *Gilbert Simondon and the Philosophy of the Transindividual*. Trans. Thomas LaMarre. Cambridge: MIT Press, 2013. Print.

Couser, G. Thomas. *Memoir: An Introduction*. Oxford: Oxford University Press, 2012. Print.

---. *Recovering Bodies. Illness, Disability, and Life Writing*. Wisconsin Studies in Autobiography. Madison: University of Wisconsin Press, 1997. Print.

---. *Signifying Bodies: Disability in Contemporary Life Writing*. Ann Arbor: University of Michigan Press, 2009. Print.

Crichton, Michael. *The Terminal Man*. 1972. *The Complete Novels*. New York: Wings Books, 1994. Print.

Cryle, Peter Maxwell. "The Aesthetics of the Spasm" *Sexuality at the Fin de Siècle: The Making of a 'Central Problem.'* Ed. Peter Maxwell Cryle and Christopher E. Forth. Newark: University of Delaware Pres, 2008. 77-92. Print.

Dallmann, Antje. "Conspiracies and Creative Paranoia: Ellis's *Glamorama*, Hustvedt's *The Blindfold*, and Whitehead's *The Intuitionist*." *Anglophonia* 19 (2006): 67-78. Print.

Davis, Lennard J. *Bending over Backwards. Essays on Disability and the Body*. New York: New York University Press, 2002. Print.

---. *The End of Normal. Identity in a Biocultural Era*. Ann Arbor: University of Michigan Press, 2014. Print.

---. *Enforcing Normalcy. Disability, Deafness, and the Body*. London: Verso, 1995. Print.

Debru, Claude. "The Concept of Normativity from Philosophy to Medicine." *Medicine Studies* 3 (2011): 1-7. Print.

Detweiler, Robert. *Breaking in the Fall. Religious Readings of Contemporary Fiction*. San Francisco: Harper & Row, 1989. Print.

Dolmage, Jay. "Between the Valley and the Field. Metaphor and Disability." *Prose Studies: History, Theory, Criticism* 27.1&2 (2006): 108-110. Print.

Eadie, Mervyn J., and Peter F. Bladin. *A Disease Once Sacred. A History of the Medical Understanding of Epilepsy*. Eastleigh: John Libbey Company Ltd., 2001. Print.

Ehlebracht, Steffi. *Gelingendes Scheitern. Epilepsy als Metapher in der deutschsprachigen Literatur des 20. Jahrhunderts*. Königshausen & Neumann, 2008. Print. Epistemata 648.

Elieff, Eden, and Thom Jones. "Interview with Thom Jones." *Mississippi Review* 27.3 (1999): 41-60.Print.

Engelhardt, Dietrich von. "Darstellung und Deutung der Epilepsie im Medium der Literatur der Neuzeit." *Das ist eine alte Krankheit. Epilepsie in der Literatur*. Ed. Dietrich von Engelhardt, Hansjörg Schneble and Peter Wolf. Stuttgart: Schattauer, 2000. 13-36. Print.

Ewart, Theodore C. "Epileptic Colonies." *BJP* 38 (1892): 212-222. Print.

Fischer-Elfert, Hans-Werner. *Abseits von Ma'at. Fallstudien zu Außenseitern im Alten Ägypten*. Ed. Hans-Werner Fischer-Elfert and Ludwig D. Morenz. Würzburg: Ergon, 2005. Print. Wahrnehmungen und Spuren Altägyptens. Kulturgeschichtliche Beiträge zur Ägyptologie 1.

Fisher, Robert S. "A Practical Clinical Definition of Epilepsy." *Epilepsia* 55.4 (2014): 475-482. Print.

Flieger, Jerry Aline. "Postmodern Perspective: The Paranoid Eye." *New Literary History: A Journal of Theory and Interpretation* 28.1 (1997): 87-109. Print.

Foucault, Michel. *The Birth of the Clinic. An Archaeology of Medical Perception*. 1963. Trans. A. M. Sheridan. London: Routledge Classics, 2003. Print.

---. *The History of Sexuality. Volume 1: An Introduction*. 1976. Trans. Robert Hurley. New York: Vintage, 1990. Print.

---. *Madness and Civilization. A History of Insanity in the Age of Reason*. 1964. Trans. Jonathan Murphy. Oxford: Routledge, 2006. Print.

---. *Psychiatric Power. Lectures at the Collège de France, 1973-1974*. London: Palgrave MacMillan, 2006. Print.

Fowler, Douglas. "Epilepsy as Metaphor in *The Crying of Lot 49*." *Notes on Contemporary Literature* 14.2 (1984): 10-12. Print.

Freud, Sigmund. "The Uncanny." 1919. Trans. Alix Strachey. *Fantastic Literature: A Critical Reader*. Ed. David Sadner, Westport: Praeger, 2004. 74-101.

Friedlander, Walter J. *The History of Modern Epilepsy. The Beginning, 1865-1914*. Westprot: Greenwood Press, 2001. Print.

Garland-Thomson, Rosemary. *Extraordinary Bodies*. New York: Columbia University Press, 1997. Print.

---. *Staring. How We Look.* Oxford: Oxford University Press, 2009. Print.

Gerigk, Hans-Jürgen. "Der Sturz als Metapher. Über Epilepsie im Gedicht." *Das ist eine alte Krankheit. Epilepsie in der Literatur*. Ed. Dietrich von Engelhardt, Hansjörg Schneble and Peter Wolf. Stuttgart: Schattauer, 2000. 51-58. Print.

Gerrig, Richard J., and Deborah A. Prentice. "Notes on Audience Response." *Post-Theory. Reconstructing Film Studies*. Ed. Bordwell, David and Noël Carroll. Madison: University of Wisconsin Press, 1996. 388-403. Print.

Goffman, Erving. *Stigma. Notes on the Management of a Spoiled Identity*. 1964 London: Penguin, 1990. Print.

Goldensohn, Eli S., Roger J. Porter, and Philip A. Schwartzkoin. "The American Epilepsy Society: An Historic Perspective on 50 Years of Advances in Research." *Epilepsia* 38.1 (1997): 124-150. Print.

Goodley, Dan. "Dis/entangling Critical Disability Studies." *Disability & Society* 28.5 (2013): 631-644. Print.

Govindaswamy, Moti Ventakarao. *Dr. M. V. Govindaswamy: Lectures and Writing*. Bangalore: Drindavan Printers & Publisher, 1970. Print.

Gross, Robert A. "A Brief History of Epilepsy and Its Therapy in the Western Hemisphere." *Epilepsy Research* 12 (1992): 65-74. Print.

Gschwind, Markus, and Fabienne Picard. "Ecstatic Epilepstic Seizures: A Glimpse into the Multiple Roles of the Insula." *Frontiers in Behavioral Neuroscience* 10.21 (2016): n. pag. Web. 17 Feb. 2016.

Günzel, Stephan, and Christof Windgätter. "Leib / Raum: Das Unbewusste bei Maurice Merleau-Ponty." Ed. Michael B. Buchholz and Günter Gödde. Gießen: Psychosozialverlag, 2005. 582-613. Print. Das Unbewusste in aktuellen Diskursen 1-3.

Hartmann, Johanna von, Christine Marks, and Hubert Zapf, eds. *Zones of Focused Ambiguity in Siri Hustvedt's Works*. Berlin: De Gruyter, 2016. Print.

Hennessy, Denis. "Thom Jones." *American Short-Story Writers since World War II*. Ed. Patrick Meanor and Joseph McNicholas. Detroit: Thomson Gale 2001. 202-210. Print.

Hirschhorn, Norbert, and Polly Longsworth. "Was It Epilepsy?: Misdiagnosing Emily Dickinson (1830-1886)." *Perspectives in Biology and Medicine* 56.3 (2013): 371-386. Print.

Hippocrates. *The Sacred Disease.* Trans. W. H. S. Jones. Ed. T. E. Page, E. Capps, W. H. D. Rouse, L. A. Post and E. H. Warmington. London: William Heinemann Ltd., 1959. Print. Hippoctates Vol. II.

Hustvedt. Siri. *The Blindfold.* London: Hodder & Stoughton Ltd, 1992. Print.

---. *The Enchantment of Lily Dahl.* New York: Henri Holt and Company, 1996. Print.

---. "Failing to Fall." *The New York Times*, 3 Mar. 2010. Web. 15 Jan. 2015.

---. *The Shaking Woman or a History of My Nerves.* London: Hodder & Stoughton, 2011. Print.

---. *The Summer Without Men.* New York: Picador, 2011. Print.

Ickstadt, Heinz. "The Creation of Normalcy." *Revue française d'études américaines* 85 (Juin 2000): 6-22. Print.

Ingold, Tim, and Gísli Pállson. *Biosocial Becoming.* Cambridge: Cambridge University Press, 2013. Print.

Jain, Satish. "Ayurveda: The Ancient Indian System of Medicine." *Complementary and Alternative Theraphies for Epilepsy.* Ed. Orrin Devinsky, Steven C. Schachter and Steven Pacia. New York: Demos Medical Publishing, 2005. 123-128. Print.

James, William. *The Varieties of Religious Experience. A Study in Human Nature. Gifford Lectures on Natural Religion Delivered at Edinburgh in 1901-1902.* New York: Random House, The Modern Library, 1929. Print.

Jameson, Alise. "Pleasure and Peril: Dynamic Forces of Power and Desire in Siri Hustvedt's *The Blindfold.*" *Studies in the Novel* 42.4 (2010): 421-424. Print.

The Young & Prodigious Spivet. Dir. Jean-Pierre Jeunet. Perf. Helena Bonham Carter, Kyle Catlett, and Judy Davis. Belga Films, 2013. Film.

Johnson, Mark. "Metaphor and Cognition." *Handbook of Phenomenology and Cognitive Science.* Ed. S Gallagher and D. Schmicking: Springer, 201ß. 401-414. Print.

---. "Mind Incarnate: From Dewey to Damasio." *Daedalus* 135.3 (2006): 46-54. Print.

---. "Philosophy's Debt to Metaphor." *The Cambridge Handbook of Metaphor and Thought.* Ed. Raymond W. Gibbs. Cambridge: Cambridge University Press, 2008. 39-52. Print.

Johnson, Tracy. "The Fear Industry: Women, Gothic and Contemporary Crime Narrative." *Gothic Studies* 4.1 (2002): 44-62. Print.

Jones, Jeffrey. "The Falling Sickness in Literature." *Southern Medical Journal* 93.12 (2000): 1169-1172. Print.

Jones, Thom. "As of July 6, I Am Responsible for No Debts Other Than My Own." *The Pugilist at Rest*. London: Faber and Faber, 1995. 131-141. Print.

---. "The Black Lights." *The Pugilist at Rest*. London: Faber and Faber, 1995. 65-85. Print.

---. "Break on Through." *The Pugilist at Rest*. London: Faber and Faber, 1995. 28-64. Print.

---. *Cold Snap*. Boston: Little, Brown and Company, 1995. Print.

---. "I Want to Live!" *The Pugilist at Rest*. London: Faber and Faber, 1995. 166-190. Print.

---. "Mosquitoes." *The Pugilist at Rest*. London: Faber and Faber, 1995. 99-112. Print.

---. "The Pugilist at Rest" *The Pugilist at Rest*. London: Faber and Faber, 1995. 3-27. Print.

---. *The Pugilist at Rest*. London: Faber and Faber, 1995. Print

---. "Rocket Man." *The Pugilist at Rest*. London: Faber and Faber, 1995. 211-230. Print.

---. "Silhouettes." *The Pugilist at Rest*. London: Faber and Faber, 1995. 142-165. Print.

---. *Sonny Liston Was a Friend of Mine*. 1999. London: Faber and Faber, 2000. Print.

---. "Unchain My Heart." *The Pugilist at Rest*. London: Faber and Faber, 1995. 113-128. Print.

---. "A White Horse." *The Pugilist at Rest*. London: Faber and Faber, 1995. 193-210. Print.

---. "Wipeout." *The Pugilist at Rest*. London: Faber and Faber, 1995. 89-98. Print.

Kelley, Nicole. "'The Punishment of the Devil Was Apparent in the Torment of the Human Body': Epilepsy in Ancient Christianity." *Disability Studies and Biblical Literature*. Ed. Candida R. Moss and Jeremy Shipper. New York: Palgrave McMillan, 2011. 201-221. Print.

Knirsch, Christian. "In a Time-Wrap: The Issue of Chronology in Siri Hustvedt's *The Blindfold*." *Current Perspectives of Postgradual American Studies* 11 (2010): no pag. Web. 9. Aug. 2016

Kreisel, Howard. *Prophecy: The History of an Idea in Medieval Jewish Philosophy*. Dordrecht: Kluwer Academic Publishers, 2011. Print.

Kristeva, Julia. *Powers of Horror. Essays on Abjection*. New York: Columbia University Press, 1982. Print.

Kurup, P. N. Vasudeva. "Bird's-Eye-View on Indigenous Systems of Medicine in India." *List of Education and Research Institutions in Traditional Systems of Medicine in India*. 3rd ed. New Delhi: Deepak Art Press, 1979. 36-44. Print.

Lakoff, George. "The Contemporary Theory of Metaphor." *Metaphor and Thought*. Ed. Andrew Ortony. 2nd ed. Cambridge: Cambridge University Press, 1993. 202-251. Print.

---. "The Neuronal Theory of Metaphor." *The Cambridge Handbook of Metaphor and Thought*. Ed. Raymond W. Gibbs. Cambridge: Routledge, 2008. 17-38. Print.

Lakoff, George, and Mark Johnson. "Metaphors We Live By." 1980. *The Production of Reality: Essays and Readings on Social Interaction*. Ed. Jodie O'Brien and Peter Kollock. 3rd ed. Thousand Oaks, California: Pine Forge Press. c2001: 124-134. Print.

Larsen, Reif. *I Am Radar*. London: Harvill Secker, 2015. Print.

---. *The Selected Works of T.S. Spivet*. New York: The Penguin Press, 2009. Print.

Laskaris, Julie. *The Art Is Long. On the Sacred Disease and the Scientific Tradition*. Ed. John Scarborough et al. Leiden: Brill, 2002. Print. Studies in Medicine 25.

Lewieki-Wilson, Cynthia, and James C. Wilson. "Disability, Rhetoric and the Body." *Embodied Rhetorics: Disability in Language and Culture*. Ed. Cynthia Lewieki-Wilson and James C. Wilson. Carbondale: Southern Illinois University Press, 2001: 1-26. Print.

Lilly, Paul R. "Male Paradigm in Thom Jones and Tom Paine." *The Postmodern Short Story. Forms and Issues*. Ed. Frahar Iftekharrudin et al. Westport: Praeger, 2008. 123-129. Print.

Link, Jürgen. "'From the Power to the Norm' to 'Flexible Normalism': Considerations after Foucault." *Cultural Critique* 57 (2004): 14-32. Print.

---. "'Irgendwo stößt die flexibelste Integration schließlich an eine Grenze' – Behinderung zwischen Normativität und Normalität." *Ethik und Behinderung. Ein Perspektivwechsel (Kultur der Medizin)*. Ed. Sigrid Graumann et al. Frankfurt: Campus Verlag, 2004. 130-139. Print.

---. *Normale Krisen? Normalismus und die Krise der Gegenwart*. Konstanz: Konstanz University Press, 2013. Print.

Linton, Simi. *Claiming Disability*. New York: NYU Press, 1998. Print.

Livingston, Samuel. *Living with Epileptic Seizures*. Springfield: Charles C. Thomas, 1963. Print.

Lombroso, Cesare. *The Man of Genius*. 1891. Ed. Havelock Ellis. 3rd ed. London: The Walter Scott Publishing, 1913. Print. The Contemporary Science Series Vol. XVI.

Lyons, Bonny, and Oliver Bill. "A Way of Feeling Better." *Passion and Craft. Conversations with Notable Writers*. Ed. Bonny Lyons and Oliver Bill. Urbana: University of Illinois Press, 1998. 112-127. Print.

Mahagin, Dennis. "Banishing The Snakes." *Grand Mal*. Bar Harbor: Rebel Satori Press, 2012. 13-15. Print.

---. "Dr Dre In Passing Bedside Manor." *Grand Mal*. Bar Harbor: Rebel Satori Press, 2012. 10-12. Print.

---. "Fare." *Grand Mal*. Bar Harbor: Rebel Satori Press, 2012. 32-33. Print.

---. "Fence Fragment." *Grand Mal*. Bar Harbor: Rebel Satori Press, 2012. 72. Print.

---. "Gilded Cage Smacks Of Sactuary." *Grand Mal*. Bar Harbor: Rebel Satori Press, 2012. 43-44. Print.

---. "Grand Mal W/ Grown Up." *Grand Mal*. Bar Harbor: Rebel Satori Press, 2012. 1-2. Print.

---. "Grand Mal W/ Landlord." *Grand Mal*. Bar Harbor: Rebel Satori Press, 2012. 96-97. Print.

---. *Grand Mal*. Bar Harbor: Rebel Satori Press, 2012. Print.

---. "Green and Yellow Relocation Villanelle." *Grand Mal*. Bar Harbor: Rebel Satori Press, 2012. 24. Print.

---. "Hitchhikers Redux." *Grand Mal*. Bar Harbor: Rebel Satori Press, 2012. 80-82. Print

---. "In A Green Dream Of Gregory Corso." *Grand Mal*. Bar Harbor: Rebel Satori Press, 2012. 73-74. Print.

---. "Jacks with Creeley." *Grand Mal*. Bar Harbor: Rebel Satori Press, 2012. 75-76. Print.

---. "The Jefferson Theater." *Grand Mal.* Bar Harbor: Rebel Satori Press, 2012. 50-51. Print.

---. "Kindle Or Something Like It." *Grand Mal.* Bar Harbor: Rebel Satori Press, 2012. 36-37. Print.

---. "Kreskin In Azure." *Grand Mal.* Bar Harbor: Rebel Satori Press, 2012. 68-71. Print.

---. "Layers & Layers Of Meaning." *Grand Mal.* Bar Harbor: Rebel Satori Press, 2012. 63-65. Print.

---. "Mr. And Mrs. Hughes Make Up And Wake the Dead." *Grand Mal.* Bar Harbor: Rebel Satori Press, 2012. 60-62. Print.

---. "Porn Star's Sunday Song." *Grand Mal.* Bar Harbor: Rebel Satori Press, 2012. 48-49. Print.

---. "Puxatawnie In His Dun Period." *Grand Mal.* Bar Harbor: Rebel Satori Press, 2012. 3-4. Print.

---. "The Reins Supreme." *Grand Mal.* Bar Harbor: Rebel Satori Press, 2012. 34-35. Print.

---. "Spill." *Grand Mal.* Bar Harbor: Rebel Satori Press, 2012. 57-58. Print.

---. "Stronger Than Dirt." *Grand Mal.* Bar Harbor: Rebel Satori Press, 2012. 8-9. Print.

---. "This Poem Has Not Been Rated." *Grand Mal.* Bar Harbor: Rebel Satori Press, 2012. 45-47. Print.

---. "Trapper Don't Look Back." *Grand Mal.* Bar Harbor: Rebel Satori Press, 2012. 25-27. Print.

Manyam, Bala V. "Epilepsy in Ancient India." *Epilepsia* 33.3 (1992): 473-475. Print.

May, Vivian M., and Beth A. Ferri. "Fixated on Ability. Questioning Ableist Metaphors in Feminist Theories of Resistance." *Prose Studies: History, Theory, Criticism* 27.1&2 (2005): 120-140. Print.

McCarron, Kevin. "'The Crack-House Flicker': The Sacred and the Absurd in the Short Stories of Dennis Cooper, Dennis Johnson, and Thom Jones." *Yearbook of English Studies* 31 (2001): 50-61. Print.

Metzel, Jonathan M. "Signifying Medication in Thom Jones's 'Superman, My Son.'" *Teaching Literature and Medicine.* Ed. Anne Hunsacker Hawkins and Marilyn Chandler McEntyre. New York: Modern Language Association, 2000. 338-43. Print.

Mieszkowski, Sylvia. "Pharmakon Zeitreise: Verborgene kulturelle Phantasmen in Audrey Niffenegger's *The Time Traveler's Wife*." ZAA 54.4 (2006): 393-408. Print.

Mitchell, David T., and Sharon L. Snyder. "Narrative Prosthesis." *The Disability Studies Reader*. Ed. Lennard J. Davis. 4th ed. New York: Routledge, 2013. 222-235. Print.

Mladenov, Teodor. *Critical Theory and Disability. A Phenomenological Approach*. Critical Theory and Contemporary Society. Ed. Darrow Schecter. London: Bloomsbury, 2015. Print.

Muhle, Maria. "From the Vital to the Social. Canguilhem and Foucault—Reflections on Vital and Social Norms." *Republics of Letters: A Journal for the Study of Knowledge, Politics, and the Arts* 2 (2014): 1-12. Print.

Murray, Stuart. "From Virginia's Sister to Friday's Silence: Presence, Metaphor, and the Persistence of Disability in Contemporary Writing." *Journal of Literary & Cultural Disability Studies* 6.3 (2012): 241-258. Print.

Niffenegger, Audrey. *The Time Traveler's Wife*. Vintage: London, 2004. Print.

Oates, Joyce Carol. "Their Bodies, Their Selves." *The New York Times*, 4 June 1995. Web. 5 Sep. 2015.

Okumara, Akihisa, at al. "Epilepsies after Pocket Monster Seizures." *Epilepsia* 46.6 (2005): 980-982. Print.

Ozer, Irma J. "Images of Epilepsy in Literature." *Epilepsia* 32.6 (1991): 798-809. Print.

Percy, Walker. "The Diagnostic Novel. On the Uses of Modern Fiction." *Harper's* 1986: 39-45. Print.

Philbrick, Rodman. *The Last Book in the Universe*. London: Usborne Publishing Ltd., 2000. Print.

Picard, Fabienne, and Florian Kurth. "Ictal Alterations of Consciousness during Ecstatic Seizures." *Epilepsy & Behavior* 30 (2014): 58-61. Print.

Poe, Edgar Allan. "Berenice." 1835. *Tales of Mystery and Imagination*. Mineola, New York: Calla Editions, 2008. 20-27. Print.

Polednischek-Veit, Ulrich. "Die epileptische Aura als zentrale Metaphor in Thomas Pynchon 'The Crying of Lot 49.'" *Das ist eine alte Krankheit. Epilepsie in der Literatur*. Ed. Dietrich von Engelhardt, Hansjörg Schneble and Peter Wolf. Stuttgart: Schattauer, 2000. 225-236. Print.

Popp, Valerie L. "'Eloquent Limbs': D. H. Lawrence and the Aesthetics of Disability." *Journal of Literary & Cultural Disability Studies* 5.1 (2011): 35-52. Print.

Pynchon, Thomas. *The Crying of Lot 49*. 1965. New York: Harper Perennial Modern Classics, 2006. Print.

Rand, Sebastian. "Organism, Normativity, Plasticity: Canguilhem, Kant, Malabou." *Continental Philosophy Review* 44.4 (2011): 341-357. Print.

Rao, Saligrama Krishna Ramachandra, ed. "The Conceptual Context of Indian Medicine." *Encyclopeadia of Indian Medicine. Vol. 2. Basic Concepts*. Bombay: Popular Prakashan Bombay, 1987. 1-15. Print.

Rolleston, J. D. "F. J. V. Broussais (1772-1838): His Life and Doctrines." *Proceedings of the Royal Society of Medicine* XXXII (January 1939): 405-413. Print.

Russel, Emily. *Reading Embodied Citizenship. Disability, Narrative, and the Body Politic*. New Brunswick: Rutgers University Press, 2011. Print.

Ryan, Marie-Laurie. "Temporal Paradoxes in Narrative." *Style* 43.2 (2009): 142-164. Print.

Sauder, Gerhard. "Sinn und Bedeutung von Krankheitsmotiven in der Literatur." *Das ist eine alte Krankheit. Epilepsie in der Literatur*. Ed. Dietrich von Engelhardt, Hansjörg Schneble and Peter Wolf. Stuttgart: Schattauer, 2000. 1-12. Print.

Schalk, Sami. "Metaphorically Speaking: Ableist Metaphors in Feminist Writings." *Disability Studies Quarterly* 33.4 (2013): n. pag. Web. 20 Mar. 2015.

Scheuer, Christina. "Bodily Compositions: The Disability Poetics of Karen Fiser and Laurie Clements Lambeth." *Journal of Literary & Cultural Disability Studies* 5.2 (2011): 155-172. Print.

Schneble, Hansjörg. *Krankheit der ungezählten Namen. Ein Beitrag zur Sozial-, Kultur- und Medizingeschichte der Epilepsie anhand ihrer Bennenungen vom Altertum bis zur Gegenwart*. Bern: Verlag Hans Huber, 1987. Print.

---. *Von der 'heiligen Krankheit' zum 'fallenden Siechtag.' Epileptologische Schriften und ihre Autoren aus Antike und Mittelalter*. Reinbeck: Einhorn-Presse Verlag, 1988. Print.

Scott, David. *Gilbert Simondon's Psychic and Collective Individuation. A Critical Introduction and Guide*. Edinburgh: Edinburgh University Press, 2014. Print.

Segal, Eyal. "Time Travel Stories as a Challenge to Narratology: The Case of The Time Traveler's Wife." *Poetics Today* 36.4 (2015): 529-560. Print.

Shakespeare, Tom. *Disability Rights and Wrongs Revisited.* 2nd ed. London: Routledge, 2014. Print.

Shildrick, Margrit. *Dangerous Discourses of Disability, Subjectivity and Sexuality*. Palgrave, 2012. Print.

---. "The Disabled Body, Genealogy and Undecidability." *Cutural Studies* 19.6 (November 2005): 755-770. Print.

Simondon, Gilbert. "The Genesis of the Individual." Trans. Mark Cohen and Sanford Kwinter. *Zone 6. Incorporations*. Ed. Jonathan Crary and Sanford Kwinter. New York: MIT Press, 1992. 297-319. Print.

---. "The Position of the Problem of Ontogenesis." Trans. Gregory Flanders. *Parrhesia: A Journal of Critical Philosophy* 7 (2009): 4-16. Web. 7 Apr. 2015.

---. *On the Mode of Existence of Technical Objects*. 1958. Trans. Ninian Mellamphy. University of Western Ontario: 1980. PDF file.

Slater, Lauren. *Lying. A Metaphorical Memoir*. London: Penguin Books, 2000. Print.

Sonntag, Carla S. "Epilepsy and Thomas Carlyle." *Dickinson Studies* 35 (1979): 23-34. Print.

Sontag, Susan. *Illness as Metaphor and AIDS and Its Metaphors*. New York: Picador, 1978. Print.

Stirling, Jeannette. *Representing Epilepsy: Myth and Matter*. Liverpool: Liverpool University Press, 2010. Print.

Stol, Marten. *Epilepsy in Babylonia*. Groningen: Postbus Styx Publications, 1993. Print. Cuneiform Monographs 2.

Tellenbach, Hubertus. *Schwermut, Wahn und Fallsucht in der abendländischen Dichtung*. Schriften zu Psychopathologie, Kunst und Literatur. Ed. Dietrich von Engelhardt, Horst-Jürgen Gerigk, Guido Pressler and Wolfram Schmitt. Hürtgenwald: Guido Pressler Verlag, 1992. Print.

Temkin, Owsei. *The Falling Sickness. A History of Epilepsy from the Greeks to the Beginnings of Early Modern Neurology*. 1945. 2nd ed. Baltimore: John Hopkins University Press, 1994. Print.

Theodorou, Stephanie. "Metaphor and Phenomenology." *Internet Encyclopedia of Philosophy*. no. pag. Web. 30 Jul. 2014.

The Time Traveler's Wife. Dir. Robert Schwenke. Perf. Eric Bana, Rachel McAdams, and Ron Livingston. New Line Cinema, 2009. Film.

Tremain, Shelly. "On the Government of Disability: Foucault, Power and the Subject of Impairment." *Social Theory and Practice* 27.4 (2001): 617-636.

Trimble, Michael R. *The Soul in the Brain. The Cerebral Basis of Language, Art, and Belief*. Baltimore: John Hopkins University Press, 2007. Print.

Turki, Amin T. "On the Normativity of the Immune System." *Medicine Studies* 3 (2011): 29-39. Print.

Turner, Bryan S. "Disability and the Sociology of the Body." *Handbook of Disability Studies*. Ed. Gary L. Albrecht, Michael Bury and Kathrine Seelman. New York: Sage Publications, 2001: 252-265. Print.

Updike, John, and Katrina Kenison, eds. *The Best American Short Stories of the Century*. Expanded ed. Boston: Houghton Mifflin Company, 2000. Print.

Vanzan Paladin, Anna. "Epilepsy in Twentieth Century Literature." *Epilepsia* 36.10 (1995): 1058-1060. Print.

Vidali, Amy. "Seeing What We Know. Disability and Theories of Metaphor." *Journal of Literary & Cultural Disability Sutdies* 4.1 (2010): 33-54. Print.

Waller, Friederike, Hans Dierk Waller, and Georg Marckmann. *Gesichter der 'Heiligen Krankheit'. Die Epilepsie in der Literatur*. Tübingen: Klöpfer & Meyer, 2005. Print.

Whitman, Walt. "Faces." *Walt Whitman. The Complete Poems*. Ed. Francis Murphy. London: Penguin Books, 2004. 475-479. Print.

Wilson, J. V., and E. H. Reynolds. "Texts and Documents. Translation and Analysis of a Cuneiform Text Forming Part of a Babylonian Treatise on Epilepsy." *Medical History* 34.2 (1990): 185-198. Print.

Wolf, Peter. "Descriptions of Clinical Semiology of Seizures in Literature." *Epileptic Disorder* 8.1 (2006): 3-10. Print.

---. "Epilepsy and Catalepsy in Anglo-American Literature between Romanticism and Realism: Tennyson, Poe, Eliot and Collins." *Journal of the History of the Neuroscience* 9.3 (2000): 286-293. Print.

---. "The Epileptic Aura in Literature: Aesthetic and Philosophical Dimensions. An Essay." *Epilepsia* 54.3 (2013): 415-424. Print.

---. "Erfahrung und Vorurteil in literarischen Epilepsiedarstellungen." *Fundamente Psychiatrica* 10 (1996): 148-155. Print.

---. "Sociocultural History of Epilepsy." *Atlas of Epilepsy*. Ed. Chrysostomos P. Panayiotopoulos. London: Springer, 2010. 35-43. Print.

Literaturwissenschaft

Carsten Gansel, Werner Nell (Hg.)
Vom kritischen Denker zur Medienprominenz?
Zur Rolle von Intellektuellen in Literatur und Gesellschaft vor und nach 1989

2015, 406 S., kart.
39,99 € (DE), 978-3-8376-3078-7
E-Book
PDF: 39,99 € (DE), ISBN 978-3-8394-3078-1

Tanja Pröbstl
Zerstörte Sprache – gebrochenes Schweigen
Über die (Un-)Möglichkeit, von Folter zu erzählen

2015, 300 S., kart.
29,99 € (DE), 978-3-8376-3179-1
E-Book
PDF: 26,99 € (DE), ISBN 978-3-8394-3179-5

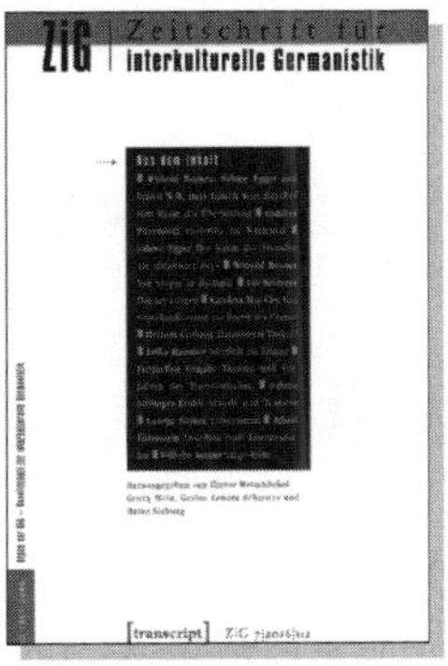

Dieter Heimböckel, Georg Mein,
Gesine Lenore Schiewer, Heinz Sieburg (Hg.)
Zeitschrift für interkulturelle Germanistik
7. Jahrgang, 2016, Heft 2: Transiträume

2016, 220 S., kart.
12,80 € (DE), 978-3-8376-3567-6
E-Book
PDF: 12,80 € (DE), ISBN 978-3-8394-3567-0

Leseproben, weitere Informationen und Bestellmöglichkeiten finden Sie unter www.transcript-verlag.de